FEMALE AGENCY AND DOCUMENTARY STRATEGIES

FEMALE AGENCY AND DOCUMENTARY STRATEGIES
Subjectivities, Identity and Activism

Edited by Boel Ulfsdotter and
Anna Backman Rogers

EDINBURGH
University Press

Edinburgh University Press is one of the leading university presses in the UK. We publish academic books and journals in our selected subject areas across the humanities and social sciences, combining cutting-edge scholarship with high editorial and production values to produce academic works of lasting importance. For more information visit our website: edinburghuniversitypress.com

© editorial matter and organisation Boel Ulfsdotter and Anna Backman Rogers, 2018
© the chapters their several authors, 2018

Edinburgh University Press Ltd
The Tun – Holyrood Road
12 (2f) Jackson's Entry
Edinburgh EH8 8PJ

Typeset in 10/12.5 pt Sabon by
Servis Filmsetting Ltd, Stockport, Cheshire

A CIP record for this book is available from the British Library

ISBN 978 1 4744 1947 5 (hardback)
ISBN 978 1 4744 1948 2 (webready PDF)
ISBN 978 1 4744 1949 9 (epub)

The right of the contributors to be identified as authors of this work has been asserted in accordance with the Copyright, Designs and Patents Act 1988 and the Copyright and Related Rights Regulations 2003 (SI no. 2498).

CONTENTS

List of Illustrations — vii
Notes on the Contributors — ix

Foreword — xiii
Kate Nash

    Introduction — 1
    Boel Ulfsdotter and Anna Backman Rogers

PART ONE   NEW MEDIA AND ACTIVISM

1. The Pencil of Identity: Instagram as Inadvertent (Female) Autobiography — 9
Kris Fallon

2. Archetype and Authenticity: Reflections on Amalia Ulman's Excellences & Perfections — 23
Cadence Kinsey

3. Blogging the Female Self: Authorship, Self-performance and Identity Politics in Fashion Blogs — 38
Monica Titton

PART TWO RELATIONALITY, SELFHOOD AND SUBJECTIVITIES

4. *'Scriptrix Narrans'*: Digital Documentary Storytelling's Radical Potential 57
   Gail Vanstone

5. Hybrid Practices and Voice Making in Contemporary Female Documentary Film 70
   Kim Munro

6. Record Keeping: Family Memories on Film – Rea Tajiri's *History and Memory: For Akiko and Takashig* and *Wisdom Gone Wild* 84
   Kerreen Ely-Harper

7. 'Not Because my Heart is Gone; Simply the Other Side': Francesca Woodman's Relational and Ephemeral Subjectivity at the Limit of the Image 100
   Anna Backman Rogers

8. Other Women: Thinking Class and Gender in Contemporary Brazilian Documentary Film 114
   Carla Maia

   Interview: 'Visualising Our Voices' – Hong Kong Scholar and Film Director Vivian Wenli Lin, in conversation with Boel Ulfsdotter 125

PART THREE IDENTITY POLITICS OF DOCUMENTARY

9. From Visceral Style to Discourse of Resistance: Reading Alka Sadat's Afghan Documentaries on Violence Against Women 137
   Anna Misiak

10. Documenting Georgia in Transition: The Films of Salomé Jashi and Nino Kirtadze 156
    John A. Riley

11. *Profession: Documentarist*: Underground Documentary Making in Iran 170
    Lidia Merás

12. 'Reflecting through Images': The Documentaries of Mercedes Álvarez 184
    Linda Ehrlich

Select Bibliography 194
Index 201

ILLUSTRATIONS

Figure 1	Amalia Ulman, *Excellences & Perfections* (*Instagram update, 5 September 2014*), 2014. Image courtesy the artist and Arcadia Missa.	25
Figure 2	Amalia Ulman, *Excellences & Perfections* (*Instagram update, 1 June 2014*), 2014. Image courtesy the artist and Arcadia Missa.	28
Figure 3	Picture of Leandra Medine, posing on a playground in her hometown, New York City, published on her blog 'The Man Repeller' (http://www.manrepeller.com/2012/06/toddler-dressing.html).	43
Figure 4	Picture of Tavi Gevinson wearing a sweater with 'Feminist' pattern published on her blog 'Style Rookie' (http://www.thestylerookie.com/2010/09/carnival.html).	47
Figure 5	Revealing secrets ... Sharon Daniel's *Public Secrets*.	62
Figure 6	Settler education: Aayu Peter in Alethea Arnaquq-Baril's *Angry Inuk*.	67
Figure 7	*Bombay Beach* [DVD], dir. A. Har'el, Ro*co Films, 2011.	77
Figure 8	*The Arbor* [DVD], dir. Clio Barnard, Artangel, 2010.	79
Figure 9	*History and Memory: For Akiko and Takashige* [DVD], dir. Rea Tajiri, USA, WMM, 1991.	87
Figure 10	*Wisdom Gone Wild* – Trailer 2:39 – 'November 2015 – LACMA on Vimeo', dir. Rea Tajiri, USA (https://vimeo.com/144466477).	95

ILLUSTRATIONS

Figure 11	*Space*, Providence, Rhode Island, 1975–8.	106
Figure 12	*Untitled*, Providence, Rhode Island, 1976.	109
Figure 13	*Milk and Iron* (*Leite e ferro*), Claudia Priscilla, Brazil, 2010.	119
Figure 14	*Like Water Through Stone* (*A falta que me faz*), Marília Rocha, Brazil, 2009.	122
Figure 15	Behind the scenes, VOW Media and IWE collaboration in Yogyakarta, Indonesia (2015).	128
Figure 16	Learning the video camera, *Displaced Daughters* (2011).	132
Figure 17	Alka Sadat.	138
Figure 18	Alka Sadat.	141
Figure 19	Segment 'Sepideh' by Sepideh Abtani.	172
Figure 20	Segment 'Sahar' by Sahar Salahshoor.	177
Figure 21	Pello Azketa.	187
Figure 22	*Parkours*.	191

NOTES ON THE CONTRIBUTORS

Anna Backman Rogers is a Senior Lecturer in Film Studies at the University of Gothenburg, Sweden. She is the author of *American Independent Cinema: Rites of Passage and the Crisis Image* (Edinburgh University Press, 2015) and the co-editor, with Laura Mulvey, of *Feminisms* (2015). Her monograph entitled 'Sofia Coppola: The Politics of Visual Pleasure' is forthcoming in 2017/2018.

Linda Ehrlich – writer, teacher, editor – has published extensively about world cinema and about traditional theatre in such journals as *Film Quarterly*, *Cinema Journal*, *Cinema Scope* and *Journal of Religion and Film*. *Cinematic Landscapes*, her first book (co-edited with David Desser), is an anthology of essays on the interface between the visual arts and cinemas of China and Japan (1994; reprint in 2008). Her second edited book, *The Cinema of Víctor Erice: An Open Window*, appeared in 2000 (with an expanded paperback edition in 2007). Her newest book, *Cinematic Reveries: Gestures, Stillness, Water*, offers a collection of prose poems about key films (2013). Linda's taped commentary on the Spanish film *The Spirit of the Beehive (El espíritu de la colmena)* appears on the Criterion DVD. She has also edited and annotated the memoirs of Juan Luis Buñuel (*Good Films, Cheap Wine, Few Friends: A Memoir*). In addition, she has published three books of poetry (*In the Breathing Time, Night Harbour, Bodegón*) and one book for young readers (*The Body is Round*). Ehrlich has taught at the University of Tennessee/Knoxville, Case Western Reserve University, and on the Semester-at-Sea programme. She received her PhD from the University of Hawaii/East-West Center.

THE CONTRIBUTORS

Kerreen Ely-Harper is a creative media researcher and filmmaker, and lecturer at Curtin University, Perth, Australia. She has written and directed a number of film projects including documentaries, short drama, dance, corporate and educational videos. She directed the virtual 3D *Foul Whisperings, Strange Matters* (2008–10), an adaptation of Shakespeare's *Macbeth* in Second Life. She is a recipient of Australian Teachers of Media (ATOM) award nominations: *Even Girls Play Footy*, nomination Best Secondary Education Resource, 2012; *Parts of a Horse*, nomination, Best Short Film, 2003; *In Her Own Words*, winner, Best Education Resource, 1997. Her research interests include the staging of personal stories and memory narratives on film.

Kris Fallon is an Assistant Professor in Cinema and Digital Media and a faculty member in the ModLab at the University of California, Davis, USA. His research focuses on documentary practices across a range of forms from photography and film to digital media including data visualisation and self-tracking. His essays and articles have appeared in *Screen*, *Film Quarterly* and a number of edited anthologies. He is currently working on a book about documentary film and digital media in the United States post 9/11, titled *Where Truth Lies: Digital Culture and Documentary Film After 9/11*.

Cadence Kinsey is Lecturer in Recent and Contemporary Art at the University of York, UK. Prior to taking up this appointment she was a British Academy Postdoctoral Fellow in the Department of History of Art at UCL, where she completed a book project about art after the Internet. Her research is primarily focused on the interrelationships between technology, subjectivity and representation.

Carla Maia lives and works in Belo Horizonte, Brazil. She has a PhD in Communication from the Universidade Federal de Minas Gerais/UFMG and was a visiting scholar at Tulane University, New Orleans, USA. Her doctoral thesis (2015) is about films by/with women in Brazilian contemporary documentary. She is currently a professor of the Communication and Arts Institute, UNA University Centre. Curator and programmer, she has organised several authors' retrospectives, including Chantal Akerman, Naomi Kawase and Trinh T. Minh-ha. She is a member of the collective Filmes de Quintal and programmer of the *forumdoc.bh: Documentary and Ethnography Film Festival* of Belo Horizonte.

Lidia Merás is film historian and an academic researcher based in London, UK. She serves as a member of the editorial staff of *Secuencias*, a peer-reviewed film journal published by Universidad Autonóma de Madrid. Merás has co-edited four volumes of *Desacuerdos: Sobre arte y política en la esfera* *pública* (2004–7). Her last contributions include the entries on *Taxi Teheran* (by Jafar Panahi) and *Seconds of Lead* (by Seyed Reza Razavi) in Parviz Jahed's *Directory of World Cinema: Iran vol. 2* (2017) and the book chapter 'The Gypsies According to No-Do', in Stuart Davis and Maite Usoz's *New Perspectives on the Modern Spanish Canon* (2017).

Anna Misiak, former Fulbright Scholar at the University of Southern California, USA, holds a PhD from the Polish Academy of Sciences. She is a Senior Lecturer and MA Film & TV Course Coordinator at Falmouth University, UK. She has authored one monograph, *Kinematograf kontrolowany* (2006), and contributed her film research to a number of peer-reviewed journals and edited collections. In 2015, she won a Leverhulme Trust Fellowship to develop her archive documentary study *Life Under Communism*. Between 2013 and 2016, Misiak also worked as an investigator on an international research project, 'Documentary in V4 Countries', which was supported by the Visegrad University Studies Grant.

Kim Munro is a filmmaker, artist and teacher from Melbourne, Australia. Her practice and theoretical research explores nonlinear documentary forms across film, installation and interactive works. She is also co-founder of Docuverse: a forum for expanded documentary practices. Her research interests include the intersections between analogue and digital processes, participation and performance, contemporary feminisms, new materialism and the use of voice and listening in documentary practice. Her current practice-led research involves collective subjectivity and aloneness.

Kate Nash is Lecturer in Media and Communication and Director of Student Education in the School of Media and Communication at the University of Leeds, UK. Her research focuses on the relationship between the cultures and practices of documentary and those of digital media. Her work has appeared in a number of leading journals including *Media Culture and Society*, *European Journal of Communication* and *Studies in Documentary Film*. She is co-editor (with Craig Hight and Catherine Summerhayes) of *New Documentary Ecologies: Emerging Platforms, Practices and Discourses* and she is currently working on a monograph on interactive documentary for Routledge.

John A. Riley is an Assistant Professor of English at Woosong University, South Korea. He holds a PhD from Birkbeck College, University of London, UK, where he completed a thesis that reconceptualised the films of Andrei Tarkovsky using contemporary film theory. His written work has appeared in a wide variety of publications, academic and otherwise. His current research interests include haunting in film and popular culture, Georgian film and documentary, and Soviet cultural theory.

THE CONTRIBUTORS

Monica Titton is a sociologist and culture critic living and working in Vienna, Austria. She holds a PhD in Sociology from the University of Vienna (2015). Her doctoral research focused on identity, collective narratives and aesthetics in fashion and street style blogs. She is a Lecturer at the University of Applied Arts and at the Academy of Fine Arts in Vienna, where she lectures across a number of areas concerning fashion theory, cultural studies and fashion history. In addition to her scholarly work, she regularly writes about fashion, style and culture for newspapers and magazines.

Boel Ulfsdotter, formerly a Senior Lecturer at the Documentary Media Production programme at Skövde University College, is an independent media scholar specialising in screen studies, and currently affiliated with the Department of Cultural Sciences at the University of Gothenburg, Sweden. Her areas of research include narrative and aesthetic perspectives in documentary and popular cinema; visual studies related to *mise en scène* and screen costuming; and visual culture in general. Her recent work has been published in the *Journal of Scandinavian Cinema*, *Journal of European Popular Culture* and *Journal of Film, Fashion and Consumption*. Ulfsdotter is also a freelancing visual arts critic at Sweden's second largest newspaper, *Göteborgs-Posten*.

Gail Vanstone is an Associate Professor in the Department of Humanities at York University, Toronto, Canada, and directs its *Culture & Expression* programme. She is the author of *D is Daring* – a cultural history of Studio D, the women's film unit at the National Film Board of Canada, and co-author, along with Brian Winston and Wang Chi, of *The Act of Documenting* (2017). Specialising in Canadian cultural production, she is currently compiling a digital archive of feminist filmmakers and other principals associated with Studio D and is researching the work of Indigenous women filmmakers in Canada.

FOREWORD

Contemporary documentary media is an expansive domain. Alongside established forms and platforms we find multifarious practices that intersect in a multitude of ways with the documentary 'project' broadly considered. Documentary, as we know, is always evolving and this is very apparent in the work collected here in this second volume of *Female Authorship and the Documentary Image*. The collection embraces this expansive and evolving domain of documentary practice, interrogating the very idea of authorship and creating a fertile dialogue between emerging and established practices and scholarship.

Organised into four thematic parts, new media and activism, selfhood and subjectivities, identity politics of documentary and the personal is political, the collection brings a fresh perspective to the study of gender and the documentary tradition. These four themes highlight a key achievement of the collection, the links it creates between contemporary documentary practices in all their diversity and the fundamental questions of film, media and documentary scholarship. The editors and contributors challenge the reader to reconsider the idea of authorship from multiple perspectives, reflecting their very different academic orientations. Key themes include: the connection between authorship, place, culture and global politics; the changing nature of collaborative authorship and the need for a more nuanced consideration of context; and the changing nature of self-representation in a digital media culture. What emerges is a picture of the fluidity and richness of female authorship today.

A particularly important strand of inquiry that runs through the collection is the importance of contexts for any attempt to understand female documentary authorship. Contributions draw attention to the intersections between gender and culture, nationality, politics, economics and personal and family histories. Female authorship admits of no 'one size fits all' theoretical or conceptual treatment. Importantly, a number of the chapters highlight the limitations of Euro-Western theoretical frameworks, drawing attention to the ways in which documentary makers skilfully negotiate and explore multiple identities and speaking positions in their work.

A particular value of the collection is, as I have already noted, its embrace of emerging platforms and practices that intersect with documentary. There are chapters on blogging, social media activism and forms of digital self-representation. In thinking through these emerging practices the writers move beyond a simplistic celebration of technological advancement to engage deeply with the practices of women who are exploring new potentials for documentary expression.

A sheer pleasure of this collection is the opportunity it affords to become immersed in the work of many vibrant and creative women from around the world who are actively pushing the boundaries of documentary representation today. While some names may be familiar, others will likely be new acquaintances, who promise to open doors to new worlds of practice that intersect productively with documentary scholarship. The editors are to be congratulated for selecting work that explores globally significant examples of female authorship that will have an impact on contemporary scholarship. This is an important work and one that I hope will spark a fresh consideration of documentaries made by women.

Kate Nash
University of Leeds

INTRODUCTION

Boel Ulfsdotter and Anna Backman Rogers

Given the new techniques and conditions of production, as well as the emerging platforms for sharing contemporary documentary footage, many scholars now agree that the conventional labels – in the form of, by way of example, *cinéma-vérité* or observational cinema – are at best inadequate, and thus call for reinvention. Now that a new group of documentarists have joined an established community of filmmakers, and a young generation of documentarists working in completely different media has rapidly emerged, it is our contention – taken as the point of inception for this volume – that this pivotal turn or paradigm shift in the production of the documentary image precipitates an urgent need for a scholarly study of the specific relationship between female authorship and the documentary image.

The book, as well as its companion volume, *Female Authorship and the Documentary Image: Theory, Practice and Aesthetics*, comprises an internationally focused study of female authorship in relation to the documentary image. Addressed by a group of scholars at the forefront of contemporary views on this issue, these two volumes are defined by a collaborative effort to map and report on authorship from a global perspective. Given the widespread interest in documenting, and indeed almost obsessional need to document, ourselves and the world around us in the contemporary moment, this two-volume monograph addresses issues as varying as: How do theory and praxis coalesce (if at all) for female practitioners within documentary image making practices? How does technology and contemporary media shape the strategies that inform female authorship and subjectivity? Has the digital turn brought about any major shifts in terms of female subject formation and activism? What is the central mode of address currently in the field? What are the key issues being dealt with? How is female authorship made manifest within a global context? Why is the notion of authorship of sustained relevance and importance to female documentary practitioners? Is female authorship always implicitly or explicitly imbricate with feminist theory?

It is commonly agreed that women's increasing claim to equal societal rights and vocalisation on a global scale have, had a decisive impact on female agency in relation to the documentation of contemporary issues. Of course, this is not a new phenomenon per se; in terms of culture and scholarship women have been seeking to establish myriad voices and perspectives on issues of gender, politics, history and selfhood throughout the various waves of social emancipation and emerging feminist agendas. Female documentary filmmakers have taken a particularly progressive stance in this practice since the arrival of lightweight equipment in the late 1950s. The 1960s women's movement further encouraged the documentation of women's lives and female agency in particular. The current impetus of an increasing globalisation, consciously reframed socio-political discourses, new technologies, not to mention developing education and job opportunities in countries outside of Western Europe and the USA, have, however, again had a decisive impact on the way women experience and document their own lives. With these books, we therefore seek to explore what female authorship is from the perspective of multiplicity and cultural diversity. What are, in fact, the theoretical, political and aesthetic discourses that contribute to female documentary practices right now? Is it possible to discern a political agenda that goes beyond problematic essentialism?

This volume addresses, implicitly, the shift from analogue to digital imagery, analogue photography being the medium so often analysed, after André Bazin (originally published 1967–71)[1] and Roland Barthes (originally published 1980),[2] in terms of the 'index', which, from the perspective of film scholars such as D. N. Rodowick (2007)[3] and Laura Mulvey (2006),[4] is thrown into crisis by the digital turn. We stress, therefore, that the notion of the documentary image addressed in this volume is altogether looser than the one in its predecessor. Our aim here is not to delimit the emerging scope and context of documentary, but rather to investigate its potential and the manifold ways in which images that pertain to 'authenticity' are being utilised to open up and question claims to truth and, by extension, power. What is offered here, then, is tentatively descriptive and not prescriptive of both notions of documentary and authorship and must be read as such. In particular, this volume centres on how self-portraiture, and contemporary manifestations such as blogging and prevalent usage of social media shape and inform female subjectivities and claims to truth. Moreover, this volume examines the scope of authorship and agency open to women using these technologies as a form of activism. Are they technologies of gender – as Teresa de Lauretis (1987)[5] has already argued of the cinematic apparatus – or are they technologies of subversion that render apparent that subjectivity is always mediated and performative within a social context? This volume, as such, does not aim to provide a historical overview of self-portraiture (although its history is addressed tangentially in a number of the essays here), but to examine the ways in which technology has hitherto mediated and informed authorship and selfhood within a specifically female context, and questions what the turn to digital imagery (dematerialisation versus activism) and social media platforms might mean for female subjectivity and authorship. This volume, like its sister volume, provides two interviews, the first of which is based on a digital conversation between Hong Kong-based scholar Vivian Wenli Lin, founder of the organisation 'Visualising Our Voices', and Boel Ulfsdotter. The second interview, which forms Chapter 12, by Linda Ehrlich, is written as an autobiographical meditation on a lifetime career as a documentary filmmaker, based on the author's dialogue with Mercedes Álvarez, one of the most experienced female documentarists in Spain. Both of these interviews seek to account for what is at stake in outlining the female authored documentary image.

The first part of this book centres on new media and activism; more specifically, the chapter addresses the ways in which new media platforms can function as potential sites of activism in terms of female authorship and critique of forms of image making that have served to disempower the female body by positing it as an object to be looked at.

Kris Fallon explores the selfie as a potential site of activism by taking into account the historical precedent of the self-portrait and the ways in which, in contradistinction to scholars who have perceived the selfie as a reinforcement of the male gaze, social media platforms such as Instagram can enable self-authorship.

Likewise, Cadence Kinsey's essay on Amalia Ulman's Instagram project *Excellences & Perfections* explores how Ulman works to open up sites of contestation in which the female documentarist can both critique and question patriarchal modes of image making and explore the postfemininst notion of authentic subjectivity via abiding feminist tropes such as presence and absence and visibility and invisibility. Kinsey suggests that Ulman seeks to move beyond debates centring on the self-image within the context of media performance in order to assert that subjectivity is already always mediated.

Monica Titton, in her analysis of the female authored blog sites 'Rookie' and 'Man Repeller', delineates fashion blogs as discursive and performative sites for the dissemination and production of fashion; in the process, she provides a critical analysis of the processes of authorship, identity and persona construction from a feminist perspective in contrast to the postfeminist ideals and attendant values of 'self-actualisation' and 'self-fashioning' so often espoused on such sites.

The second part of this book centres on notions of relationality, selfhood and subjectivity and opens with Gail Vanstone's provocative delineation of the concept of *'scriptrix narrans'*, which draws on the tradition of *(cin)écriture feminine* (after Cixous and Agnès Varda) to open up alternatives to canonical patriarchal narratives. By way of filmmakers Varda, Sharon Daniel and Alethea Arnaquq-Baril, Vanstone offers intricate readings of films that work to foreground notions of intersubjectivity, community and collaboration at play within any 'authorship'.

Kim Munro's essay examines voice making in contemporary female documentary practice; she explores how feminist filmmaking techniques embody the explicit construction of identity through a shared and collaborative approach to subject participation and performance in relation to ideas about the 'voice'. By highlighting the use of 'hybrid' practices and border-crossing in film, as well as art processes, she identifies how strategies of participation and performance allow for non-binary complexities and voice making to emerge.

Following on from this, through a close reading of Rea Tajiri's *History and Memory: For Akiko and Takashig* (USA, 1991), Kerreen Ely-Harper, in her contribution, proposes to demonstrate how Rea Tajiri moves through three stages in her filmmaking process: (1) embodiment, (2) distillation and (3) re-representation. These processes (as distinct from the commercial stages of producing a film) can be seen to parallel the narrative and trauma theory models of transformation from incoherence to coherence through the reconstruction of the autobiographical memory narrative.

Anna Backman Rogers' essay on the photographic self-portraiture of Francesca Woodman re-positions Woodman's work as an act of mediation between self and other and self and apparatus. Woodman's work has commonly been read in light of her depression and tragic suicide at the age of just twenty-two, in particular as the figuration of (or rehearsal for) an act of disappearance; this essay aligns itself with more recent scholarship on Woodman and argues that, in actual fact, Woodman stages a precise dissection of what it means to be both the subject and object of her own gaze. As such, Backman Rogers answers to and echoes both Fallon's and Kinsey's essays in this volume by contrasting Woodman's imagery with that of the phenomenon of the selfie and parsing out how subjectivity comes into being *for* an 'other' (whether that other is an apparatus or an observer).

Focusing on the relationality in documentary film, Carla Maia's chapter proposes to consider such films as examples of filmmaking *with* women rather than films *of* women. In essence, the shift to *in-between spaces* – between the subject and the camera and the viewer and the film – precipitates reflection on the aesthetic, ethical and political potential that a cinema marked by different women's perspectives can bring to light.

Concluding this part is Boel Ulfsdotter's interview with Hong Kong-based scholar and activist Vivian Wenli Lin. This conversation focuses on her organisation 'Visualising Our Voices', which encourages disenfranchised women in Southeast Asia to make their voices heard through various forms of documentary filmmaking. Lin's organisation provides them with the necessary skills for making documentary films for free.

The final part of this volume is given over to issues of identity politics and how, more specifically, such a politics informs contemporary documentary practice.

Anna Misiak's chapter explores Alka Sadat's documentary tactics of granting the voice to oppressed and displaced Afghan women through a number of visual and textual strategies of distanciation. It also shows that Sadat's films offer multilayered analyses of systemic violence against women alongside the lamentable disempowerment of Afghan women's rights activists.

John A. Riley utilises the films of Salomé Jashi and Nino Kirtadze as examples of the multivalent ways in which Georgian female documentarists have conceptualised Georgia as a country in the midst of complex transition. Jashi and Kirtadze are the country's key female documentarists and by situating their work within a socio-political and cultural context, they make visible the arbitrary nature of Georgian identity politics since it became an autonomous country.

In the last essay in this volume, Lidia Merás uses the Iranian omnibus production *Profession: Documentarist* (2014) and its diary-style format as a case study for her delineation of the collective practices, aesthetics and narrative interests of contemporary female documentarists in Iran. Through study of the professional barriers involved in documentary filmmaking in the country today, especially the hard censorship laws, the menace of political retaliations as well as gender discrimination, Merás contends that the diary-style format is, although often the sole option available, a powerful tool in the hands of these female practitioners.

Bringing the volume to conclusion is Chapter 12, Linda Ehrlich's interview with the Spanish documentary filmmaker Mercedes Álvarez. Written up as a reflection on a long professional career as one of Spain's most renowned female documentarists, this essay foregrounds Álvarez's ongoing aspirations and experiences in the field.

Together with its twin volume, *Female Authorship and the Documentary Image: Theory, Practice and Aesthetics*, this collection of essays is the first response to a call for an international scholarly study of female authorship and the documentary image. We would like to express our gratitude to Edinburgh University Press, especially Gillian Leslie, for giving us the opportunity to explore this topic. We also extend our appreciation to all contributors for having engaged with the remits of our project with such enthusiasm, generosity and outstanding expertise. We hope these books inspire both scholars and filmmakers to take the implications of our findings further.

Notes

1. André Bazin, *What is Cinema*, vols 1 and 2 (Berkeley, CA: University of California Press, 2004). First published 1967–71.
2. Roland Barthes, *Camera Lucida* (London: Vintage Books, 2000). First published 1980.
3. David N. Rodowick, *The Virtual Life of Film* (Cambridge, MA: Harvard University Press, 2007).
4. Laura Mulvey, *Death 24 × a Second* (London: Reaktion, 2006).
5. Teresa de Lauretis, *Technologies of Gender* (Bloomington, IN: Indiana University Press, 1987).

PART ONE

NEW MEDIA AND ACTIVISM

1. THE PENCIL OF IDENTITY: INSTAGRAM AS INADVERTENT (FEMALE) AUTOBIOGRAPHY

Kris Fallon

> With smartphone in hand, we can now share with others how our narcissism looks to us. The selfie chronicles a counter-Copernican revolution ... everything once again revolves around us.[1]

Of the cultural objects generated by the rise of ubiquitous digital media, few are perhaps more loathed than the selfie. The simple act of taking your own picture and distributing it via social media to the public is apparently symptomatic of any number of social and individual ills. It has been deemed the icon of social narcissism, an emblem of our collective tendency to get lost in ourselves. It has also been classified as a symptom of mental illness and a risk indicator for suicide, evidence of an overwhelming lack of a sense of self.[2] Generationally, they seem to be the cultural product of the so-called me-me-me-generation (*Time* magazine's update on the derisive title given to baby boomers), those digital millennials who grew up overly coddled by protective, helicoptering parents who provided them with plenty of self-esteem but little self-reliance.[3] Even the act of taking a selfie, posing with one's arm stretched in front of oneself, has become an object of scorn. Locked in a face-to-face interaction with one's screen and the mirror image it offers, the self who authors a selfie is a poster child for the sort of digital insecurity and obsessive insularity that writers such as Sherry Turkle, Nicholas Carr and Mark Bauerlein have described.[4]

But this obsession with the selfie misses a larger point. In the course of photographing ourselves, we seem to have opened up a new mode of authorship that enables and encourages everyone to document the world around themselves. As image capture becomes a common cultural practice, it alters the relationship between the self and the world, inviting one to view the world, if not photographically, then at least as it might be photographed. These interactions with the world and others seem to obviate the apparent self-centredness and narcissism of the selfie.

To see this at work we need to consider the selfie in its native habitat, on the social networking site Instagram, and place the site within the longer history of autobiography, photography and social networking of which it is a part. With over 500 million users (nearly 60 per cent of whom identify as female), Instagram's critics charge that it perpetuates the same destructive cult of beauty and celebrity endemic to wider mainstream culture. Admittedly, certain elements of the selfie culture on Instagram do clearly fit what Rosalind Gill and others have described as the emergence of a postfeminist sensibility.[5] Over the course of the last decade, Gill has astutely, and devastatingly, charted the nature of this sensibility within popular media and culture across a range of texts, from fashion and advertising to reality television and other mainstream contexts. She contends that a move towards self-surveillant policing of both female bodily appearance and interior affective states masquerades as an ethos of neoliberal self-empowerment that encourages women to do what 'feels right', ultimately concluding that 'it appears that the ideal disciplinary subject of neoliberalism is feminine'.

While the broader paradigm that Gill and others have described is undoubtedly accurate, in what follows I will describe several points of divergence, or even resistance, to these trends. The first lies in the range of images beyond selfies that one finds on Instagram, an expanded lexicon that I contend enables autobiographical expression without necessitating self-exposure or self-policing. Shifting focus from the selfie reveals a broader spectrum of images that appear alongside of them as well as narrative threads that emerge within and between images as they form a larger stream or feed. Here the selfie comprises one element in a larger serial, autobiographical narrative, one socially authored by the self and the wider world. The second point is that Instagram provides a platform for expressing and exploring a range of subjects and subjectivities beyond the heterosexual feminine ideal that Gill so trenchantly identifies within mainstream popular culture. In popularising a novel form of self-authorship open to anyone with a smartphone, Instagram challenges the traditional definition of whose story is worth sharing, and who gets to tell that story. The ubiquity of this practice has further destabilised the traditional power relationships that govern what constitutes a legitimate subject (in both senses of the term) enabling a wider spectrum of selves to participate. As we shall see, some of the most prominent (if not widespread) uses of Instagram have directly involved questions of gender and identity. Considering the platform and the image feed it produces shifts the focus from one particular image, or even one particular genre of image, over into the mode of inscription and recording that the tool itself seems to produce. Rather than heralding the doom of enlightened culture as its critics contend, here the selfie contributes to a novel form of non-fiction serial narrative that captures the nature of the self in the digital world.

Autobiography

Considered individually, the selfie of course draws on the longer lineage of portraiture in painting and art photography. Historically, the gesture of the self-portrait hovers somewhere between self-expression and self-definition while bearing a strong imprint of the culture in which a given portrait is created. As Joseph Koerner's study of Albrecht Durer demonstrates, Durer's self-portrait of 1500 arrives in a historical moment when categories of self, man, artist and creator are being reworked in the broader tension between the Renaissance and the Reformation.[6] And Durer is not unique. Indeed, an entire cottage industry within art history exists to situate specific styles culturally and socially within specific moments and locations in history. This same case has been made in other periods, including seventeenth-century Dutch portraiture or twentieth-century feminist painting.[7] Thus, we see modes of self-presentation at work in artists such as Rembrandt and Van Gogh as a reflection of both individual technique and prevailing styles but also as reflections of shifting definitions of subjectivity in the societies in which they were created.

The move from painting to photography in the nineteenth century quickly ushered in the first photographic self-portraits, thereby dating our current fascination with the selfie back to the earliest daguerrotypes. Throughout the late nineteenth and twentieth centuries, the self-portrait became a standard gesture amongst artists and art-photographers. Thus a rich tradition of self-representation and self-performance stretches from Bayard's 1840 portrait as a drowned man through to Trish Morrissey's 2007 portrait project *Front*, in which Morrisey poses with other people's families wearing their clothes. The clear connections between the current wave of selfies and the longer history of self-portrait photography is well-travelled ground for scholars working on selfie culture (here I would point to the extensive work being done through sites like the Seflie Research Network at www.selfieresearch.com) and I will therefore focus on the shift that photography initiates in the broader history of the portrait.

The shift from painting to photography brought with it an air of objectivity, that is, of seeing the self from an outside perspective, as an objective observer might. As the art historian Amelia Jones has argued, this makes self-portrait photography what she calls a 'technology of embodiment, if a low tech one', that 'produces and mediates subjectivities in the contemporary world'.[8] Its use by artists to explore this possibility hence indicates its dual nature as expressive tool and objective record, what Blake Stimson and Robin Kelsey describe as its 'double indexicality'.[9] Indeed, the nineteenth-century debate over photography's status as either art or science provides fertile ground for considering the status of the selfie within the context of a social network.[10] On one hand the expressive, artistic side of the selfie bears the imprint of the author/artist; it is literally a product of the hand at work capturing the self. Whatever filters and digital manipulation it undergoes are further interventions and evidence of the aesthetic sensibility of the creator on the raw digital information captured by the device. On the other hand, the objective record of the photograph offers a view of the individual subject as a group of outsiders might see her, thereby enabling the group to reach its own conclusions about the evidence that is provided.

Unlike the unified, agential autonomous 'picture' of the subject that Durer offered, photographic self-portraiture divides subjectivity between individual expression and group observation. The dynamic between these competing forces and the impact they have on a newly fractured subjectivity is complex. The normative influence of snapshot culture and the widespread homogeneity of amateur photographs have long been noted, an impact that would only seem to widen with the ubiquity of placing these images online.[11] But as scholars working on contemporary selfie culture demonstrate, the genre contains the potential to capture and reveal complex dimensions of identity including sexuality, gender, taste, class and power.[12] Here the performative rather than normative dimension of selfie culture emerges, placing the genre in line with the rich historical lineage of performative political documentary work that emerged in the 1980s and 90s around issues of identity, gender and sexuality. In the same way that the Marlon Riggs's landmark autobiographical film *Tongues Untied* (Marlon Riggs, US, 1989) raised the issue of race and homosexuality before a mainstream, PBS audience in the 1990s, so the various feeds and memes documenting gender reassignment and transformation bring the issue on scene before a widespread audience on Instagram. Riggs's film, moreover, appeared alongside a number of similar texts which blended personal, autobiographical stories with broader social and political issues, including Rea Tajiri's *History and Memory* (Rea Tajiri, US, 1991), Tom Joslin and Mark Massis's *Silverlake Life* (Tom Joslin and Peter Friedman, US, 1993), Marlon Fuentes's *Bontoc Eulogy* (Marlon Fuentes, US, 1995), as well as others.

Photography

The Instagram chapter within the history of photography and documentary demonstrates its clear connection to the longer technological and cultural evolution of the medium. As a widespread amateur practice it follows from the roll film and the $1 Brownie camera that Kodak introduced at the turn of the century. As Patricia Zimmerman points out, these innovations both pushed photography from a specialised technology utilised by professionals to a widespread practice of amateur hobbyists, a group we would now refer to as 'users'.[13] For Adam Levin its square format and 'instant' results owe an obvious debt to the handheld, all-in-one ease of the Polaroid.[14] These historical precedents demonstrate that still photography was in many ways the first mass market form of mass media. The move by entrepreneurs such as George Eastman and Charles Land to simplify photographic technology and market it to a mass public, in modern terms democratising or consumerising the technology, makes it an important precursor to the emergence of device-driven user-generated content over the last decade. Indeed, the strategy within social media to allow for mass content sharing relies of course on the ability of the masses to create and distribute content easily and cheaply. Tools like the Brownie, and eventually the Polaroid, solved the first part of this equation. Their handheld descendent, the smartphone, solved the second.

But while current practice owes a solid debt to this historical legacy, it is also critical to attend to the radical shift that tools like Instagram signify. It is difficult to overstate the impact of social media and mobile technology on photographic practice, not to mention the industry behind it. While the break between the analogue and digital phases of photography generated a great deal of discussion about the 'nature' of photography and the fate of indexicality, the break between the digital camera and the cameraphone is equally dramatic. Since the emergence of the iPhone in 2008, Apple has claimed that it makes the world's number one camera, and Kodak and Polaroid have both gone into bankruptcy. Where the move to digital eliminated the relatively high cost of analogue film and provided instant feedback, the cameraphone ensures ready access to a camera at all times. As Heidi Rae Cooley points out, the move towards 'mobile screenic devices' troubles the easy distinction between amateur/professional (now everyone can 'publish' their work) and alters standards of aesthetics and subject matter.[15] Cooley's account of early mobile imaging, published presciently in a pre-iPhone era, argues that users of early cameraphones and other handheld devices participate in a form of 'self-evidencing', incessantly capturing fragmentary and ephemeral images of experiences and objects in their environments 'tactile vision'. While this might have produced an accumulation of autobiographical fragments, for Cooley these collections operated according to the logic of the database rather than the logic of the linear narrative. This emphasis on the database logic of online photography is one that persists throughout discussions of its evolution, but one that I argue Instagram directly overturns.

Indeed, as the barriers between the moment of capture and the moment of exhibition slowly fell away, several distinct phases in online digital photography emerged. Where early sites like Ofoto and Snapfish enabled users to upload digital and analogue images into albums for printing or sharing via email, later sites like Flickr emerged in the early days of social networking as platforms for users to upload, share and comment on one another's photos. Instead of treating user uploads like private material, Flickr approached them as parts of a massive, open user-generated database of content, allowing novel combinations and collections of images to emerge.

Instagram, on the other hand, conceived of and launched in a post-Facebook, post-iPhone moment, flips the group/individual hierarchy. Unlike Flickr and other sites intended to be the final destination for images that had travelled from camera to computer to website, Instagram emerged on the mobile iOS platform as a way for users to quickly edit photos shot on their iPhones and share them to other social networks like Twitter and Facebook. Rather than a large pool of curated images tagged by users according to specific subjects, the core of Instagram is the image stream and the strong connection between a particular image and an individual's profile on whatever social platform it might eventually populate. The introduction of the wide angle, front facing camera on the iPhone 4 and other competing devices on the Android platform, turned the screens of these devices into mirrors, enabling users to compose at arm's length and capture until the device was full. Connected to a profile driven channel of distribution, the selfie, as we currently think of it, was born.

Social Networking

The selfie's rise to prominence as a cultural form can be attributed to the simultaneous rise of social networking as both a dedicated activity and a general mode of online engagement. Beyond the major platforms like Facebook and Twitter, social engagement is now a constituent part of digital culture more broadly. As José van Dijck points out in her history of social media, what she calls the 'culture of connectivity' stretches from the larger sources of user-generated content like YouTube and Wikipedia, to what she calls trading and marketing sites like Amazon, Ebay, Groupon and Craigslist, to what she further identifies as the play and game sites like SIMS, World of Warcraft, Second Life and others.[16,17] While this already encompasses a major portion of the webtraffic today, it still ignores the social angle built into other major sites like Netflix and Spotify which invite us to connect and share with friends, not to mention the longstanding social environment that emerges in various community forums and usergroups. As this last example illustrates, the history of sociality in online media is much longer than the history of social media proper, stretching all the way back to the earliest newsgroups and discussion boards.[18]

While few if any of these particular sites or communities identifies itself as a social network in a strict sense, they all invite or enable individuals to come together and interact in some fashion through networked technologies, and as part of this require each user to create a unique identity or profile. A constituent part of the current profile is the inclusion of an image or icon to identify oneself visually, hence the need for picture of the self, or a selfie. As the Internet has become increasingly social, the selfie itself has risen to prominence as an icon of the necessary individuation the culture of connectivity requires.

Given its focus on photography, Instagram is perhaps the natural environment for the selfie to thrive apart from the social networking trend that propelled it to prominence. But beyond Instagram's relationship to photography more generally, it is worth lingering on the relationship between social media and the culture of narcissism which the selfie has come to symbolise. Social media as a cultural phenomenon suffers from a somewhat mixed reputation. While the longer history of social media is beyond the scope of my discussion here, I would briefly point to the emergence of Web 2.0, often cited as the starting point of modern social network, which engendered a great deal of utopian theory about the power that novel technologies like blogs, wikis and other platforms gave individuals.[19] The honeymoon, however, was short-lived, as the criticism heaped on the selfie I described earlier indicates. Like the wider Internet which preceded it, social media seems to have fallen into the same contradictory paradox that Wendy Chun first described in *Control and Freedom: Power and Paranoia in the Age of Fiber Optics*, inspiring a mixture of mutually reinforcing optimism and loathing. As Trebor Scholz and others have pointed out, user-generated content is in many ways synonymous with free labour, turning newly birthed 'authors' and creators into 'products' sold to advertisers. And as Evgeny Morozov has demonstrated, its apolitical nature is perhaps more suited to 'solutions' than 'revolutions'.[20]

Instagram, moreover, is the most apolitical of social networks. Unlike Twitter and Facebook, Instagram has never been credited, even rhetorically, with spawning a social revolution.[21] It seems more a 'selfie' network than a social network, self-obsessed rather than outwardly, politically focused. While I do not hope to answer all of the charges laid at the feet of social media, it is worth keeping in mind who is implied when the label of narcissism is applied. As the historian Elizabeth Lunbeck demonstrates, the diagnosis, like so many other psychopathologies, comes down to us from Sigmund Freud, who primarily associated the problem with women and a feminised quality in men.[22] As narcissism transformed from an individual pathology to a social malady in the consumer culture of mid-century America, critics like Christopher Lasch maintained the gendered distinction, counting among its symptoms stereotypically female obsession with physical appearance, fashion, shopping and celebrity gossip. These became the outward symbols of a generationally inward focus. According to Lunbeck, this is the interpretive legacy in which our contemporary understanding of narcissism originates. Her discussion is critical to understanding who the selfie's critics are targeting when they dismiss the selfie as an outward sign of self-obsession rather than an empowered act of self-expression and authorship.

And this same gendered association holds with social media more generally. Consider, for example, contemporary anxieties around adolescent social media. According to the parenting advice site Common Sense, social media's 'redflag' behaviours include 'pitfalls such as drama, cyberbullying, and oversharing (sexting)'.[23] While these dangers can obviously affect teens regardless of gender, it is difficult not to hear overtones of mean girls and teen porn. Lest we miss the cue, the article is helpfully illustrated with an image of a young woman sitting outside and staring anxiously at her phone. If the selfie is an emblem of all that is wrong with social media and our wider culture more generally, then it seems we have young millennial women to blame.

Instagram as Serial Autobiography

The expressive power of the individual image to capture an individual's identity now leads us to consider the narrative threads that begin to emerge when a stream of these images are linked together. Instagram's emphasis on the photo stream, and its 'instant' appearance on other social media timelines, binds it more firmly with a traditional notion of individual identity, temporal linearity and serial progression. While Nadav Hochman and Lev Manovich recently pointed out the inherent fuzziness in Instagram's presentation of this timeline (for example, there are no timestamps), it remains nonetheless bound to a fixed temporal progression from past to present.[24] This temporal dimension of the platform as well as its exclusive organisation of the profiles of individual users outlines a fundamental oversight of much of the scholarship on digital photography. That is, discussions tend to focus on either the individual image, that is, the selfie, or they focus on the broader collection, that is, the database. Occasionally, a project like Manovich's own SelfieCity.net will even attempt to do both, that is collecting a database of individual selfies and organising them by city. While both approaches have their merits, neither is entirely able to account for the way in which Instagram privileges the stream over the individual image and centralises this stream around the individual user. This emphasis is what enables Instagram's autobiographical potential. But it also underscores the need to look beyond established categories towards other organisational schema to account for the mode of expression we encounter there.

Outside of the #hashtag, a self-tagging system borrowed from Twitter, there is no way to sort or search images on Instagram other than the default timeline offered on a user's profile. And while the #hashtag loosely resembles Flickr's more robust tagging feature, it operates on the logic of the meme which it was intended to capitalise on and facilitate. As spontaneous trends which emerge and either catch on or fade away, memes are a transitory, amorphous collection of practices that have no single author. This would seem to put memes at odds with the strong identity connection that I am claiming Instagram engenders. Indeed, as Kriss Ravetto-Biagioli has pointed out, memes associated with the group Anonymous are intended to destabilise established categories of individuality, collectivity and recognisable identity.[25] Instagram memes, of which the selfie trend is a prime example, are the polar opposite. Rather than acting as a cover to shield one's identity, trending hashtags are often used to raise one's profile or collect additional followers. Participation in memes like #bestofsummer or #newyears are opportunities to distinguish one's individuality even as they signify participation in an ephemeral collective. Instagram emphasises the 'me' in meme, as it were.

But this desire for greater visibility on the site further enhances the autobiographical potential of the timeline. One actively and consistently populates one's stream (an individual user's contributions) in order to remain an active presence in the feed of one's followers (the flow of images comprising contributions by the group one follows). The push to 'feed one's followers' gives the images the same ephemeral, disposable feel that for many defines digital photography.[26] And yet, these frequent updates also add to the permanent size of the individual photostream, giving additional depth to the record of one's activities and experiences. While the focus is always on a permanent sense of 'now', the by-product is a more complete documentary record of one's output arranged from past to present. In the grid view, this record offers a type of timelapse portrait of one's activity. One might even experience a stream comprised exclusively of selfies as a sort of timelapse progression of physical fitness, ageing, pregnancy and as I mentioned earlier, gender transformation.

The typical Instagram stream, moreover, is far more varied than a simple set of selfies. While the selfie is a common, prominent mode, one often finds them tucked in alongside images taken of and with friends and family members, landscapes and other more traditional genres of amateur, domestic photography. Once again, there is no denying that these images often evince the same travel trophy collecting or bourgeois badging that has been present throughout the history of photography. A picture of oneself in front of some a landmark like the Eiffel Tower or posing with one's friends on a ski lift are obvious attempts to mark one's belonging to particular social class or sub-group.[27] Certain genres of images mark, or perhaps market, a specific lifestyle, hobby or personality in the same manner that video shot with a GoPro camera signifies identification with an active lifestyle and participation in a variety extreme sports. People who practise yoga, for example, will often post photos documenting a specific pose for the amusement, imitation and encouragement of their followers. Such images simultaneously demonstrate specific achievements as well as an ongoing process of aspirational becoming. They simultaneously declare 'I did this' but also 'I am the type of person who does these types of things'. This development over time and the effort to define oneself marks the resonance between the Instagram stream and other modes of autobiographical narrative.

This wider variety also critically distinguishes the Instagram stream from the photo-a-day for x number of days type projects that Jill Walker Rettberg describes in her recent book on digital autobiographical practice. Rettberg places the work of established photographers like Suzanne Szucs as well as the amateur practitioners who aggregate selfies into timelapse videos on YouTube in a genre she calls the 'serial selfie'.[28] Unlike the prescribed, rigidly defined temporality and format of such projects, the ephemera captured on Instagram feels far more varied but also far more intentional. Rather than a strict regimen that dictates a temporal requirement (a photo per day) or outlines a specific subject matter (all of one's meals), all of the images in one's Instagram feed are a product of the desire to share something with a wider audience. This is where the gram in the name Instagram becomes a critical component. Whereas Insta is an obvious connection to the 'Instamatic' tradition in photography and its roots in the Polaroid (something also echoed in the app's icon), the gram indicates a connection with the telegram, pointing to a mode of communication and, in the context of social networking, broadcasting. Rather than a private daily diary or set of recordings at pre-defined instants, Instagram photos are intentionally broadcast to an audience as a series of narrative instalments.

But if, as I am claiming, the stream is more narrative than database in its form, what particular narrative form does it adopt? The open-ended, unfolding self-documentation it offers resembles in many ways the modern serial narrative, a form currently enjoying a resurgent moment of cultural popularity as evidenced by high-concept series like *Breaking Bad* (US, 2008), *Mad Men* (US, 2007) or *The Wire* (US, 2002), or in audio form in podcasts like the *This American Life* spinoff 'Serial'. As Christine Geraghty has pointed out, serial narratives work against the dominant Aristotelian form of a clean narrative arc of beginning/middle/end within a digestible time format by offering complex alterations of temporality, spatiality and causality.[29] Studying the long form serial narrative of the soap opera, Geraghty demonstrates that characters can appear and disappear almost at will, forcing entire narrative threads to be re-written or re-imagined. Seen in this light, the Instagram stream offers, in fits and starts, a set of similar instalments that follow the adventures of a particular protagonist as they move through disparate spaces alongside an array of minor characters and props. As relationships are documented, these other characters can appear and play a prominent role in the images for an extended period, only to suddenly disappear and reappear. Searching for the hashtag #breakup and following some of the profiles found there will confirm what I am referring to here. The brute uncertainty of the future further mimics a type of mini-cliffhangers – forcing us to ponder 'what will happen next? will this image be the last image?'

The irregular appearance of Instagram instalments combined with the ready availability of one's past output further mimics the production and consumption of many modern serial texts. As critics have pointed out, the move away from a rigid broadcast schedule demanding as many as twenty-six episodes per season has allowed series like *The Sopranos* (US, 1999) or *The Wire* to focus on quality over quantity. This has also resulted in irregular production and release schedules, with several months or years separating seasons of these series. Similarly, many Instagram feeds progress in fits and starts, with long periods of no output being punctuated with brief bursts of high activity. The ability to quickly flip through an entire profile of images recorded over a series of months or even years simulates the practice of binge watching an entire series on DVD or through streaming services such as Netflix.

Beyond form, the Instagram stream also resembles the content of the serial narrative. As Jeffrey Sconce has argued in relation to contemporary serial television, long form narrative engages in what he argues is a form of world-building, establishing alternative narrative spaces for audiences to explore and inhabit like the recreated world of 1960s New York in *Mad Men*, or the fantasy world of vampires and other creatures in *Buffy the Vampire Slayer* (US, 1997).[30]

The documentary impulse at work on Instagram puts a non-fiction spin on the form of serial world building, offering us access not to a fictional world but rather to the social and historical worlds of its users, to paraphrase Bill Nichols's well known distinction between fiction and documentary.[31] Indeed, wandering through the profile of some users we can get a clear sense of that particular user's world, a world that is built out and expanded as further images are added. This sense of place does not itself manifest in the totalising, comprehensive view we can access through tools such as Google Earth and Google Street View. Instead, it arrives filtered via the particular, individual experience of the photographer, an amalgamation of world building and worldview as it emerges from a particular aesthetic sensibility. Looking at the profile of miss_etc, a graphic artist who records images in and around her home in Bordeaux, France, gives us an impression not so much of France per se, but rather of the very particular French world that her images describe and document. Although she never appears in the images on her feed (there is not a single selfie), one comes away with a sense of her particular world view, if not some facet of her identity. Somewhere between self-portrait and fiction, the aspirational narrative is a story that it is difficult to imagine taking shape on some other platform.

Even those only tangentially acquainted with Instagram will have noted by now that there is a prominent dimension of the site that I have thus far ignored, namely the benefit these images and their attendant metadata have for both Instagram and other agencies with access to this data. While acknowledging the potential for surveillance (and, following Gill, self-surveillance) that Instagram clearly offers, I would contend that this is not unique to this particular tool. Nor would I deny that users of the site enter into the same Faustian bargain of selling data and identity in exchange for the 'free services' that it offers, but this too is not unique to Instagram. The ubiquity of image making spawned by the cameraphone has enabled social media to function to some extent as 'socialised media': allowing alternative, image driven forms of social interaction even as it profits large corporations through the free labour of its citizens. This type of push–pull between community and commodity (or, community as commodity) has always haunted photography, marketed throughout much of the twentieth century as a way to preserve memories and those 'Kodak moments'.[32] At once a tool of artistic expression and state surveillance and control, photography offers a complex historical lineage as it moves onto new platforms powerfully capable of both extremes. But as I hope I have shown here, Instagram draws on a broader set of historical references than photography alone, integrating elements of non-fiction narrative as it has developed in literature and film. While the selfie may work as an emblem of this emergent mode of autobiography, isolating the selfie does not reveal the whole picture. Finally, the long history of autobiographical practice alerts us to the importance of considering the type of subjectivity that such gestures reveal, from Durer through to today. That is, we may not like the selfie and the broader culture of self-performance and self-branding that it symbolises, but we cannot ignore the extent to which this particular portrait is, after all, a portrait of ourselves.

NOTES

1. Galen Guengerich, 'Galen Guengerich: "selfie" culture promotes a degraded worldview', *Washington Post*, 31 January 2014. Available at <http://www.washingtonpost.com/local/galen-guengerich-selfie-culture-promotes-a-degraded-worldview/2014/01/31/cb444130-8942-11e3-916e-e01534b1e132_story.html > (last accessed 10 September 2015).
2. Victoria Wollaston, 'Selfies are "damaging" and leave young people vulnerable to abuse, claims psychologist', *Mail Online*, 2013, <http://www.dailymail.co.uk/sciencetech/article-2401017/Selfies-damaging-leave-young-people-vulnerable-abuse-claims-psychologist.html> (last accessed 18 September 2016).
3. Cindy Perman, 'Are millennials really the "me" generation?', *USA Today*, 2013, <http://www.usatoday.com/story/money/business/2013/08/24/millenials-time-magazine-generation-y/2678441/> (last accessed 18 September 2014).
4. Mark Bauerlein, *The Dumbest Generation: How the Digital Age Stupefies Young Americans and Jeopardizes Our Future (Or, Don't Trust Anyone Under 30)* (New York: TarcherPerigee, 2009); Sherry Turkle, *Alone Together: Why We Expect More from Technology and Less from Each Other* (New York: Basic Books 2012).

5. Rosalind Gill, 'Postfeminist media culture elements of a sensibility', *European Journal of Cultural Studies*, 10/2, 2007, pp. 147–66; Rosalind Gill and Andy Pratt, 'In the social factory? Immaterial labour, precariousness and cultural work', *Theory, Culture and Society*, 25/7–8, 2008, pp. 1–30.
6. Joseph Leo Koerner, *The Moment of Self-Portraiture in German Renaissance Art* (Chicago, IL: University of Chicago Press, 1993), pp. xv–xviii.
7. Celeste Brusati, 'Stilled lives: self-portraiture and self-reflection in seventeenth-century Netherlandish still-life painting', *Simiolus: Netherlands Quarterly for the History of Art*, 1990, pp. 168–82; Marsha Meskimmon, *The Art of Reflection: Women Artists' Self-Portraiture in the Twentieth Century* (New York: Columbia University Press, 1996).
8. Amelia Jones, 'The "eternal return": self-portrait photography as a technology of embodiment', *Signs*, 27/4, 2002, pp. 947–78.
9. Robin Kelsey and Blake Stimson (eds), *The Meaning of Photography*, The Clark Symposium (Williamstown, MA, and New Haven, CT: Sterling and Francine Clark Art Institute, 2008).
10. Alan Trachtenberg, *Classic Essays on Photography* (New Haven, CT: Leete's Island Books, 1980).
11. Geoffrey Batchen, 'Snapshots', *Photographies*, 1/2, 2008, pp. 121–42; Alice E. Marwick, *Status Update: Celebrity, Publicity, and Branding in the Social Media Age* (New Haven, CT: Yale University Press, 2013).
12. Theresa M. Senft and Nancy K. Baym, 'Selfies introduction ~ what does the selfie say? Investigating a global phenomenon', *International Journal of Communication*, 9, 2015, p. 19.
13. Patricia Rodden Zimmermann, *Reel Families: A Social History of Amateur Film* (Bloomington, IN: Indiana University Press, 1995), p. 32.
14. Adam Levin, 'The selfie in the age of digital recursion', *InVisibile Culture: An Electronic Journal of Visual Culture*, 20, 2014.
15. Heidi Rae Cooley, '"Identify"-ing a new way of seeing: amateurs, moblogs and practices in mobile imaging', *Spectator*, 21/1, 2004, pp. 65–79; Heidi Rae Cooley, 'It's all about the fit: the hand, the mobile screenic device and tactile vision', *Journal of Visual Culture*, 3/2, 2004, pp. 133–55; Heidi Rae Cooley, 'The autobiographical impulse and mobile imaging: toward a theory of autobiometry', in *Workshop Pervasive Image Capture and Sharing: New Social Practices and Implications for Technology at Ubicomp*, 2005, v, 11–14, <http://www.ht.sfc.keio.ac.jp/~tailor/ubicomp/mirror/ubicomp2005web/Ubicomp%202005/www.spasojevic.org/pics/PICS/autobiographical_impulse_and_mobile_imaging.pdf> (last accessed 14 September 2014).
16. José van Dijck's list of playable game sites includes things like Farmville and others; it seems to me that she misses the virtual world sites outside of the SIMS, a notable omission from her otherwise very comprehensive discussion. Suffice it to say that I think Instagram is another notable omission, for reasons which this article hopes to make clear.
17. José van Dijck, *The Culture of Connectivity: A Critical History of Social Media* (Oxford: Oxford University Press, 2013), p. 8.
18. Howard Rheingold, *The Virtual Community: Homesteading on the Electronic Frontier*, rev. ed. (Cambridge, MA: MIT Press, 1993); Fred Turner, *From Counterculture to Cyberculture: Stewart Brand, the Whole Earth Network, and the Rise of Digital Utopianism* (Chicago, IL: University of Chicago Press, 2008).
19. Clay Shirky, *Here Comes Everybody: The Power of Organizing Without Organizations* (New York: Penguin Press, 2009).
20. Trebor Scholz (ed.), *Digital Labor: The Internet as Playground and Factory* (New

York: Routledge, 2012); Evgeny Morozov, *The Net Delusion: The Dark Side of Internet Freedom* (New York: Public Affairs, 2011); Evgeny Morozov, *To Save Everything, Click Here: The Folly of Technological Solutionism* (New York: Penguin Books, 2014).
21. The potential for social networks to initiate, enhance or enervate existing social movements is a topic of ongoing debate. See *The Internet and Democracy - Evgeny Morozov, Jillian York, Deirdre Mulligan*, 2011, <http://www.youtube.com/watch?v=vbDFWWSyR38&feature=youtube_gdata_player> (last accessed 12 January 2012).
22. Elizabeth Lunbeck, *The Americanization of Narcissism* (Cambridge, MA: Harvard University Press, 2014), pp. 11–14.
23. Christine Elgersma, '9 social media red flags parents should know about', 2016, <https://www.commonsensemedia.org/blog/9-social-media-red-flags-parents-should-know-about> (last accessed 16 October 2016).
24. Nadav Hochman and Lev Manovich, 'Zooming into an Instagram city: reading the local through social media', *First Monday*, 18/7, 2013, <http://firstmonday.org/ojs/index.php/fm/article/view/4711> (last accessed 15 September 2014).
25. Kriss Ravetto-Biagioli, 'Anonymous social as political', *Leonardo Electronic Almanac*, 19/4, 2013, pp. 179–95.
26. Susan Murray, 'Digital images, photo-sharing, and our shifting notions of everyday aesthetics', *Journal of Visual Culture*, 7/2, 2008, pp. 147–63.
27. Marwick, *Status Update*.
28. Jill Walker Rettberg, *Seeing Ourselves Through Technology* (Basingstoke: Palgrave Macmillan, 2014), pp. 33–44, <http://www.palgraveconnect.com/doifinder/10.1057/9781137476661> (last accessed 1 January 2015).
29. Christine Geraghty, 'Continuous serial – a definition', in Richard Dyer et al., *Coronation Street* (London: British Film Institute, 1981).
30. Jeffrey Sconce, 'What If? Charting Television's New Textual Boundaries', in *Television after TV: Essays on a Medium in Transition*, ed. Lynn Spigel and Jan Olsson (Durham, NC: Duke University Press, 2004).
31. Bill Nichols, *Representing Reality* (Bloomington, IN: Indiana University Press, 1991), p. 112.
32. Nancy Martha West, *Kodak and the Lens of Nostalgia* (Charlottesville, VA: University Press of Virginia, 2000).

2. ARCHETYPE AND AUTHENTICITY: REFLECTIONS ON AMALIA ULMAN'S *EXCELLENCES & PERFECTIONS*

Cadence Kinsey

Between April and September 2014, the Argentine-born artist Amalia Ulman presented herself online as an 'Instagram Girl'.[1] Using popular hashtags from micro-celebrities on the social network, Ulman created a three-part performance work that explored how women present themselves online. Entitled *Excellences & Perfections*, the project saw Ulman take on the roles of 'cute girl', 'sugar baby' and 'life goddess', characters that were chosen, Ulman says, because 'they seemed to be the most popular trends online (for women)'.[2] By the final post of the project on 19 September 2014, Ulman had amassed 88,906 followers. At this point, Ulman revealed that the project had been a performance, rather than a record of real life, attracting criticism from individuals who had followed her account in good faith and posted messages of support in times of crisis. Feeling that they had in some way been lied to, these followers expressed what Ulman has described as a 'glitch' in social media: the concept of authenticity.[3]

In this chapter, I want to consider the importance of authenticity as a category for mediating the construction of gendered identity online. In particular, I want to think about how this category relates to the notion of performativity and the significance of this relationship for recent feminist art practices that engage modes of technological, and specifically digital, mediation. Focusing on Ulman's *Excellences & Perfections*, I hope to argue that current engagements with social media generate a series of tensions between presence and absence, visibility and invisibility, which are of long-standing and core concern within feminist art practice. Despite the fact that the discourses of social media from the last ten years have displaced the narrative that the Web offered a sphere of representation that is inherently detached from a material, physical or 'real' world, I do not wish to argue that platforms such as Facebook or Instagram now produce a friction-free relationship between on- and offline modes of representation. Instead, I hope to demonstrate that digital technologies continue to serve as a site of conflict, difficulty and ambiguity in relation to the question of representation.

Performing Authenticity

Amalia Ulman's Instagram performance *Excellences & Perfections* (Figure 1) began on 19 April 2014 with an post that stated simply 'Part 1', and was captioned 'Excellences & Perfections'. Constructed as a three-part narrative, the first stage of the performance featured a series of photographs characterised by their use of pale colours, white linen and daylight. Fresh-faced, and posing in delicate lingerie, the artist appears in these images adorned with the trappings of kawaii culture: rabbits, ribbons and strawberry-based cakes. Then, on 20 June, a post is made, featuring a photograph of Ulman in a toilet mirror with slicked, wet hair and a white dress, and a caption which reads 'Aw going on fancy date with my favourite person. some cocktails on the roof n swimming pool soooo excited.' This 'fancy date' turns out to be the setting for a break up, and later in the evening another post is made: 'don't be sad because its over, smile because it happened ~ after 3 years it has been time to move on i guess. there have been good and bad moments but i will remember the best bits. life goes on.'

At this point the performance moved into its second phase, marked by a change in the tone and style of the posts. The pastel colours are gradually replaced by darker shades of brown and gold, and we see images of the artist in increasingly sexually suggestive scenarios. Post break-up, Ulman appears to have begun working as an escort, and begins to share images of cash, gifts and drugs, as well as postoperative photographs from a breast augmentation surgical procedure. However, this new lifestyle rapidly appears to be unsustainable and, by 8 August, Ulman appears to reach crisis point. She posts short videos of herself crying, followed a few days later by a photograph of a heart drawn in snow accompanied by a message of apology to all those she had 'offended'. 'Everything came out from a soul full of pain, anger and darkness', the post reads, 'Thank you so much for being patient with me'.

Thus, the project had entered its third phase: recovery. Images depicting inspirational mottos, family time and avocados on brown toast are used to illustrate Ulman's desire to heal and amend her ways. She is now her 'real' self: neither the super-cute blonde girl who spends her time taking pictures of baby animals that she was during her relationship, nor the gold-digging pole dancer

Figure 1   Amalia Ulman, *Excellences & Perfections* (*Instagram update, 5 September 2014*), 2014. Image courtesy the artist and Arcadia Missa.

she became in the aftermath of the break-up. Instead, Ulman is now the kind of girl who wraps up in oversized cardigans with a latte in hand, looks after her baby cousin, and enjoys nourishing superfoods.

The performance winds down as Ulman enters into a new relationship. 'Isn't it nice to be taken care of', one post reads, accompanying a photograph of the artist and her supposed new boyfriend in matching fluffy white robes. His face is partially obscured, but Ulman stares into the smartphone held in front of her, wearing a fragile expression as they pose for a joint selfie; we do not meet her gaze. The performance finishes on 19 September, marked by a blank: a simple grey square. This post receives 142 likes.

At the centre of *Excellences & Perfections* are the comments that were posted to Instagram by Ulman's followers throughout the duration of the performance. Reading through them, it is clear that many of Ulman's followers reacted to the images that she was posting at face value. For example, in response to one post about the breast augmentation surgery, the comments included 'Sending ultra-healing vibes girl!', 'Well done, Kid. Rest', and 'How much did it cost'. Unaware that it was a performance, these followers did not know that the surgery had been simulated and these particular images cribbed from the social media feeds of other profiles. What I would like to suggest is that the comments are central to the performance because they reveal the forms of belief and expectation that structure our engagement with social media, which we might think about in the context of authenticity.

Authenticity has become a central motif within discussions of social media platforms because they generally require – or at least encourage – the use of real names and a single identity across integrated platforms in order to produce a one-to-one relationship between the online and the offline self.[4] Crucially, this relationship is often consolidated through the photographic image: both the profile photograph and the 'selfie' establish an interplay between text and image that invokes authenticity in its appeals to a specific, embodied identity. This marks a significant shift in ways of thinking not only about the Web but about digital modes of representation more generally. While the early Web was predominantly text-based and prioritised anonymity – a perceived site of privacy and piracy bolstered by the theoretical distinction between a 'real' world and a world of digital representations – the development of social media platforms around the mid-2000s reconfigured the Web as a regulated space built on the twin axes of trust and honesty.[5] As Mark Zuckerberg, the founder of Facebook, famously proclaimed: 'You have one identity . . . The days of you having a different image for your work friends or co-workers and for the other people you know are probably coming to an end pretty quickly . . . Having two identities for yourself is an example of a lack of integrity.'[6]

As the disjunction between the images of the fake surgery and the earnest comments suggest, *Excellences & Perfections* pushes against this narrative of consistency and coherence; something which has been discussed by the curator Melanie Bühler in terms of an undoing of the tropes of immediacy and intimacy associated with the 'selfie'.[7] What I would like to suggest, however, is that the performance should not simply be thought of as a fake or false representation: the postoperative images did not feature Ulman but they did show *someone*. But, perhaps even more significantly in the context of this discussion, the artist actually drew upon elements of her pre-existing social media output in order to construct the narrative, stating that she 'went for the artsy-tumblr-girl aesthetic first because it was closer to home and wouldn't be like too suspicious of a transformation'.[8] Thus, the suggestion here is that the 'one identity' paradigm is not simply undermined or overturned so much as used to exploit expectation and test trust. What is interesting about *Excellences & Perfections*, therefore, is not that it merely proposes the inauthenticity of social media, in contradistinction to an authentic offline world, so much as problematise the very concept of authenticity itself: hence the idea of a 'glitch'.

In this respect, it is significant that Ulman frames *Excellences & Perfections* specifically as a performance, since it invigorates the category with its multiple associations and inherent frictions and contradictions. Bühler, for example, has considered *Excellences & Perfections* alongside Sven Lütticken's theory of 'general performance', summarised as the 'normalized imperative to work at our lives while living to/through work'.[9] But, in troubling the concept of authenticity, *Excellences & Perfections* also plays with the notion of performance as attached to both originality in art – as per Peggy Phelan's model of 'representation without reproduction'[10] – and the forms of imitation or simulation associated with the theatre. The artist's body is used to both invoke presence while simultaneously inhabiting a persona. This is important because bringing together apparently contradictory models of performance in this way chimes with recent discussions around the representation of the self on social media. In the literatures of anthropology and sociology, the categories of authenticity and performativity are rarely opposed to one another but are rather understood as existing in dynamic, so that performative practices of self-representation in fact become integral to constructions such as the 'authentic self'. As the anthropologist Daniel Miller has argued,

> We need to move from overwrought, moralistic and simplistic arguments based on a dualism between online and offline to an appreciation that most people now engage with a mix of communication and identity platforms which usually include a multiplicity of online and offline identities without any clear break between these ... As studies become more contextualised it seems that the real lesson of online identity is not that it transforms identity but that it makes us more aware that offline identity was already more multiple, culturally contingent and contextual than we had appreciated.[11]

Of note here is the suggestion that we should not think of the 'one identity' paradigm as promoting a single or stable subject, authenticated by the body, so much as a way of locating authenticity in the degree of coherence between online and offline performance.[12] One important consequence of this is that it resists theorising authenticity in terms of essentialising categories: although the 'one identity' paradigm encourages a re-synchronisation of online and offline practices of self-identification, you do not have to define yourself online according to your biological being. Thus, on social media platforms, authenticity is not necessarily produced through the embodied specificity of one's physical being, but through the extent to which performative practices of self-actualisation cohere across multiple sites, whether that may be on- or offline.

This way of thinking authenticity through the notion of performance is also a recurring motif in the work of a number of other artists of Ulman's generation. For example, a Facebook status update posted by the New York-based artist Bunny Rogers in March 2014 reads: 'Performing yourself should fit like a well-tailored suit. Should feel loose in the shoulders, should feel natural stop conflating acting with insincerity as if honesty exists.'[13] As with *Excellences & Perfections*, there is a sense here in which we are being asked to consider more than a straightforward division between authenticity and performativity, structured through a prior separation between the online and the offline. What

I would like to suggest is that the self-image is central to this formulation, serving both as a site that authenticates experience through presence while simultaneously drawing attention to how that experience was always already mediated through culture. This, of course, has a strongly gendered dimension and in what follows I want to further develop the construction of the concept of authenticity on social media in relation to the gendered archetypes explored by Ulman.

Described as responding to the demands of social media to act in a certain way, *Excellences & Perfections* can be said to illustrate the way in which authenticity, or coherence between on- and offline performance, is constructed not simply through representation but through expectation.[14] In the realisation of the performance narrative, Ulman made extensive and judicious use of stylistic markers – such as types of clothes, food or music – in order to reproduce highly gendered paradigms: the naif, the 'empowered' pole dancer, and the life-goddess. Although distinct, these were unified through a dominant, and indeed defining, aesthetic logic that has become the axis around which much of Ulman's practice has revolved: prettiness.[15]

This is directly figured in several moments from the performance, for example in a post made on 1 June featuring the artist posing in front of a mirror wearing a floral headband and a white T-shirt, with the words 'pretty please' in pink and black block lettering across the front (Figure 2). Or in the comments thread attached to a post from the 24 August, which exclaim 'Perfect!

Figure 2   Amalia Ulman, *Excellences & Perfections* (*Instagram update, 1 June 2014*), 2014. Image courtesy the artist and Arcadia Missa.

Pretty :-)' in response to an image of the artist sitting in what she describes in the post as an '#ethnic #eclectic' café. As in other works by Ulman – including the exhibition *Moist Forever* (2013) held at Future Gallery in Berlin and the Skype-lecture-performance 'Buyer, Walker, Rover' (2013) held at the Regional State Archives in Gothenburg – prettiness serves as an indicator of taste that is connected to both gender and class. It represents an aspirational but ultimately bland femininity: that which is simply 'pretty' possesses a sub-visibility that is not only the mark of the historical association of femininity with passivity, but also of acceptability, moderation and restraint. In this, prettiness stands for the exertion of a violent normativity that is, ultimately, exclusionary. As such, it is an aesthetic logic that belies its ugly core values.

What I would like to suggest is that it is this logic of prettiness that frames the entire narrative of *Excellences & Perfections*, which follows the fall and redemption of the 'good girl'. Opposite to the 'bad boy', the 'good girl' stands for a form of correctness that permeates the entire performance, evidenced by the number of comments posted by Ulman's followers that read simply 'good' or 'this is good'. Here, correctness is correlated to the construction of authenticity since by doing the 'right' thing, or behaving in the 'right' way, Ulman's Instagram account presented a believable character, achieving significant popularity and visibility along the way. Basing her characters on the most popular trends online for women, Ulman had fleshed out a blueprint of femininity that was subsequently valued, in a tautological loop, according to its alignment with these pre-existing ideals: the more closely the images that Ulman posted corresponded to an existing trope or paradigm, the more her popularity increased. Paradoxically, then, it was Ulman's ability to replicate an ideal type that lent the project credibility: according to Ulman, relying on a character and a narrative that had been seen before allowed 'people to map the content with ease'.[16] As the project description stated, 'These images are excessive, but also believable – because they're so familiar.'[17] In *Excellences & Perfections*, Ulman thus presents an interesting tension in that her use of feminine archetypes, fleshed out through a familiar narrative and the appropriate props and apparel, paradoxically invoked an idea of authenticity.

The reproduction of specific types in *Excellences & Perfections* is particularly important because it resonates closely with the idea that the interface architectures of social media structure identity by funnelling user profiles through increasingly standardised formats: one may add various items of personal information (name, date of birth, hometown, school, gender, likes and dislikes) but there is relatively little control over *how* that information is presented by the platform.[18] Although this kind of 'drop down identity' represents a form of heteronomy that might appear to run counter to the very narratives of authenticity and self-determination promoted by social media platforms, this should not be thought of simply as a top-down process. After all, individuals will already have made decisions about the selection and presentation of certain kinds of information, often in relation to the imagined quality and quantity of the responses that the information may elicit. Notably, standardisation has a role to play in this since it facilitates the accrual of likes and shares on social media by enhancing connectivity, particularly through devices such as the hashtag. In other words the standardisation, and subsequent homogenisation, in the architecture of social media profiles should be thought of in tandem with social, cultural and commercial pressures, such as the predetermined selections one makes based on the acceptable genres, ideas and modes of expression of one's peers. As a 2013 study published in the journal *Media Psychology* argued, organising one's self-presentation according to expectation is unlikely to generate heterogeneity.[19] Thus the presentation of oneself as conforming to a particular type or trope on social media is often self-reflexively instituted as a normalising procedure, and not merely imposed by the platforms themselves. The London-based artist Jesse Darling, who is represented by the same gallery as Ulman, has described this process as a 'form of Stockholm Syndrome: when the captive learns to love the captor as a mechanism of survival'.[20]

This replication, or even intensification, of a normalising, homogenising process of constructing the subject has been most acutely problematised in the arena of gender. As multiple analyses of Web use over the last twenty or so years have argued, the Web tends to reflect and even amplify highly traditional narratives, behaviours and forms of expression in relation to gender.[21] By reproducing some of the most enduring and problematic representations of the female subject – which, although derived from popular Instagram hashtags, correlated to offline stereotypes such as the 'sugar baby' – *Excellences & Perfections* therefore illuminates something of this process. This can be thought of as an area of long-standing interest for Ulman, as other projects have also explored the way in which certain images gain popularity online over and above others. In her 2012 essay 'f/f', for example, Ulman looked at the circulation of images of the female body on the South American social networking sites Fotocumbia and Fotolog.[22] However, where *Excellences & Perfections* is perhaps distinct is that it additionally presented a sharp reflection of Ulman's own role as the artist *ingénue*. Launching the project at Frieze Art Fair in London as part of the New Museum's First Look programme in October 2014, Ulman asked in a performance-lecture: 'How is a female artist supposed to look like? How is she supposed to behave? The prices of artworks grow in relation to your looks.'[23] Given the global interest in *Excellences & Perfections* from museums and galleries and the art press, we might argue that, perhaps, little difference may lie between how power, privilege and prestige are constructed on the online networks of social media and those of the art world.

How Not to Be Seen

Although I have been arguing that *Excellences & Perfections* highlights this deeply regressive, and indeed aggressive, system of rewarding such normative representations, the performance nonetheless drew criticism for failing to exceed problematic tropes of representation and exploiting the already privileged visibility of a body that is young, white, female and attractive. This apparent inability or unwillingness to irritate gendered and racialised paradigms of representation has generated significant debate not only in relation to Ulman but a much wider circle of artists who have also explored the relationship between the 'social Web' and the self-image. In the following section, what I therefore want to focus on is the contemporary significance of the debate around visibility and its relationship to historic iterations, and situate *Excellences & Perfections* in this larger context.

Although *Excellences & Perfections* has perhaps achieved the greatest visibility, including articles in the mainstream press and inclusion in major museum exhibitions, it is one of a number of works of performance that have utilised social media.[24] Ann Hirsch's early and important work *Scandalishious* (2008–9), for example, comprised a series of performances based on her research into online modes of self-representation. This research took the form of YouTube videos which the artist made of herself, at times dancing provocatively – and often humorously – and at others offering diaristic commentary on her everyday experiences in the tradition of the vlog. Posting as 'Caroline', a Syracuse University freshman, Hirsch was able to retain a degree of anonymity in an otherwise highly exposed situation. As with *Excellences & Perfections*, Hirsch's *Scandalishious* has been discussed in terms of both a discrepancy between life on- and offline and a parodic representation of the so-called 'camwhore'. However, as Hirsch has described in interviews, the YouTube videos were not produced as a parody but as explorations of the artist's own desire to be represented as desirable.[25] What is significant about this is that *Scandalishious* incorporated a critical negotiation of the artist's own relationship to such gendered paradigms.

Nevertheless, Hirsch, like Ulman, has been included in exhibitions that have appeared to uncritically replicate these paradigms. Notable examples include *Body Anxiety* (2015), an online exhibition curated by Leah Schrager and Jennifer Chan, and *Lonely Girl* (2013), which was held at Martos Gallery in New York. Upon opening, both of these exhibitions were framed by discussions around so-called 'selfie feminism' and the concomitant criticism that it has resolutely failed to speak with, to or for intersecting categories such as race, since the majority of the artists included in both of these exhibitions were young, white and cis female.[26] As such, the presentation of these artists together as a bloc served merely to reinforce the visibility of this type, rather than critique or undo it. As Aria Dean has recently written in a much-cited article for *The New Enquiry*,

> there is a shared belief that the control afforded through the act of self-imaging is invaluable; nothing less, in fact, than *the primary* feminist tool for resistance ... I don't intend to advocate for a politic of anti-representation or a fundamental refusal of the image. However, being of the mind that to be Black in particular is to be at once surveilled and in the shadows, hypervisible and invisible, an either/or theory of representation seems unhelpful. So long as the feminist politic with the most traction enjoys this uncomplicated relationship to visibility, it will only sink further into aestheticisation and depoliticisation. As long as its framework is derived primarily from its racist, classist, capitalist 'lean-in' equality-core (#freethenipple) predecessor, we – specifically Black women, but also perhaps all of us here whose bodies and selves are failed by a second-wave capitalist, classist, racist, cissexist, ableist feminism – do ourselves a disservice by considering it in the least bit viable.[27]

Indeed, by replicating an image of the artist that conformed to highly normative or idealised categories these exhibitions appeared to replay some of the most entrenched tropes of second-wave feminism. This was particularly acute in the exhibitions' overwhelming emphasis on the self-image. For a number of performance artists of the 1960s and 1970s, the self-image had served as a reparative within a discursive framework that was largely structured around a subject–object binary, in which, for example, a subject split between public and private duties might be reconciled through the overarching category 'work' – sublimating reproduction into production – or in which a subject whose naturalised condition as 'embodied' was nonetheless simultaneously perceived as absent, mediated by processes of acculturation that substituted for its lack. Within such debates, the self-image could be utilised as a tool for reconciling a subjectivity that was at once both an active agent (the subject who *makes* art) and an objectified body (the subject *of* art); a slippage captured, for example, by Carolee Schneemann's statement that 'I am both image maker and image' or in Hannah Wilke's notion of a 'performalist self-portrait'.[28] However, in such examples, the self-image confronted a subject–object binary through relatively homogeneous categories of identity that neglected those at the margins of those categories, particularly in relation to the concept of work.[29] As such, the self-image was, and still is, simply not able to sufficiently problematise the issue of visibility and the inherent privileges associated with it.

This, of course, is where a work such as *Excellences & Perfections* is differentiated in that it actually stresses the *limitations* of the self-image in this respect. After all, there is little that appears redemptive in Ulman's use of the device. Nevertheless, the work has the potential to lend itself to these debates as an easy shorthand for the reinscription of this problematic. Thus, in recent years the question of visibility has become central to this generation of artists working with or around networked communications technologies such as the Web, with many producing work in which the image of the body is not merely represented but doubled, diffused or dispersed in some way. Key examples in this respect include Hannah Black's video *My Bodies* (2014), Hito Steyerl's *HOW NOT TO BE SEEN: A Fucking Didactic Educational .MOV File* (2013), Jesse Darling's performance *Habeas Corpus Ad Subjiciendum: Or, Body of Work? You're Looking at It* (2012), Bunny Rogers' installation *Self Portrait (Mourning Mop)* (2013), and Andrea Crespo's series *SIS* (2015–16). Posed against works such as *Excellences & Perfections* and *Scandalishious*, these perhaps invite the observation that recent art that engages with questions of identity and representation should be thought about in terms of a tendency to either *use* or *refuse* the image of the body.

However, what I would like to argue is that these two strategies are much less readily opposed than might initially appear. Rather than collapsing into a strategy of either/or, decisions about whether to use or refuse the image of the body might be more productively read as a dialogue around the conditions of representation of the body. Indeed, what all of these practices are grappling with is not a binary of exposure and concealment, of visibility and invisibility, of public and private, but a subject interpellated through technological and cultural mediation: these artists share a concern not only with the construction of gender online, the sexualisation of online culture and, even, the narratives of feminism itself, but also with drawing attention to a highly ambiguous politics of visibility and the relation of categories of identity to embodiment. In this respect, it is precisely the idea of performativity that unites them in their exploration of a subject always already mediated by social and technological infrastructures. Certainly, these infrastructures provide a very particular framework for the difficulty in reconciling with visibility, since the Web is itself often understood through a binary of visibility–invisibility, where issues of privacy and surveillance exist in parallel with the internalisation of visibility as ideal condition. As the curator Katrina Sluis has argued,

> Giving up one's anonymity is increasingly a necessary precondition for social participation, under technological conditions in which security and marketing progressively go hand in hand. This has become possible because, as Zygmunt Bauman suggests, '[t]he condition of being watched and seen has . . . been reclassified from a menace into a temptation'.[30]

As we have already seen, this regime of visibility is foregrounded in *Excellences & Perfections* through Ulman's exploitation of popularity rankings by playing to type. Thus, the thematics of visibility in such a work criss-crosses the formation of the subject within late capitalism, the production of art and the mechanics of historic feminist performance. As with the notion of authenticity, the exploration of visibility is an exploration of how regimes of identity intersect with wider socio-technological structures. Although *Excellences & Perfections* might not be able to overturn or resolve the problematic relationship between the self-image and a particular politics of visibility, it is important to recognise that the performance is not blindly complicit with that politics.

To conclude, then, I would like to suggest that *Excellences & Perfections* reaches beyond the debates around the critical purchase of the self-image within feminist performance to be suggestive of a more pervasive condition of the mediated subject. By drawing attention to a 'glitch' in social media, Ulman's performance sets centre stage the way in which categories such as authenticity and performativity do not readily map over a divide between the on- and the offline. As such, Ulman's work can be understood as part of a widespread dismantling of the so-called digital divide not only in art, as artists work with increasing fluidity across or between digital and physical media, but also in digital culture more broadly, as smart phones, mobile Internet and Cloud computing have integrated the Web into our everyday lives to an extent previously unknown.[31] In undermining any simplistic opposition between the two realms, Ulman challenges us to consider not just the technological but also the social forces that feed into problematic and uncomfortable representations of the female subject. At the heart of this problematic is the familiar story of a body produced not only through fantasy but the fantasy of reality, figured here as a tension between authenticity and archetype. Although authenticity is usually more commonly understood as an intensification of the individual, while the archetype could be seen as an eradication of it, it is precisely the tension between the two that is central to the functioning of social media and perhaps even constitutes the defining condition of the subject on such platforms.

Notes

1. The performance has been captured in its entirety by the social media archiving tool Colloq, developed by the organisation Rhizome. It is available to view via the following weblink: <http://www.newmuseum.org/exhibitions/view/amalia-ulman-excellences-perfections> (last accessed December 2016).
2. Cadence Kinsey, 'The Instagram artist who fooled thousands', *BBC Culture*, 7 March 2016. Available at <http://www.bbc.com/culture/story/20160307-the-instagram-artist-who-fooled-thousands> (last accessed December 2016).
3. Ulman used the term 'glitch' in an artists talk given at Showroom MAMA in Rotterdam on 22 May 2015 as part of a two-day symposium entitled *The Internetional*. In this talk, Ulman described how her followers felt that they had somehow been tricked. Further descriptions can be found in Cadence Kinsey

and Rózsa Farkas, 'Being visible', *Photoworks Annual*, issue 22, pp. 82–95; and Melanie Bühler, 'Remnants of the index: hanging on to photographic values – the selfie', *Still Searching...*, 20 April 2015. Available at <https://www.fotomuseum.ch/en/explore/still-searching/articles/27009_remnants_of_the_index_hanging_on_to_photographic_values_the_selfie> (last accessed December 2016).
4. For a discussion of authenticity in relation to social media see Georgia Gaden and Delia Dumitrica, 'The "real deal": strategic authenticity, politics and social media', *First Monday*, 20/1, 5 January 2015. Available at <http://firstmonday.org/ojs/index.php/fm/article/view/4985> (last accessed December 2016).
5. The anthropologist Daniel Miller has outlined this historic shift, taking into account specific technological changes such as the introduction of social networking sites in distinction to a broadly undefined 'Internet'. For this discussion see Daniel Miller, 'What is the relationship between identities that people construct, express and consume online and those offline?', *Future Identities: Changing identities in the UK – the next 10 years* (London, Government Office for Science, January 2013). For an example of how digital media have previously been thought about in the context of an abstraction from the physical world, see Kevin Robbins, 'The virtual unconscious in post-photography', *Science as Culture*, 3/1, 1992, pp. 99–115.
6. Mark Zuckerberg, quoted in in David Kirkpatrick, *The Facebook Effect: The Real Inside Story of Mark Zuckerberg and the World's Fastest Growing Company* (New York: Simon and Schuster, 2010), p. 199. For a discussion of the 'one identity' paradigm see José van Dijck, '"You have one identity": performing the self on Facebook and LinkedIn', *Media, Culture and Society*, 35/2, 2013, pp. 199–215.
7. See Bühler, 'Remnants of the index', p. 2.
8. See Kinsey, 'The Instagram artist'.
9. See Bühler, 'Remnants of the index'.
10. For a discussion of this see Peggy Phelan, *Unmarked: The Politics of Performance* (London: Routledge, 1993).
11. See Miller, in *Future Identities*.
12. For a further discussion of this see Rob Cover, 'Performing and undoing identity online: social networking, identity theories and the incompatibility of online profiles and friendship regimes', *Convergence*, 18/2, 2012, pp. 177–93.
13. Bunny Rogers quoted in Rózsa Zita Farkas, 'Bunny Rogers', *Cura Magazine*, no. 19, Winter 2015, pp. 124–37.
14. The press release for the performance reads: 'For three months, [Ulman] allowed her profiles to be exactly what social media seems to demand – that she be a "Hot Babe"'. See 'Amalia Ulman Excellences & Perfections' [press release]. No date. Available at <http://www.newmuseum.org/exhibitions/view/amalia-ulman-excellences-perfections> (last accessed December 2016).
15. For a further discussion of the concept of 'prettiness' in Ulman's work see Cadence Kinsey, 'Taste-y: an essay & interview in two parts (w/Amalia Ulman)', in Rózsa Farkas and Tom Clark (eds), *Networked, Every Whisper is a Crash Upon My Ears* (London: Arcadia_Missa Publications, 2014), pp. 56–73.
16. This was the description used by Ulman in a performance lecture for Frieze Art Fair in London, which was hosted by Rhizome as part of the talk series *Do You Follow? Art in Circulation*. See Amalia Ulman, *Do You Follow? Art in Circulation #3* [panel discussion], Selfridges Old Hotel, London, 15 October 2104. Available at <https://www.youtube.com/watch?v=EgSlxB3bwO8> (last accessed December 2016).
17. See 'Amalia Ulman Excellences & Perfections' [press release], no date.
18. For a discussion of these ideas see van Dijck, '"You have one identity"'; Heather Horst, 'Aesthetics of the self: digital mediations', in Daniel Miller (ed.), *Anthropology and the Individual* (London: Bloomsbury, 2009), pp. 99–115;

and Maria Bakardjieva and Georgia Gaden, 'Web 2.0 technologies of the self', *Philosophy & Technology*, 25/3, September 2012, pp. 399–413. As van Dijck has argued, one reason for this trend toward standardisation is that it improves the capture of data, since 'standardizing data input guarantees better results'. See van Dijck, '"You have one identity"', p. 202.
19. Cong Li and Sriram Kalyanaraman, '"I, me, mine" or "us, we, ours?": the influence of cultural psychology on Web-based customization', *Media Psychology*, 16/3, 2013, pp. 272–94.
20. Tom Clark and Rózsa Farkas, 'Self compression: an interview with Jesse Darling', *MetaMute*, 20 June 2012. Available at <http://www.metamute.org/editorial/articles/self-compression-interview-jesse-darling> (last accessed December 2016).
21. The sociologist Lynn Jamieson, for example, has connected the way in which current opportunities for practices of self-construction have tended to conform to conventional tropes, behaviours and relationships. See Lynn Jamieson, 'Personal relationships, intimacy and the self in a mediated and global digital age', in Kate Orton Johnson and Nick Prior (eds), *Digital Sociology – Critical Perspectives* (London: Palgrave Macmillan, 2013), pp. 13–33. See also Eileen Green, '"Gendering the digital": the impact of gender and technology perspectives on the sociological imagination', in Orton Johnson and Prior, *Digital Sociology*, pp. 34–50; and Miller, *Future Identities*, p. 5.
22. Amalia Ulman, 'f/f', *Pool*, 5 April 2012. Available at <http://pooool.info/f-f/> (last accessed December 2016).
23. Ulman, *Do You Follow?*.
24. For example, in the UK *Excellences & Perfections* was profiled in the *Telegraph* newspaper, *Elle* magazine, and on the *BBC Culture* Web platform. The work was also included in the major exhibition *Performing for the Camera*, held at Tate Modern, London, in 2016.
25. See, for example, Cadence Kinsey et al., 'Becoming camwhore, becoming pizza', *MetaMute*, 8 November 2012. Available at <http://www.metamute.org/editorial/articles/becoming-camwhore-becoming-pizza> (last accessed December 2016).
26. The following artists were included in the exhibition *Body Anxiety*: Andrea Crespo; Saoirse Wall; Victoria Campbell; Endam Nihan; Aurorae Parker; Mary Bond; RAFiA Santana; Ann Hirsch; Nancy Leticia; Georges Jacotey; Erika Alexander; Hannah Black; Randon Rosenbohm; Rachel Rabbit White; Faith Holland; Kate Durbin; Angela Washko; Leah Schrager; Marie Karlberg; Alexandra Marzella; and May Waver. And the following in *Lonely Girl*: Al Baio, Petra Cortright, Maggie Lee, Greem Jellyfish, Bunny Rogers, Analisa Teachworth and Amalia Ulman.
27. Aria Dean, 'Closing the loop', *The New Enquiry*, 1 March 2016. Available at <http://thenewinquiry.com/essays/closing-the-loop/> (last accessed December 2016).
28. See Carolee Schneemann, untitled, no date. Available at <http://www.caroleeschneemann.com/eyebody.html> (last accessed December 2016).
29. Here my use of the term 'margin' is intended to invoke the important criticism of second-wave feminism mounted by bell hooks in *Feminist Theory: From Margin to Center* (Cambridge, MA: South End Press, 1984).
30. Katrina Sluis, 'Image recognition', *either and*, no date. Available at <http://eitherand.org/exhibitionism/image-recognition/> (last accessed December 2016). Likewise, in an article for the journal *New Media & Society*, Taina Bucher has argued that EdgeRank, the algorithm that structures the flow of information of Facebook's 'News Feed', is akin to Michel Foucault's model of surveillance, arguing that participation is not constituted through an all-seeing vision machine but through the fear of disappearing, and the loss of material and social rewards

concomitant with that disappearance. See Taina Bucher, 'Want to be on the top? Algorithmic power and the threat of invisibility on Facebook', *New Media & Society*, 14/7, 2012, pp. 1164–80.
31. A widely cited discussion of this tendency was presented by Nathan Jurgenson in the essay 'Digital dualism and the fallacy of web objectivity', published on *Cyborgology*, 13 September 2011. Available at <https://thesocietypages.org/cyborgology/2011/09/13/digital-dualism-and-the-fallacy-of-web-objectivity/> (last accessed December 2016).

3. BLOGGING THE FEMALE SELF: AUTHORSHIP, SELF-PERFORMANCE AND IDENTITY POLITICS IN FASHION BLOGS

Monica Titton

Since the mid-2000s, the rise of fashion bloggers who create their own small fashion media universes has fostered a new space for the enactment and performance of fashionable identities. Fashion blogs are online fashion diaries or journals, usually run by a single person who writes about her or his views on current or past fashion trends and shares stories about her or his daily dressing habits, beauty regimes or their latest, fashionable purchases.[1] Today, a select crowd of the most successful fashion bloggers and other 'digital influencers' has reached the upper echelons of the fashion industry's social hierarchy and sits in the front row of the most sought-after fashion shows in Paris, Milan, London and New York. With their self-made, self-styled microcosms, fashion bloggers challenge the division between the discourses and idealised femininities invoked by fashion media[2] and the experiences of anonymous consumers of fashion and dress.[3] Due to the fact that the majority of fashion bloggers are female, fashion blogs represent social spaces pertinent to feminist discourses on privacy and domesticity, identity politics and female experiences of fashion media authorship and consumption. This paper examines the narrative and performative practices set forth by the two fashion bloggers and feminist media entrepreneurs Leandra Medine and Tavi Gevinson and discusses the transformation of female authorship and self-construction within digital culture.

Performing Gendered Identities on Fashion Blogs

On fashion blogs, individual practices of self-fashioning combined with autobiographical texts and pictures (self-portraits and photographs of the bloggers) are broadcast online, where they become part of the fashion and popular culture media imagery and circulate as collective narratives. Fashion blogs can therefore be theorised as cultural spaces that revolve around routines of self-display and self-presentation mediated through fashion, dress and beauty. In his famous study *The Fashion System*, Roland Barthes argues that fashion 'constructs itself (. . .) as a program of behaviour'[4] by producing idealised biographies of women who inhabit the worlds of fashion. For Barthes, fashion magazines are equal to all works of mass culture insofar as they propagate the 'dream of identity (to be oneself, and to have this self be recognised by others)'.[5] Fashion bloggers actualise the cultural script of fashion media by enacting and performing their own, fashionable identity created and maintained for the purpose of their blogs. With the concept of 'fashionable persona', I suggest a theoretical model of authorship that shows how collective fashion narratives become interwoven in processes of self-creation and identity construction on fashion blogs.[6] By recurring to their everyday experiences, personal musings, biography and opinions as a trope for their writing about fashion, style, health and beauty, and by combining these texts with pictures of themselves that illustrate and validate their texts, fashion bloggers constantly actualise and re-inform their presentation of self and engage in the construction and enactment of an online version of themselves. Fashion bloggers thus construct a 'fashionable persona', a 'situated, narrative and performative character developed specifically for their blogs that is anchored simultaneously in the blogger's self-identity and biography and in the enactment of collective cultural narratives'.[7] Fashion bloggers access knowledge about fictional subjectivities when constructing their own personal fashion narratives and through the adoption of a 'fashionable persona', they negotiate the effects of this narrative and performative process on their self-identity. The 'fashionable persona' is theorised as a concept about the amalgamation of self-identity, practices of narrative and performative authorship and the embodiment of collective body discourses through photographs. On fashion blogs, the construction of self is interwoven with the production of autobiographical texts and pictures. Images are pivotal for the visual *Gestalt* of fashion blogs and they fulfil a double function: on the one hand, they provide the illustration and documentation of the written text, and on the other hand, they are the basis for the performative enactment of the 'fashionable persona'.[8] Barthes wrote that the photograph initiates 'the advent of myself as other'.[9] He argues that photography disassociates the consciousness and the body from self-identity,[10] and it is precisely in this in-between space that the performative aspect of fashion blogging can be located. The practice of producing documentary fashion images of themselves becomes a routine of self-creation for fashion bloggers. Self-portraits belong to those social techniques of the body that revolve around reflexive identity politics and the performance of identity. Peggy Phelan underlines the reflexivity set in motion by portrait photography, arguing that 'photography is fundamentally performative'.[11] As much as the maintenance of a narrative unity is required for a coherent sense of self-identity, also the maintenance of a consistent sense of embodiment of oneself is a precondition for self-identity. 'The self', as Anthony Giddens puts it, 'of course, is embodied'.[12] Through the photographs on their blogs, fashion bloggers locate their self-identity and their blogger persona in a network of visual meaning about fashion, style, beauty, femininity, class, race and ethnicity. The act of taking 'selfies' or being photographed institutes the reflexive experience and cognition of self, in the same way as autobiographical writing feeds into the constitution of self-identity.

The fashion bloggers' performance of their personae is situated in the context of fashion media, and this performance thus inherently partakes in the reproduction, production and affirmation of representations of idealised identities related to gender, but also related to class, race, ethnicity and sexuality. Erving Goffman understands gender as the result of culturally and socially learned performances and argues that 'there is no gender identity. There is only a schedule for the portrayal of gender'.[13] Femininity and masculinity are thus conceived as ritualised routines of identity performance. Goffman argues that with gender being the cultural construct resulting out of biological sex differences, gender display 'refers to conventionalised portrayals of these correlates'.[14] Exaggerated and highly stylised versions of gender stereotypes are perpetuated by the media, and particularly, by advertisements, because their goal is to quickly and convincingly deliver commercial messages.[15] Fashion and women's magazines are the main outlets of fashion advertisements and are therefore privileged spaces for the analysis of gender displays and 'culturally sedimented gendered dualities', to speak with Susan Bordo.[16] By replicating the 'iconic' poses seen in fashion media, fashion bloggers not only re-affirm existing rituals of gender display in Goffman's sense, but also empower themselves to claim and inhabit the 'idealised world' of fashion. Just as gender is, as Judith Butler writes, 'instituted through the stylisation of the body, and hence, must be understood as the mundane way in which bodily gestures, movements, and enactments of various kinds constitute the illusion of an abiding gendered self',[17] so the fashionable persona as a situated narrative and bodily practice relies on the enactment of a set of body postures. Following Goffman's and Butler's notion of gender identities resulting out of performances, the posing routines of fashion bloggers are conceived as performative actions contributing to the ongoing process of persona creation. By discussing the blogs of two young women who have started out as fashion bloggers and have transitioned into the broader realm of feminist media production, I show that the identity work and permanent concern with one's own self-image that comes with the activity of fashion blogging bears an inherent potential of feminist politicisation. I contend that this potential lies in the practice of autobiographical authorship and of producing photographs of oneself.

Repelling Men between Subversion and Affirmation of Gender Stereotypes

Leandra Medine's blog 'Man Repeller' represents an interesting example for a feminist critique of fashion blogs because it was conceived by Medine as a forum to present fashion that 'repels' men (hence the name of her blog), that is, clothing that does not make women more attractive to men but is worn by women because they want to celebrate their personal, idiosyncratic style. Founded in 2010 by Leandra Medine as a hobby project, in the past six years the once one-woman enterprise has grown into a small media company with twelve full-time employees (as of August 2016) and an office space in Manhattan. In its early years, the blog 'Man Repeller' centred exclusively on Leandra's quirky and offbeat outfit pictures, but today 'Man Repeller' has evolved into a website that covers a variety of topics ranging from 'style, feminism, culture, beauty, wellness, relationships and careers'.[18] Medine's enterprise grew through a combination of advertising, sponsored blog posts, appearance fees, designer collaborations and publishing deals (she published her first book in 2013) and today she ranks among the most successful fashion bloggers worldwide. The development of her blog was marked not only by the transition from a one-person corporation to a small company, but also, interestingly, by a shift from a focus on personal fashion to a wider range of topics that fall into the typical domain of women's magazines, framed by a commitment to feminism and body positivity.

Before it was gradually re-defined as a website over the past two years and when she was still running the blog on her own, the distinguishing feature of Medine's blog was her humour that permeated both her texts and her pictures. In the quote underneath, it becomes tangible what a fundamental difference self-portraits or pictures depicting the fashion blogger make for them and their self-understanding as bloggers. Leandra Medine writes about how she began to form a persona for her blog when she included photographs of herself:

> Initially, The Man Repeller was a commentary on culture. I wasn't the man-repeller, I was just making the observations. Over time, I started putting images of myself on the site, sort of took on this role and created a persona.[19]

Medine reconstructs the crucial importance of photographs for the development of her blogging persona, and argues that her activity as blogger involves the performance of a part that only became realised through its visual representation and her embodiment in photographs.

The expressivity and particularity of her exaggerated poses set Medine apart from fellow fashion bloggers from the outset of her blogging career, as she assumed poses in her outfit pictures that conformed neither with the conventions of posing on fashion blogs nor with the conventions of poses depicted in fashion magazines. Since she started her blog, she has been making fun of the fashion industry for producing clothing that looks ridiculous or impossible to wear on the street, yet at the same time she appreciates the creative potential and beauty of these clothes. Her blog has been characterised since its inception as a playful, ironic meta-commentary on the imagery of the fashion industry and this mode of authorship separates her from the masses of fellow fashion bloggers. By photographing herself in poses that express her astonishment and bafflement with the design of particularly avant-garde clothes or accessories, she subverts the very idea of the fashion model. Medine inhabits the garments and reacts to their unusual cut, fabric or texture by translating her commentary into a particular pose and facial expression. She uses the performative space enabled by photography to complete her persona adoption on a visual level. Fashion bloggers enact their fashionable persona not only through writing, but also through their self-portraits, and they have to make their visual appearance align with their written self-presentation. That is to say that their whole outer appearance in terms of fashion, style and 'look' has to correspond and be consistent with their writing style and the authorship position they construct in their texts.

Medine's blog is a very good example of the meaning of pictures, and particularly the importance of posing, as a form of embodiment for the construction and maintenance of a gendered fashionable persona. In a blog post from 2012 entitled 'Toddler Dressing', Medine went to a playground in New York City and staged a fashion photo shoot. The text of her blog post revolved around her description of her personal style, which she characterised as follows: 'little boy meets little girl – this is often followed by, and then Hell's Angel motorcyclist kidnaps them'.[20] The text was accompanied by four photographs of Leandra Medine in which she was depicted wearing an outfit that fitted into her description of her personal style as 'toddler dressing': a pair of widely cut, light blue shorts, a loosely cut cream top with a large round collar, a necklace resembling a collar and a pair of nude high heel platform sandals (Figure 3). While on the first three pictures, Medine was smiling and assumed the poses of a happy, playful child climbing on the playground equipment, on the fourth picture she made the desperate face of a crying child.[21]

With this fourth picture she pushed the analogy between young woman and child so far as to turn it into a parody and thus made fun not only of

Figure 3 Picture of Leandra Medine, published on her blog 'The Man Repeller', posing on a playground in her hometown, New York City (http://www.manrepeller.com/2012/06/toddler-dressing.html).

herself, but also of those fashion magazines that feature fashion shoots on playgrounds and fetishise the child-woman in fashion media imagery in general.

Goffman describes the depiction of women in child-like poses as belonging to the category of gender displays concerned with 'the ritualisation of subordination', and writes about the implications of this depiction: 'Given the subordinate and indulged position of children in regard to adults, it would appear that to present oneself in puckish styling is to encourage the corresponding treatment. How much of this guise is found in real life is an open question; but found it is in advertisements'.[22] Medine is well aware of the way in which fashion media reaffirm stereotypical notions of gender identities and situates her mock fashion shoot in the realm of parody and the absurd. With her hyperbolic exaggeration and parody, Medine undermines the popular woman-child-analogy and unveils its artificiality and its inherently sexualised core. Medine's performance recalls Butler's discussion of the subversive potential of drag performances. Butler argues that 'drag is subversive to the extent that it reflects on the imitative structure by which hegemonic gender is itself produced and disputes heterosexuality's claim on naturalness and originality'.[23] With Butler, Medine's performance can be interpreted as a conscious, ironic rupture with the imitative structure by which fashion photography mediates gendered bodies and inscribes specific notions of heteronormative femininity. Medine playfully subverts the gender stereotypes of fashion both on a visual level with her pictures and on a textual level by satirising the invocation of idealised characters or personae in fashion writing. In fact it is through her ongoing humourous and absurd performances of an excessively and absurdly fashionable femininity that Medine created her own fashionable persona of 'Man Repeller'.

On her blog, Medine defined the term 'man repeller' as follows:

> 'man·re·pell·er [mahn-ree-peller]
> —noun
> outfitting oneself in a sartorially offensive mode that may result in repelling members of the opposite sex. Such garments include but are not limited to harem pants, boyfriend jeans, overalls (see: human repelling), shoulder pads, full length jumpsuits, jewelry that resembles violent weaponry and clogs. [24]

From this mock lemma it becomes clear that Medine thinks of a specific style of dress as the vehicle through which women can for a time refute being part of the circuit of heterosexual desire and eschew the male gaze. However, her definition is itself based on biased stereotypes about heterosexual men as being only attracted to women who wear clothing that enhances their beauty (the definition of which is totally arbitrary) and heterosexual male desire as homogenous and undifferentiated. At the same time, the definition of 'man repeller' also presupposes the stereotype that women who wear clothes that might be liked by men are only doing it to please men and not themselves or their female peers (thereby not only excluding the existence of a heterosexual female gaze but also effectively foreclosing any form of lesbian or bisexual desire). The tongue-in-cheek humour of the definition of 'man repeller' did not prevent it from reinforcing the very gender stereotypes it superficially claimed to subvert.

As her blog rose to fame, the term 'Man Repeller' entered the Internet's fashion vernacular and Medine leveraged her persona into both a commercially successful personal brand and a subject position that other girls and women could identify with. The shift went hand in hand with a re-definition of 'Man Repeller' so as to encompass multiple contributors, new topics and a diversity of features such as an online shop, a video channel and a podcast channel.

In the new text for the 'About' section of the website, the word 'Man Repeller' is no longer used as a term intended to denominate a character but rather as a brand name, in the same way as the masthead for a newspaper or magazine:

> Man Repeller isn't just a website. It's an award-winning multi-media business and a global community of bright, interested and interesting people who know that fashion, humour and intelligence are not mutually exclusive.
> Our founding tenet is the belief that style is a meaningful form of self-expression. And the most empowering thing you can share is your point of view: through clothes, through words, through whatever wacky and wonderful shape it might take. It's by offering up our genuine selves that we can actually connect with others.[25]

The readers of 'Man Repeller' are included in the definition of the website and are addressed as producers ('community') and as part of the website's success and mission. An active audience is indeed crucial for the economic viability of online media as their contribution in the form of likes, shares and comments are translated into quantifiable metrics and the basis for calculations of the return on marketing investment for advertising agencies or other potential commercial partners.[26] What is presented to the readers of 'Man Repeller' as an invitation to join a community of like-minded women and express their inner selves is in fact an economic imperative for Medine and her investors. The text furthermore conveys the notion that style is the means for individual self-expression and hence empowerment and connection. With this statement of purpose, 'Man Repeller' adheres to similar statements of purpose or letters from the editor in fashion and women's magazines that each single out their 'own specific configuration of both forbidden and acceptable arenas of enjoyment', yet only to 'find a means of containing these pleasures, harnessing them to consumerism', as Ellen McCracken writes.[27] In the case of 'Man Repeller', the promise of self-fulfilment and feminist empowerment is tied up with the act of consumption and with it, radical self-expression. The feminist vision propagated on 'Man Repeller' revolves around self-acceptance, body-positivity and the realisation of dreams and ambitions that are accomplished through acts of fashion consumption or other, related lifestyle choices (make-up, styling, nutrition, exercise, etc.). However, this perception of feminism is deeply apolitical, as, with its focus on individual self-realisation, it ignores structural gender inequalities and how they intersect with other structural inequalities such as racism, classism and homo- and transphobia.[28] Many feminist scholars such as Rosalind Gill,[29] Nancy Fraser,[30] Angela McRobbie[31] and Nina Power[32] have pointed to the failure of so-called 'postfeminism' to articulate a systematic critique of capitalism and its entanglement with gender inequality.

Rosalind Gill argues that postfeminist media culture is characterised by 'the almost total evacuation of notions of politics or cultural influence' that can be seen in 'the ways in which every aspect of life is refracting through the idea of personal choice and self-determination'.[33] In her book *The One-Dimensional Woman* Nina Power coined the term 'Feminism™' for this commodified version of feminism, articulating her concern about the capitalistic core of 'contemporary feminism'.[34] Writing about Jessica Valenti, founder of the feminist blog 'Feministing', Power argues: 'Slipping down easily as a friendly-bacteria yoghurt drink, Valenti's version of feminism, with its total lack of structural analysis, genuine outrage or collective demand, believes it has to compliment capitalism in order to effectively sell its product.'[35] Although Power's critique ignores the diversity of contemporary feminism, particularly in online media such as Tumblr, Twitter and on blogs, her argument can be extended to 'Man Repeller', where feminism is equated with personal empowerment and self-fulfilment through clothes, grooming and unrelenting self-involvement, echoing Nancy Fraser's verdict that in a post-fordist economy, 'the dream of women's emancipation is harnessed to the engine of capitalist accumulation'.[36]

Over the years, Leandra Medine's involvement with fashion and the production of her own fashionable persona and of her own representation of fashionable femininity has resulted in an intensification of her processes of introspection and public emotional self-exploration.

Becoming a Feminist: Style Rookie and the Politics of Girlhood

A contrasting example is represented by Tavi Gevinson, whose career trajectory also saw her moving away from fashion blogging to the field of popular culture and feminist activism, but under different premises than Medine (Figure 4). The distinguishing trait in the early years of Tavi Gevinson's blogging career was her exceptional young age, which in combination with her unusual styling made her stand out from the fashion crowd, but also from the blogger community.[37] The very nature of digital success stories makes it hard to reconstruct the precise timeline of her ascent to the fashion circus, but within a couple of years, she rose to fame as a fashion blogger wunderkind to become today's poster child of American pop-feminism. Gevinson founded her blog 'Style Rookie' in 2008 at the age of eleven, and when she was thirteen she was invited to sit in the front row of the Dior Haute Couture fashion show, causing a media frenzy for wearing a big bow-shaped hat given to her by hat maker Stephen Jones.[38] In 2011, Gevinson launched the first issue of her feminist online magazine 'Rookie Magazine'; the first print issue of the magazine ('Rookie Yearbook') was published in 2012. In recent years, Gevinson added acting and singing to her already prolific professional activities, thus fully embracing the requirements of neoliberal capitalism, which, as Luc Boltanski

Figure 4 Picture of Tavi Gevinson wearing a sweater with 'Feminist' pattern published on her blog 'Style Rookie' (http://www.thestylerookie.com/2010/09/carnival.html).

and Ève Chiapello argue, promotes new forms of labour based on temporary projects demanding flexibility and innovation, but also on notions of self-management and self-surveillance.[39]

During most of her teenage years, taking pictures of herself was an almost daily habit for Gevinson and the pictures published on her blog documented not only her countless fashion choices but also her growing, changing body and its transition from adolescence to early adulthood. Her self-portraits were an important medium for Gevinson's self-realisation as a fashion blogger and supported her practice of authorship through enabling the performative embodiment of her narrative subject position. Gevinson is known for her unconventional, unique point of view on fashion – which she successfully capitalised – and through her posing and self-styling captured in her self-portraits, she created a visual commentary for her own fashion narrative. With her idiosyncratic taste in fashion and her cool and unruffled poses, Tavi Gevinson rejected the overtly sexual female poses enacted in mainstream fashion magazines and in popular culture, and situated herself outside of the mainstream fashion media discourse through her performative persona enactments.[40]

At the same time, her visual self-presentation was placed at the centre of the discursive construction of Gevinson as both a curiosity and an anomaly in the media: journalists and media commentators inexorably stressed Gevinson's young age and no newspaper article or report about her failed to comment on the minutiae of her looks, which were always discussed in relation to her age. Jessalynn Keller maintains that the constant recourse to Gevinson's age and in particular, her small stature, serve 'to link Tavi's physicality with a state of disempowerment, a position of dependence, and a lack of agency – qualities that are often problematically associated with children – and specifically girls – in dominant social discourses and media representations'.[41] Gevinson, however, defied the ascription of these diminishing attributes with the next step in her career. With 'Rookie Magazine' and 'Rookie Yearbook', Gevinson has created a diverse forum for the articulation of feminism that, as Keller argues, echoes the media production of 1990s girl zinesters and riot grrrls.[42] Her gradual shift away from fashion to feminism began in the summer of 2010, when Gevinson was invited to speak at the 'ideaCity10' conference in Toronto and instead of talking about fashion, as had been announced, she spoke about feminism, girlhood and the representation of women in the media.[43] In July 2010, Gevinson published an open letter to 'Seventeen Magazine', in which she condemned the magazine for the sexist and fat-shaming headline 'The party drug that can make you fat & ugly' on the cover of its June/July 2010 issue.[44] The headline, she wrote in her letter, implies that 'the worst thing that can happen to your average reader, a teenage girl, as a result of drug use, is not that she will have any damage done to her brain or become unhappy, but that her appearance will suffer (again, being fat does not mean bad appearance, but that is what you imply)'.[45] With this criticism, Gevinson articulated her discomfort with the messages sent to young women by mainstream media and at the same time asserted her subject position as female author and media producer. In September 2011 Gevinson announced the launch of 'Rookie Magazine', an online publication dedicated to pop culture and 'built around the celebration and cultivation of a feminist girlhood'.[46] In contrast to Medine's generic use of the term 'feminism' and her frequent use of the term 'empowerment' instead, Gevinson specifically positions 'Rookie Magazine' as a feminist media outlet that discusses issues such as sexual harassment, sexuality and LGBTQ issues, body politics, female friendships and feminist activism.[47] While on

'Man Repeller' feminism is narrated in conjunction with fashion and always inherently coupled with consumption, 'Rookie Magazine' proposes a version of feminism that actively encourages its readers to be critical of mainstream media, to participate in political activism and to challenge blind consumerism through DIY practices and crafting, but also a version of feminism that can be reconciled with tropes associated with heteronormative femininity such as make-up, dating advice, fashion, music, TV and film. The defining traits of 'Rookie Magazine' are texts written by often semi-anonymous contributors (only the author's first names are disclosed) in the same confessional, personal and autobiographical tone Tavi had already established in her fashion blog 'Rookie'. By encouraging female authorship and self-writing about topics such as mental disorders, physical or sexual abuse, gender identities and teenage angst in general, Gevinson created an alternative space for forging feminist solidarity among girls and young women based on sharing their intimate, everyday experiences. With its critical attitude towards mainstream representations of girlhood and femininity and the creation of an online space for the performance and exploration of feminist and queer identities, 'Rookie Magazine' fosters practices of media production that, as Keller argues, 'are politically significant in and of themselves, as they demand a new framework for understanding feminist girls as positive and agential figures of social change'.[48] It was only possible for Gevinson to access and explore this feminist agenda once she had 'abandoned' the realm of fashion blogging, as her systemic critique of the fashion industry and its media would not have been accepted by the brands that paid for advertising on her blog. Despite the fact that fashion plays a minor role on 'Rookie Magazine' in terms of content and advertising partners, Gevinson has been keeping to work as a model for fashion and beauty advertising campaigns. It is precisely her rebellious, nonconformist and authentic attitude that makes her interesting for fashion and cosmetic brands that want to rejuvenate their image and reach younger customer segments.

Conclusion: Female Authorship between Self-creation and Neoliberal Co-optation

Fashion provides a rich imaginary with real and/or symbolic spaces, subjectivities, temporal categories and situations which nurture the narratives of self-creation and female authorship on fashion blogs, but never yield closure or the sense of 'arrival'. Barthes described this temporal loop of fashion as 'an amnesiac substitution of the present for the past'.[49] In a much more critical vein, McRobbie postulates that global neoliberal economic policies have set forth a new kind of female subject who is caught in a 'state of non-identity',[50] to which the fashion industry responds by generating dissatisfaction and projecting aspirations. Fashion bloggers like Medine and Gevinson use fashion and dress to structure their autobiographical narratives and photographic self-portraits, but they have both moved beyond this mode of sartorial self-creation. While Medine chose to magnify her personal self-exploration by opening up about her private life and further emotionalising her fashion choices, Gevinson mostly distanced herself from fashion by criticising its sexist and consumerist messages and by re-inventing herself as a feminist. Both Medine and Gevinson started out as fashion bloggers and both transformed their blogs into online magazines with a shared (yet different) emphasis on female empowerment and feminism. While the editorial direction of 'Man Repeller' falls largely within the realm of women's fashion and lifestyle media, 'Rookie Magazine' is aimed at teenage girls and thematises alternative modes of girlhood, pop culture, identity politics, music, fashion and feminism, echoing the media production of 1990s girl zinesters and riot grrrls.[51] Despite their editorial differences, both Medine and Gevinson have been embraced by the fashion industry as role models for a new femininity and both have starred in advertising campaigns for international fashion brands. What fashion brands value in Medine and Gevinson is their authenticity, uniqueness and recognisability, modes of authorship that they have systematically constructed through their writing and which they have successfully monetised through self-branding. The construction of an 'authentic' self-brand coheres with the requirements of the digital economy and its culture of entrepreneurship, which 'rewards those who are entrepreneurial, positive, self-motivated, and who provide information-rich content', as Alice Marwick writes.[52]

From a feminist perspective, Tavi Gevinson as the figure of the young, pretty and web-savvy digital media entrepreneur and pop cultural icon recalls McRobbie's description of the production of girlhood in postfeminist discourses.[53] McRobbie argues that liberal feminist principles of the 1960s and 1970s were incorporated in neoliberal narratives of female self-realisation and that in this post-feminist cultural milieu, the young woman has become 'an intensively managed subject of post-feminist, gender-aware biopolitical practices of new governmentality'.[54] The fashion industry is singled out by McRobbie as one of the key institutions which promote the project of female individualisation, generate bodily dissatisfaction and thus encourages young women to 'embark on a new regime of self-perfectibility (i.e. self-completion)', within which 'the fearful terrain of male approval fades away and is replaced instead with a new horizon of self-imposed feminine cultural norms'.[55] With McRobbie's considerations in mind, Medine and Gevinson become apparent as archetypal personifications of post-feminist femininity, entangled in a web of reciprocal, hence (potentially) monetised relationships with fellow bloggers, their audience, journalists, advertisers and PR agents working for fashion and beauty brands, and in the case of Gevinson, a larger pop-cultural audience. As fashion bloggers, Medine and Gevinson engaged in an ongoing dialogue about their fashion choices, habits and body image with these different groups of people who formed their horizon of 'self-imposed feminine cultural norms' that McRobbie mentions.[56] Medine and Gevinson made capital out of their practice of female authorship that is embedded in their private, quirky, homely fashion orbits – they embraced the values of the digital economy by leveraging their carefully curated 'fashionable personae' into lifestyle brands and perform as 'economically active female citizens'.[57] Gill has pointed out the similarities between the psychological requirements bestowed upon individuals in neoliberalism and the construct of the autonomous post-feminist self in contemporary media culture. She writes: 'At the heart of both is the notion of the "choice biography" and the contemporary injunction to render one's life knowable and meaningful through a narrative of free choice and autonomy, however constrained one actually might be.'[58] In this context, both Medine and Gevinson exemplify how the production of neoliberal subjectivity is effected through the practice of (fashion) blogging as it relies on the feminine self as a malleable, transitory and somehow always incomplete project. Gevinson's explicit critique of mainstream representations of girlhood and femininity and her promotion of feminist and queer identity politics became incorporated into her public persona and into her brand. Having essentially grown up online, Gevinson's personal development from a prepubescent fashionista with dorky glasses to a multi-faceted pop-cultural entrepreneur coincides largely with the evolution of her 'brand', which has consistently been co-opted by the fashion and beauty industry as a precious commodity. This comes as no surprise since in contemporary capitalism, as Ulrich Bröckling argues, the requirement to be different and unique at all costs has turned into what he calls 'the tyranny of alterity' on highly competitive labour markets, but also in other realms such as romantic relationships and markets structured by the distribution of attention, like the creative industries.[59] The blogosphere and social media economy can also be described as subject to this Foucauldian 'tyranny of alterity' insofar as aspiring blogger and Instagrammers are advised to develop a 'personal brand' tailored to their own self-identity, and they are encouraged to capitalise on their individuality. On the feminist fashion blogs discussed in this chapter, the neoliberal discourse of individualising liberation converges with the fashion media discourse of female lives as permanently unfinished and insufficient projects, confirming Fraser's argument of a deep affinity between neoliberalism and second-wave feminism.[60]

Despite these structural dynamics of neoliberal co-optation, it is important to stress that on the level of individual agency, fashion bloggers contribute to the formation of a collective counter-discourse to mainstream representations of fashionable femininities by embarking on projects of self-discovery and personal emancipation through their autobiographical writing and the production of documentary images of themselves.

Notes

1. Over the past couple of years, the social media platform Instagram has come increasingly to replace fashion blogs as a blogging platform, and while many fashion bloggers keep their blogs active in addition to their Instagram and Snapchat accounts and use their blogs as a kind of 'repository' for their digital content, many rising 'fashion influencers' exclusively use Instagram as their blogging platform. Even if in this text I mainly refer to fashion bloggers, the analysis presented here can equally be applied to Instagrammers as the basic social mechanisms remain the same across different digital platforms.
2. Roland Barthes, *The Fashion System* (Berkeley, CA: University of California Press, 1990); Agnès Rocamora, *Fashioning the City: Paris, Fashion and the Media* (London: I. B. Tauris, 2009).
3. Joanne Entwistle, *The Fashioned Body: Fashion, Dress and Modern Social Theory* (Cambridge: Polity Press, 2000); Sophie Woodward, *Why Women Wear What They Wear* (Oxford: Berg, 2007).
4. Barthes, *The Fashion System*, p. 291.
5. Ibid. p. 255.
6. Monica Titton, 'Fashionable personae: self-identity and enactments of fashion narratives in fashion blogs', *Fashion Theory*, 19/2, 2015, pp. 201–20.
7. Ibid. p. 202.
8. Ibid. p. 215.
9. Roland Barthes, *Camera Lucida: Reflections on Photography* (New York: Hill and Wang, 1981), p. 12.
10. Ibid. p. 9.
11. Peggy Phelan, *Unmarked: The Politics of Performance* (London: Routledge, 1996), p. 35.
12. Anthony Giddens, *Modernity and Self-Identity: Self and Society in the Late Modern Age* (Stanford, CA: Stanford University Press, 1991), p. 56.
13. Erving Goffman, *Gender Advertisements* (New York: Harper Torchbooks, 1987), p. 8.
14. Ibid. p. 1.
15. Ibid. p. 27.
16. Susan Bordo, *Unbearable Weight: Feminism, Western Culture and the Body* (Berkeley, CA: University of California Press, 2003).
17. Judith Butler, 'Performative acts and gender constitution: an essay in phenomenology and feminist theory', *Theatre Journal*, 40/4, 1988, p. 519.
18. 'What is Man Repeller?', *Man Repeller*, <http://www.manrepeller.com/what-is-man-repeller> (last accessed 27 September 2016).
19. Leandra Medine, 'The Man Repeller', in William Oliver (ed.), *Style Feed: The World's Top Fashion Blogs. Selected by Susie Bubble* (Munich: Prestel, 2012), p. 31.
20. Leandra Medine, 'Toddler dressing', *Man Repeller*, 11 June 2012, <http://www.manrepeller.com/2012/06/toddler-dressing.html> (last accessed 27 September 2016).
21. <http://www.manrepeller.com/2012/06/toddler-dressing.html> (last accessed 28 November 2016).
22. Goffman, *Gender Advertisements*, p. 48.
23. Judith Butler, *Bodies That Matter: On the Discursive Limits of 'Sex'* (New York: Routledge, 1993).
24. Leandra Medine, 'What is a Man Repeller?', *Man Repeller*, 25 April 2010, <https://web.archive.org/web/20121015020555/http://www.manrepeller.com/2010/04/what-is-man-repeller.html> (last accessed 27 September 2016).

25. 'What is Man Repeller?', *Man Repeller*, <http://www.manrepeller.com/what-is-man-repeller> (last accessed 27 September 2016).
26. Alice E. Marwick, *Status Update: Celebrity, Publicity, and Branding in the Social Media Age* (New Haven, CT: Yale University Press, 2013), p. 105.
27. Ellen McCracken, *Decoding Women's Magazines: From Mademoiselle to Ms.* (Houndsmill, UK: Macmillan, 1993), p. 136.
28. Jessalynn Keller, *Girls' Feminist Blogging in a Postfeminist Age* (London: Routledge, 2016), p. 103.
29. Rosalind Gill, 'Postfeminist media culture: elements of a sensibility', *European Journal of Cultural Studies*, 10, pp. 147–66.
30. Nancy Fraser, *Fortunes of Feminism: From State-Managed Capitalism to Neoliberal Crisis* (New York: Verso, 2013).
31. Angela McRobbie, *The Aftermath of Feminism: Gender, Culture and Social Change* (London: Sage, 2009).
32. Nina Power, *One-Dimensional Woman* (Winchester: O Books, 2009).
33. Gill, 'Postfeminist media culture', p. 153.
34. Power, *One-Dimensional Woman*, p. 27.
35. Ibid. p. 30.
36. Fraser, *Fortunes of Feminism*, p. 221.
37. Keller, *Girls' Feminist Blogging*, p. 161.
38. Jenna Sauers, 'Tempest in a trilby: fashion blogger Tavi Gevinson's hated hat', *Jezebel*, 25 January 2010. Available at <http://jezebel.com/5456560/tempest-in-a-trilby-fashion-blogger-tavi-gevinsons-hated-hat> (last accessed 27 September 2016).
39. Luc Boltanski and Eve Chiapello, *The New Spirit of Capitalism* (New York: Verso, 2005), p. 191.
40. <http://www.thestylerookie.com/2010/09/carnival.html> (last accessed 28 November 2016).
41. Keller, *Girls' Feminist Blogging*, p. 162.
42. Ibid. p. 71.
43. Ibid. p. 170.
44. Tavi Gevinson, 'An open letter to Seventeen Magazine, also, WHY ARE YOU UGLY WHAT IS WRONG WITH YOU', *The Style Rookie*, 13 July 2010, <http://www.thestylerookie.com/2010/07/open-letter-to-seventeen-magazine-also.html> (last accessed 27 September 2016).
45. Ibid.
46. Keller, *Girls' Feminist Blogging*, p. 173.
47. Ibid. p. 173.
48. Ibid. p. 40.
49. Barthes, *The Fashion System*, p. 289.
50. McRobbie, *The Aftermath of Feminism*, p. 62.
51. Keller, *Girls' Feminist Blogging*, p. 71.
52. Marwick, *Status Update*, p. 192.
53. McRobbie, *The Aftermath of Feminism*.
54. Ibid. p. 60.
55. Ibid. p. 62.
56. Ibid. p. 62.
57. Ibid. p. 58.
58. Gill, 'Postfeminist media culture', p. 154.
59. Ulrich Bröckling, 'Jenseits des kapitalistischen Realismus: Anders anders sein', in Sighard Neckel (ed.), *Kapitalistischer Realismus: Von der Kunstaktion zur Gesellschaftskritik* (Frankfurt am Main: Campus, 2010), p. 283.
60. Fraser, *Fortunes of Feminism*, p. 224.

PART TWO

RELATIONALITY, SELFHOOD AND SUBJECTIVITIES

4. 'SCRIPTRIX NARRANS': DIGITAL DOCUMENTARY STORYTELLING'S RADICAL POTENTIAL

Gail Vanstone

To have voice is to have power.
Ron Marken, Foreword, in Maria Campbell's
Stories of the Road Allowance People

Agnès Varda

Agnès Varda, the highest ranked female director in *Sight and Sound*'s 2014 poll of greatest documentaries in 'Best Documentaries of All Time',[1] embraces a mode of activist cinema in her *Les glaneurs et la glaneuse/The Gleaners and I* (2000) that subverts classical theory through a unique *'cinécriture'*, according to Delphine Bénézet. Together with 'a visual and verbal emphasis on female embodiment', Varda's documentaries offer what Bénézet characterises as 'a voice of resistance [in] her commitment to resist norms of representation and diktats of production'.[2] Hers is the voice of the 'subject' as 'agent' proudly claiming her own filmmaking.

The Gleaners and I examines the act of gleaning in a contemporary light, introducing viewers to a rich cross-section of the French population (a chef, an artist, a language teacher, low-income wage earners, the homeless), people who forage for their better-offs' leftovers. In one instance, Varda herself, searching for heart shaped-potatoes, gleans with foragers collecting misshapen potatoes – market rejects – dumped in the field by farmers, her hands appearing on screen 'not only as authoring agent, but as subject matter'.[3] Throughout the film, Varda achieves a singular bricolage, cobbling together a narrative from her many hours of footage (much of which includes herself), self-reflexively acknowledging her own role as a 'gleaner of images': *la glaneuse*, as Virginia Bonner puts it.[4]

Declaring that she wants to explore the problems of consumption – waste, the eating of food discarded by the well-off – Varda shuns the role of 'sociolgue' or 'ethnographe' with its whiff of class imbalance between filmmaker and filmed. Instead Varda inserts herself into her own film, she is one who interviews subjects precisely as an inquiring subject. For Homay King, Varda and her modern-day gleaners 'recover, save and collect things, not in order to embalm them, but to use them, in the sense of putting them into practice and circulation'.[5] Here, Varda, 'flâneuse with a portable camera ... embodies a transitional, peripatetic mode of subjectivity' that is at once 'materialist, feminist, phenomenological and political'.[6] Aware that she is asking her subjects to reveal personal details, Varda thinks it only fitting that she reciprocates: 'I thought that the film should also reveal a little about the filmmaker, that I should use a little bit of myself in it'.[7]

Varda's methodology, as Bonner notes, underscores the fact that documentary filmmaking itself is always a form of gleaning, but what makes Varda's methodology unique is her persistent manipulation of address as she goes about doing this. Bonner makes a compelling case that, 'By modifying the modes of address, identification, and narration particular to the documentary genre', Varda hails both her viewers and the people she films – including herself – as active participants'.[8]

Varda achieves this unusual approach to film address by combining first and second person voice. This mixed-address voice-over encourages an intersubjective dialogue with those she films. As filmmaker, Varda gleans 'acts, gestures and information', while at the same time she allows the filmed gleaners to condition her text, revealing their diverse motives (anticipated and otherwise): poverty and adversity are played out against resourcefulness, tradition, art and activism. Her gleaners emerge, not as abject victims, but inventive subjects. This process reflects what Trinh T. Minh-ha sees as: 'a different way of working with freedom in experiencing the self and the world'.[9] Her act of 'filmer en femme', a phrase Varda coins, produces works that are both, as Bonner sees it, 'feminist and political in their conception and message ... a perspective shift better understood as "an opening up of critical space".'

Varda might be said to be taking a leaf out of strategies practised by avant-garde poet and writer Nicole Brossard, who seeks a truer rendering of female experience in language and form. Brossard does this by interrogating and refiguring European history and traditions of narrative and voice from a female point of view, an act theorists label *écriture feminine,* invoking Hélène Cixous's term coined in 'The Laugh of the Medusa'.[10] This term, often taken (wrongly) to refer exclusively to women's writing, is more generous. Cixous makes it clear that *écriture feminine* can be produced by men or women writers (filmers), as masculinity and femininity exist in every human being.[11] Varda's work as *(cin)écriture féminine*, is not then simply a matter of gender. Rather, it is that the constricted *homo narrans* of the closed readerly text gives way to an unbounded, what I want to call '*scriptrix narrans*', creating and amending an open, writerly alternative.

The *scriptrix narrans* is a different sort of auteur, committed to breaking out of the constraints of traditional 'patriarchal' narrative, supportive of hierarchies, divisions, etc. She is one who, facing in one direction, enables those she films to become *scriptrix narrans* and, who, facing in the other direction, produces what Roland Barthes describes as *scriptible*, writerly, as opposed to *lisible*, readerly texts.[12] Her approach – her *cinécriture* – is, in fact, transformative.

To voice one's story is to commit an act of agency but, for Sophie McCall, the act of voicing involves a necessary 'interpenetration of authorship and collaboration', recognising the relationship between the 'voice' of the storyteller and the 'recorder' of the story.[13] Noting that this relationship navigates ground from empowerment to appropriation, she draws our attention to the 'subtle shifts of the balance of power' between the speaker and the 'recorder' of the narrative, a hybrid body of 'as-told-to forms, techniques and arenas'.[14]

To act with agency traditionally appealed to feminists as a liberatory manoeuvre, countering patriarchal domination. Lois McNay suggests that the increasingly complex, plural and unstable nature of late-capitalist societies necessitates a reconceptualisation of both notions – subjectification and agency: 'The conceptualization of gender identity as durable but not immutable has prompted a rethinking of agency in terms of the inherent instability of gender norms and the consequent possibilities for resistance, subversion and the emancipatory remodeling of identity.'[15] McNay argues for a theory of agency that 'yields an understanding of a creative or imaginative substrate to action' that, likewise, takes into account 'a more precise and varied account of agency that explains the differing motivations and ways in which individuals and groups struggle over, appropriate and transform cultural meanings and resources'.[16]

Within this framework the old dichotomies of domination and female subordination wane in the face of emerging inequalities drawn around generational, class and racial lines, where, to paraphrase McNay, structural divisions among women are as significant as divisions between women and men:

> With regard to issues of gender a more rounded conception of agency is crucial to explaining both how women have acted autonomously in the past despite constricting social sanctions and also how they may act now in the context of processes of gender restructuring.[17]

In the face of more recent examples of documentary filmmaking by women what effect does a shifting in digital media have? How are questions of voice and agency affected? Does *scriptrix narrans*, as a concept, make meaning in this new environment?

Sharon Daniel

Video-artist and activist Sharon Daniel is an early and exciting example of what possibilities the rich tools this evolving environment offers for feminist scholars, artists and collaborating activists intent on unsettling and resisting coercive, centrist and colonialist forms of knowledge construction. She is, of course, not alone: as works such as Shelly Jackson's *Patchwork Girl* (1995); Caitlin Fisher's *These Waves of Girls* (2001); Stephanie Boluk's *Dwarven Epitaphs* (2006); Michelle Citron's *Mixed Greens* (2016) attest. Their often unruly practices perfectly illustrate non-fiction storytelling's radical potentials. Central to emerging methods and models are interdisciplinary collaborations particularly dedicated to unleashing authentic 'voice'. Spectators/participants are invited to unpack seductively familiar formulae, collaboratively rising to the challenges of building transformative, critical community capacity. In terms of feminist narratology, such practices in digital media, installation art and performance art, ruffle and challenge the ways we engage intellectually.

Working at the nexus of art and activism, theory and practice, Daniel has produced two distinct but related forms of Internet art – participatory media platforms and interactive new media documentaries, all catalogued on her website: www.sharondaniel.net. The core of her practice is the development of innovative online interfaces to databases of original interviews and other participant-generated content.

Over the last fourteen years, this body of new media documentary work is animated by a series of questions:

- Does new media matter at sites of social injustice?
- Can information architecture expand the public sphere, reveal human rights abuses, represent marginalised communities, enable new political subjects and expose social injustice at critical 'sites' of public interest and responsibility?
- Can new media effectively provide the public of the 'first' world with an immersive experience of the 'third' world within it – our 'secret publics'?

Daniel asks: 'what is the political efficacy of art? How might we re-imagine the political and the aesthetic, in tandem?'[18]

This preoccupation underscores all of her projects, documenting and analyzing testimony and evidence of 'how state institutions, social structures and economic conditions connect in a causal chain (from inequality in health care and education to racial and economic discrimination in the justice system) that fosters and perpetuates social injustice'.[19]

Public Secrets was triggered by Daniel's volunteering at an HIV prevention programme that ran an open needle exchange programme three nights a week close to where she lived in east Oakland – 'a post-industrial wasteland' is how Daniel saw it. Her interactive interface explores the troubled intersection of criminal and social justice as experienced by a group of women living mainly on the street. Based on an audio archive of hundreds of statements made by these formerly incarcerated women, the interface unmasks the secret injustices of the war on drugs, the criminal justice system and the 'prison industrial complex' (http://www.sharondaniel.net/#about-1). These women had no official identification, either because of a criminal record or having no fixed address, thereby being denied access to 'basic civic rights or social services'. From one woman she met who used the needle exchange, Daniel learned – her words – 'a lot about the third world inside the first'; about how 'realities of poverty, racism, social isolation, past trauma, sexual abuse and sex-based discrimination can make a person, even an extraordinarily intelligent person, vulnerable to addiction and psychosis.[20] Moved by the fundamental injustice of the women's invisibility – 'a kind of public secret' (Figure 5) – Daniel created the interactive interface to unleash 'a critical dialogue about crime and punishment and challenge the assumption that imprisonment provides a solution to social problems'.[21] It is as much constructed as a system for collaborative and collective authoring online as it is, overall, a predetermined narrative.

At the i-DOCS conference in Bristol, UK, 2013, Daniel revealed in conversation with conference organiser Sandra Gaudenzi how closely her methodology echoes the *scriptrix narrans* model. Daniel's words:

> Using digital media and creating an interactive interface that allows the audience to navigate a large number to interviews/stories as opposed to telling just one story in linear form allows me to take the focus off individual responsibility and helps the viewer to understand and recognize that the stories, together, represent the experience of a subjugated or oppressed 'class' – as opposed to seeing the 'exemplary' story as a tragic, but isolated, narrative. It takes more than one story.
>
> For me *design is a form of argument and the navigation is a form of inquiry* so in my work the design of the interface and information architecture constitute a form of 'argument'.

Figure 5   Revealing secrets . . . Sharon Daniel's *Public Secrets*.

Indeed, this is a remarkable relinquishing of the maker's voice. She creates the platform *in order that* the voices of her subject may sound. One may think of this as being, rather than a *single* road across that site to get from point A to point B, the kind of interface that sets the viewer down *within* the boundaries of this territory – allowing, encouraging her to find her own way. These practices tease out exactly how digital media can be organised around a non-linear agenda. This is the *scriptrix narrans* again, like Varda, speaking and allowing her subjects to speak, but using new digital technology to do so.

Inside the Distance, a subsequent Daniel project, is organised around the metaphor of a boxing match – 'distance' referring to the scheduled length of a fight. As Daniel says, 'for the boxer, as for all of us, the goal is to stay standing':

> *Inside the Distance* is a victim–offender mediation conducted in Belgium where restorative justice is institutionalized within the criminal justice system. It looks at mediation as a potential alternative to dominant retributive modes and theories of punishment. Mediation almost always begins with a focus on details – victim and offender wanting to reconfirm each other's understanding of what happened – who was hurt and why.[22]

It uses filmed mediation re-enactments, interviews with mediators, criminologists, victims and offenders. For Daniel, criminal acts are rents in the fabric of the social order – expressions of something that does not fit.[23] Better to understand these rents, her *Inside the Distance* presents reconstructions of the crime and the processes of mediation as recalled by victim, mediator and offender.

These digital works exemplify (and broadcast) Daniel's concern with the criminal justice system, illuminated through first-hand testimony and evidence given by individuals who become implicated. But Daniel does more than give voice. Her purpose is to share the agency she has as a privileged artist, allowing these people to become her co-creators. Daniel's treatment illustrates just how the *scriptrix narrans* transforms subject positions.

Alethea Arnaquq-Baril

Daniel explores what digital affordances add to Varda's feminised *cinécriture* but such *scriptrix narrans* potentials can further transform voice and agency not only for women but for the doubly marginalised, in this case, Indigenous women. The crucial element remains – the rethinking of the creator function, exactly that which the digital most easily affords.

Angry Inuk (2016), Alethea Arnaquq-Baril's hotly anticipated documentary film, shares much common ground with Varda and Daniel. Founder of her own production company, Unikkaat Studios, the celebrated Inuit filmmaker is based in Iqaluit, Nunavut Territory in Canada's Arctic. Arnaquq-Baril has already established herself as a first-rate director with a series of films (documentary, animation and *Arctic Rescue* – a film and an interactive game she produced with John Walker) illuminating and celebrating Inuit culture and language. As she tells it, her motivation was pressing:

> Inuit didn't have a writing system before European contact, and to this day, there is a serious lack of Inuktitut reading materials. We are an oral culture, and so that means our culture and history, up until recently, has mostly been undocumented, or documented by outsiders. This is changing slowly, but there is an enormous amount of knowledge and history that needs to be documented in a short period of time, while the last elders that lived traditionally out on the land are still alive. Filmmaking is such a natural and easy way for Inuit to do this important work.[24]

But as well as the preservation of orality and the traditional record for the community, an equally urgent spur for the filmmaker is the need to communicate with the outside world – to communication in an Inuit voice. Arnaquq-Baril's own words: 'Probably the most powerful thing I could do for myself and my fellow Inuit is to be a documentary filmmaker, because I don't know how else I can contribute to helping our voices be heard on the world stage, on issues that are critical to us.'

In 2003, the Maori filmmaker and theoretician Barry Barclay proposed a 'Fourth Cinema' for Indigenous peoples in contrast to the long-established oppositional concept of a Third Cinema to give agency to filmmakers in the developing world:[25] 'It seems likely to me that some Indigenous film artists will be interested in shaping films that sit with confidence within the First Second and Third cinema framework . . . to shape a growing Indigenous cinema outside the national orthodoxy.'[26] The Fourth Cinema he proposed for indigenous filmmakers does not privilege the creation of new cinematic language as a given which Solanas and Getino did in the 1960s. Rather it seeks to rework cinematic language, proposing the expression of Indigeneity *within* the norms of First, Second and Third Cinemas. Indigenous eyes will find their traditional core values reworked with vitality and richness, whereas, for the non-Indigenous, reception will be through more accurately calibrated eye-glasses (as it were).

For Neal McLeod (Saskatchewan Cree/Danish), this manifests the working of a kind of Indigenous poetics: 'a theoretical activity grounded in narrative and language [and] the embodiment of Indigenous consciousness'.[27] McLeod draws on a number of Indigenous voices from his book to explain the power of the embodied poetic consciousness: 'one of its most important functions . . . is to help decolonise the imagination by bridging the ideological boundaries that often separate the beneficiaries of colonialism from those who are objectified and impoverished by it';[28] more specifically, it can be 'a way of retrieving the feminine'.[29] In sum, Indigenous poetics can 'puncture holes in the expectations and understandings of contemporary life' of both Indigenous and 'settler' society.[30] In *Angry Inuk*, Arnaquq-Baril heeds, with fresh urgency, Sophie McCall's warning that '"voice" remains a central point of struggle for "Aboriginals" and that "Aboriginal/non-Aboriginal" interactions are overshadowed by colonial legacies'.[31] Arnaquq-Baril's ambitious *cinécriture* expresses both the need of her own community to find public voice *and* the agency to address the global community as a whole in that voice.

The Indigenous voice validates cultural integrity in the face of counter-world views. Arnaquq-Baril and her friend and co-activist Aaju Peter, a lawyer, stand in Aaju's kitchen, looking at fridge magnet photo of two grinning toddlers sitting on a floor. It is the classic 'birthday cake shot' with icing smeared everywhere except, here, there is no icing. The clothes, faces and hands of the children – Aaju's – are smeared in blood and, from their smiling faces, they are delighted. Laughing, Anaquq-Baril asks: 'That's "them" eating seal meat? That's a proud Inuit photo!' 'Yes', Aaju replies. 'Their grandfather used to come home with seal and they were just like huskies, they'd dive right into the meat.' 'Headfirst apparently!' Alethea responds. More laughter.

Aaju: 'It would be scary to any other culture but to us it's (the two in unison): *so cute*'.

This exchange reflects Arnaquq-Baril's drive to voice her culture. But it also constitutes a transgressive act confronting the world. It is a direct take-down of anti-sealing propaganda (the all too familiar shot of white baby seals lying in a pool of blood). Here is the filmmaker messing with this iconography. Although doubly disadvantaged, Arnaquq-Baril, as an Inuit woman, seizes agency to execute a filmic 'jujitsu',[32] re-purposing a Western technology to make a case against Western inflictions on indigenous life. Arnaquq-Baril is in the business of taking agency back. As she says in the film: 'At some point in my childhood, I realised there are people out there who didn't like seal hunting ... Every spring I'd watch people on the news call seal hunters horrible things.' The drive to record culture in *Angry Inuk* also furnishes the materials to correct the outside world's – the 'settler's' – stereotyping of it.

Arnaquq-Baril was in Aaju Peter's kitchen in Iqaluit because:

> I wanted to make this film because it bothered me when animal welfare groups portrayed seal-hunting as an evil and greedy thing. The images and messages they put out don't reflect the seal-hunting I know – they don't even mention the Inuit – but my friend Aaju Peter is fighting to change that.

Peter, not only lawyer but also sealskin clothing designer, is a longtime activist for seal hunting rights. These are most threatened currently by a 2009 ban on the sale of seal products – all products, even meat and oil – in the twenty-seven-nation bloc of the European Union. Peter is launching a legal challenge to this legislation, the progress of which Arnaquq-Baril will document.

Thereby the film also becomes a tool for this second motivation – speaking Inuit truth to power. Moreover, in doing so as a *scriptrix narrans* Arnaquq-Baril makes no more pretense at being a sociologist or an ethnographer (or a journalist) than did Varda in *Les glaneurs*. It is not a usual patriarchal position: 'Many examples of digitial activism, whether strategic or non-strategic, are not self-consciously performative and insist on non-ironic position of agency and approaches to authentic voice.'[33] Anarquq-Baril, in contrast, is a key figure in her own film, a melded filmer/filmed subject *and* agent. She is far from 'non-ironic'. No supposedly 'objective' observer, she is – within in terms of her own culture which finds the open expression of anger extremely problematic – an 'angry Inuk': 'Politicians seem to have a hard time seeing us as part of the commercial market. They're still picturing Eskimos and igloos with no need for money.' And they certainly do not understand that, food apart, seal products and skins are a major source of revenue for Inuit communities.

But animal protection agencies (Greenpeace, WWF, IFAW) also need money and the image of a baby seal is easy to exploit. The filmmaker finds archive footage of a Greenpeace worker candidly explaining on the radio that: 'The ban is all about not killing seals – not because they are endangered (they are not) – but because they are cute.' Using social media, Arnaquq-Baril films herself tracking down Annemeike Roell, former IFAW manager, and films their Skype conversation. Roell tells how she was fired by IFAW when she challenged her employer for perpetuating a picture of sealing not in line with reality: 'They were not interested in ending the ban – it brings in millions of dollars in donations.'

Peter and Arnaquq-Baril take a group of Inuit political science students who have been researching the realities of the seal ban to Paris and Brussels to meet with EU government ministers to present arguments appealing the ban. For Lee Maracle, the telling of a story is a distinctly Aboriginal vehicle of instruction central to the oral traditions of Aboriginal culture – 'the listener is as much a part of the story as the teller'.[34] The students are story-tellers – story-tellers with facts. Their targeted audience, the agents of the ban, are interpolated into the Inuit activists' story. It is 'settler' education in action (Figure 6). As one student says on camera:

> At the very least, we ask that you educate your people about the nature of the propaganda of the animal rights groups. Hunting feeds us and selling skins gives us an income. We want economic equality and to achieve that we have to stop the prejudice imposed on us.

A politician tells the students they have had better success in explaining the matter than the Canadian embassy 'in four years'; another notes that seal hunting is sustainable and environmentally responsible, unlike artificial fur coats made from oil (non-renewable petroleum) – 'you have a hell of a time to get rid of them'.

Like Varda, Arnaquq-Baril is a central figure in her film, but she is no *homo narrans*. *Angry Inuk* is the product of collaboration, affecting filmer and filmed. It delineates the working of a collective *scriptrix narrans*. It uses the accessibility of digital technology to give voice and agency to the previously excluded. Arnaquq-Baril's bricolage presents both a cultural celebration for Inuit and instruction for the non-Indigenous, effectively shifting the film's emphasis into new territory. In this sense, *Angry Inuk* is deeply activist proposing 'new forms of agency in the interface of digital activism, where words, images and narratives matter'.[35]

But, more than this, the *scriptrix narrans* points the way for a final melding – not only that of the filmer and the filmed but also that of the filmed-filmer and the viewer. Interactivity – from navigating a website through to upload-

Figure 6 Settler education: Aayu Peter in Alethea Arnaquq-Baril's *Angry Inuk*.

ing materials to the point of co-creation – is, thus far, not much explored. Interestingly, early work – such as that of Sharon Daniel – comes from women pioneers. We are only at the beginnings of the road where this might lead. As Australian scholar Kate Nash points out, the traditional civic functions of documentary from educational films, through Grierson to investigative journalism – the terrain of *homo narrans* – no longer represent a boundary. But with interactive documentary – collaboratively created by *scriptrix narrans* – these traditional functions can be readily augmented by attempts to build community and foster all forms of civically oriented participation (private communication). In this article I have wanted to suggest that the ways in which this can be done are favoured by *filmer en femme*.

Notes

1. 'Best documentaries of all time', *Sight and Sound*, 2014, <http://www.bfi.org.uk/sight-sound-magazine/greatest-docs> (last accessed 7 January 2017).
2. Delphine Bénézet, *The Cinema of Agnès Varda: Resistance and Eclecticism* (New York: Columbia University Press, 2014), p. 6.
3. Homay King. 'Matter, time, and the digital: Varda's The Gleaners and I', *Quarterly Review of Film and Video*, 24/5, 2007, p. 422.
4. Virginia Bonner, 'The radical modesty of *Les Glaneurs et La Glaneuse*', in Corinn Columbar and Sophie Mayer (eds), *There She Goes: Feminist Filmmaking and Beyond* (Detroit, MI: Wayne State University Press, 2009), p. 120.

5. King, 'Matter, time, and the digital', p. 439.
6. Ibid. pp. 426, 422.
7. Richard Havis, 'Varda gleans DV style', *2-pop: The Digital Filmmaker's Resource Site Online*, 30 May 2001, <http://www.2-pop.com/library/articles/2001_05_30.html> (last accessed 9 May 2016).
8. Bonner, 'The radical modesty of *Les Glaneurs et La Glaneuse*', p. 120.
9. Trinh T. Minh-ha, *The Digital Film Event* (New York: Routledge, 2005), p. 28.
10. Hélène Cixous, 'The laugh of the Medusa', in Marta Segarra (ed.), *The Portable Cixous*, trans. Keith Cohen and Paula Cohen (New York: Columbia University Press, 2010), p. 4.
11. Cixous, Hélène (2010). 'The laugh of the Medusa', *The Portable Cixous*, trans. Keith Cohen and Paula Cohen, ed. Marta Segarra, *The Portable Cixous* (New York: Columbia University Press, 2010), p. 4.
12. Roland Barthes, *S/Z* (New York: Farrar, Straus and Giroux, 1991), p. 4.
13. Sophie McCall, *First Person Plural: Aboriginal Storytelling and the Ethics of Collaborative Authorship* (Vancouver: University of British Columbia Press, 2011), p. 2.
14. Ibid. p. 2.
15. Lois McNay, *Gender and Agency: Reconfiguring the Subject in Feminist and Social Theory* (Cambridge: Polity Press, 2000), p. 7.
16. Ibid. p. 8.
17. Ibid. p. 9.
18. Sharon Daniel, 'Argument, inquiry and political narrative', in Matt Soar and Monkia Gagnon (eds), *Database | Narrative | Archive*, 2014, <http://dnaanthology.com/anvc/dna/aesthetics--politics?path=case-study-public-secrets-and-blood-sugar> (last accessed 7 January, 2017).
19. Ibid.
20. Sharon Daniel, 'Collaborative systems: redefining public art', in Margot Lovejoy, Christiane Paul and Victoria Vesna (eds), *Context Providers: Conditions of Meaning in Media Arts* (Chicago, IL: University of Chicago Press 2010), p. 56.
21. Sharon Daniel, *Public Secrets*, <http://www.sharondaniel.net/#about-1> (last accessed 7 January 2017).
22. Sharon Daniel, 'Inside the distance'. Recorded presentation Western Humanities Alliance, 6 November 2013, University of California San Diego, <https://www.youtube.com/watch?v=ZcBkHIVBm3I> (last accessed 7 January 2017). Sharon Daniel (n.d.), 'Inside the Distance', <http://www.sharondaniel.net/#inside-the-distance> (last accessed 7 January 2017).
23. Ibid.
24. Arnakuk-Baril 'About', <http://www.unikkaat.com> (last accessed 2 August 2016).
25. Fernando Solanas and Octavio Getino, '*Hacia un terce cine*' *Tricontinental 13* ['Towards a Third Cinema', 1969], in *25 Years of the New Latin American Cinema* (London: British Film Institute), <http://documentaryisneverneutral.com/words/camasgun.html> (last accessed 7 January 2017).
26. Barry Barclay, 'Celebrating fourth cinema', *Illusions Magazine*, July 2003, p. 6, <http://www.maoricinema.com/wp-content/uploads/2014/02/BarclayCelebratingFourthCinema.pdf> (last accessed 8 January 2017).
27. Neal McLeod (ed.), *Indigenous Poetics in Canada* (Ottawa: Wilfrid Laurier University Press, 2014), p. 4.
28. Warren Cariou, 'Edgework: Indigenous poetics as re-placement', in Neal McLeod (ed.), *Indigenous Poetics in Canada*, p. 32.

29. Lesley Belleau, 'Stretching through our watery sleep: feminine narrative retrieval of cihcipistikwân in Louise Halfe's *The Crooked Gain*', in Neal McLeod (ed.), *Indigenous Poetics in Canada*, p. 337.
30. McLeod, *Indigenous Poetics in Canada*, p. 6.
31. McCall, *First Person Plural*, pp. 2–3.
32. Ella Shohat and Robert Stam, *Unthinking Europcentrism: Multiculturalism and the Media* (London: Routledge, 1994), p. 307.
33. Carrie Prei and Maria Stehle, *Awkward Politics: Technologies of Popfeminist Activism* (Montréal/Kingston: McGill-Queen's University Press, 2016), p. 123.
34. Lee Maracle, *Sojourner's Truth and Other Stories* (London: Press Gang Publishers, 1990), p. 11.
35. Prei and Stehle, *Awkward Politics*, p. 8.

5. HYBRID PRACTICES AND VOICE MAKING IN CONTEMPORARY FEMALE DOCUMENTARY FILM

Kim Munro

INTRODUCTION

> The voice is elusive. Once you've eliminated everything that is not the voice itself – the body it houses, the words it carries, the notes it sings, the traits by which it defines a speaking person, and the timbres that colour it, what's left? What strange object, what grist for poetic outpourings?[1]

Voice has been written about from various perspectives in documentary, from Nichols's conceptualisation of the 'voice of documentary'[2] to situating it as a social function in enabling the previously unrepresented a measure of agency. In documentary film, voice can also refer to modes of address in narration or how interviews are used. Underpinning many of these ideas around voice have been gendered concerns about who speaks, who is spoken of and how the speaking occurs, revealing issues of representation, identity and power.

The concept of voice continues to be, as Chion muses, a 'grist for poetic outpourings' not least because of its inability to be fully grasped and defined. More recent theories of voice have continued to explore and dissect meaning and ontologies around ideas of collaboration as well as a focus on process-orientated documentary theory. With these ideas in mind, and taking the concept of voice to be both nebulous, and situated across film theory and filmic strategies, I wish to study both sites of the 'voice of the participant' and the 'voice of the film'. Underlying this examination are questions pertaining to how we might think about voice as representative of more collaborative and reflexive modes of filmmaking, and how this allows documentary subjects to participate in the construction of their (self) representation.

Drawing on a genealogy of both theories around voice and practices of female documentary filmmaking, this chapter focuses on a range of filmmaking techniques that challenge the concept of documentary authority in constructing voice. In distinguishing between various methodological approaches taken by female filmmakers concerning the 'coming to voice', I will explore how these co-constructed forms contribute to self-representations. We shall see how the strategies used by these filmmakers also highlight elements of how truth, narrative and identity are constructed through the hybrid filmmaking practices used by Gillian Wearing, Clio Barnard, Alma Ha'rel and Carol Morley.

Speaking of Voice

'The grain is the body in the voice as it sings, the hand as it writes, the limb as it performs.'[3]

As Barthes describes the grain of the voice, so too the 'documentary voice' can be theorised as more than the sum of the voices it represents. According to Nichols's seminal essay, 'Voice is perhaps akin to that intangible, moiré-like pattern formed by the unique interaction of all a film's codes'.[4] Nichols likens the 'voice' to documentary's version of film style, with the additional components of its place in the historical world and the presentation of the perspective of the filmmaker through their address to the audience.[5] It is the combination of style, the translation of perspective, and the interaction with the participant. It also includes all the formal filmmaking decisions including cutting, editing, and equipment.

While the concept of voice is multi-layered and complex, Nichols's idea of voice still largely pertains to the singular unified perspective of the filmmaker rather than positioning the subject as part of their own representation. Although Nichols has contemporised his theory on voice over the years, the focus on the dominance of the film as text is still predicated on this singular concept of voice. Arguing that the commercialisation of documentary filmmaking has resulted in the muting of the filmmaker's voice, Gibson and Leahy further equate voice with the stance (attitude, tone, perspective) taken to the subject, something like the filmmaker's point of view expressed by all the techniques the documentary maker uses to create meaning.[6]

Trish FitzSimons further supports the claim that funding institutions and their dictates form a component of the film's voice in her significant contribution to the field of documentary voice and discussion of her own documentary filmmaking practice.[7] Presenting a more practice-led interpretation of voice in her essay, FitzSimons uses the term 'coming into voice' to speak of a more active process of meaning making in the concept of a film's voice.[8] FitzSimon's use of the term 'braided voice' is apt when applied to the multiple roles women have played in the making of films, not to mention the obvious craft associations and 'women's work'. From early films such as *Man With a Movie Camera* (1929), women are shown 'stitching' the film together in the edit suite. Patricia Zimmermann also highlights the importance women have played in other film-related behind-the-scene roles such as organisers, curators and other collaborators working to create collective experiences in film events.[9] Additionally, while women have traditionally been more dominant in documentary production, it is the hybrid spaces that have allowed for approaches less dictated by dominant paradigms of film production. This 'braiding' becomes evident in the pulling together from many places and disciplines to create the voice of the film, thus expressing a shared authorship. While Nichols presents a unified and hierarchal concept of documentary voice, FitzSimons argues for a more complex understanding stemming from critical theory positions such as post-structuralist and subaltern studies.[10] This braided voice also emerges from her position as a practising filmmaker.

The Filmmaker's Voice Outsourced

'You should've spent the money they gave you to make this film on therapy.'[11]

With easier access to filmmaking equipment and handy-cams in the 1980s and a turn towards an interest in identity politics, the under-represented or traditional objects of documentary gained access to means that enabled them to represent themselves and their communities. The object became the subject and traditional minorities began to speak for themselves and each other, countering long-standing absences and silences. This includes autobiography and self-portraiture as well as more experimental approaches to the construction of identity. It also conflates the concept of voice as both emerging from the filmmaking practice as well as from the subject of the film.

Carol Morley's *The Alcohol Years* (2000) positions the filmmaker as both subject and object. In this film, she returns to Manchester in an attempt to remember, or at least recover lost memories caused by her heavy alcohol use between 1982 and 1987. Eliciting participation by posting an advertisement in a local newspaper, she calls for people who knew her during this period to come forward and testify to her behaviour, activities and general character at that time. The film is largely constructed of these talking head interviews, looking straight down the barrel of the camera in direct address to both the filmmaker and the audience. These testimonies are intercut with constructions, which in the absence of memories fulfil the role of the documentary re-enactment. These have the appearance and aesthetic of grainy archival footage and impressionistically illustrate the anecdotes and narrative that unfold. The voices of the uncaptioned interviewees (with names only listed in the end credits) leave the audience to guess at the relationship they once had, and may still have. One of these acquaintances clearly expresses his anger in a barely veiled accusation of indulgent narcissism, 'You should've spent the money they gave you to make this film, on therapy'. Apparently he is not aware of the Renovian term 'techno-analysis', or using autobiographical filmmaking as a way to make sense of one's place in the world. Renov refers to this as 'the displacement of the analyst by the apparatus itself, resulting in a kind of do-it-yourself psychotherapy'[12] to describe the turn towards autobiographical filmmaking made possible with easier access to filming and editing equipment.

Autobiographical films have contributed significantly to what Julia Lesage calls a feminist film canon.[13] These films were seen as ways to vocalise what had been silenced. Morley uses these voices to recover the gaps. This project calls into question to what extent the filmmaker is able to construct their own identity through editing together these interview responses. The trope of the unreliable narrator is well known in literature as well as first-person filmmaking. We do not hear Morley speak, except in brief off-camera responses to participants, yet her identity is constructed through these informal accounts as they recall memories of her promiscuity and unreliability. This results in the dual voice construction of outsourcing of subject positioning, yet mediated by the filmmaker. Thomas Waugh claims that the documentary identity (voice) is constructed through this relationship between participant and filmmaker.[14] The voice presented by *The Alcohol Years* then is tense and fraught, built not on a collaborative dialogue but an uncomfortable intimacy.

The metaphor of the ventriloquist's voice is often used in thinking about ideas of the filmmaker's voice. Documentary subjects and participants are at times engaged to speak what the filmmaker wishes to say, but cannot. Rick Altman cites Hutton's thoughts on the role the dummy plays in speaking the unconscious, claiming the dummy speaks repressed desires, as the filmmaker speaks through the film.[15] The fundamental relationship between the dummy and its human is, however, one of contrasting perspectives, or at least what the use of the dummy permits the ventriloquist to say. The throwing of the voice to the cipher displaces the speaking body and supplants it into this vessel, which is also used as a way to distance what is said from the speaker. In her more recent discussion of the use of the ventriloquial voice, FitzSimons claims that while also a loaded term, it may be useful to use the metaphor of the ventriloquist in situations 'where one entity's expression is subordinated to another'.[16] Giving the construction of Morley's identity to these interviewees troubles the question of 'who speaks for whom'.

The idea of 'giving voice' is questionable here as while these subjects clearly speak their minds, with little evident self-censoring, the complicated relationship with the subject is evident. Morley's *The Alcohol Years* is autobiographical and the participation is controlled through the premise of the film. Jill Daniels claims that 'by withholding her own voiced responses to the interviewees, Morley creates an identity of considered detachment, distinction and a discomforting absence at the heart of the film'.[17] Morley uses the effective strategy of the documentary filmmaker never filling the silence with her voice so that the subject will continue to speak, to fill the void, to betray more of their thoughts and feelings.

While it is often claimed that art (and film) is at its core autobiographical, the idea of getting others to speak in the place of the 'author' is a strategy used for various ends. Doubting the legitimacy of her own voice, Gillian Wearing explicitly states 'I'm more interested in how other people can put things together, how people can say something far more interesting than I can . . . attempting to address what I couldn't verbalise'.[18] In *Signs that say what you want them to say and not Signs that say what someone else wants you to say* (1992–3), the work for which she became famous, she asks people to write down what they 'really' want to say . The title of this work suggests the enabling of a voice that has been repressed, marginalised or inhibited. Barry Schwabsky claims that Wearing's voice is the 'estranged voice' and that our self-estrangement is shared through the voicing of it.[19] Through her own estrangement she is also able to access this trait in her participants.

Coming to Voice as Therapy

'Would you like to be in a film? You can play yourself or a fictional character. Call Gillian.'

What would compel someone to respond to such an invitation? Apparently around 2,000 such people were interested enough to call Gillian, with seven being invited to participate in Wearing's first feature *Self Made* (2010). Much like Morley's newspaper advertisement, this request for participation frames the opening sequence in this hybrid film, which is part art project process, part dramatised events, part talking head interviewees, and part acting-workshop documentation. The first glimpse we have into the participants is their self-introductions, possibly from their audition tapes. Throughout the film, these participants take part in three weeks of method acting workshops with drama teacher Sam Rumbelow. These sessions assist in preparing the participants for the short filmic scenes they will realise at the end of the intense and cathartic experience. The workshops give the participants tools so that they can craft their own narrative reflected in the short film made. Some of them draw from their own experiences or their suppressed fears or desires, while others adapt from established texts. This therapy-like process allows them to manifest something dormant in their lives. The use of cinematic techniques and higher production values in these scenes are self-consciously contrasted with both the observational footage of the workshops and the unflatteringly lit documentary interviews.

Vestiges of Wearing's other work and her art practice can be seen in *Self Made* though she appears to have relinquished some of the artist's control by allowing the participants some agency in the creation of their set-pieces. The use of the human voice is a common trope of Wearing's work, manifesting itself differently in each of her projects. During the acting workings, the participants in *Self Made* are shot from many angles, but they are also imbricated in a larger representation of themselves. These workshops are a kind of talking cure with the 'coming to voice'[20] of the participants demonstrated metaphorically through a literal coming to voice. In the beginning of the process, the sounds the participants express are primal and guttural, moaning and emanating from the body. With Rumbelow acting as surrogate therapist and interviewer, soon the participants are verbalising difficulties in their lives around childhood, family and intimate relationships. One participant, Dave reveals that he has decided that on a certain day in the future he will die, and has thus begun the process of distancing himself from people close to him, effectively and painfully closing himself down. This confession seems to appear unannounced and yet he is able to articulate this to camera as he workshops improvised encounters at his workplace and takes part in other dramatic scenes with other participants. It is also prudent, though, to consider what has occurred off-camera here, and to what degree performance plays a part.

The movement from the more traditional documentary strategies of observation and interview towards the stylised short films or 'end pieces' positions the participants as co-authors or collaborators in the construction of their films. This contrast recalls Trinh T. Minh-ha's deconstructive and much theorised *Surname Viet Given Name Nam* (1989). In the first half of this film, amateur Vietnamese-American actors voice words taken from transcribed interviews with Vietnamese women. They provide a body from which these words can be spoken. In the second half of this film, the filmmaker affords a degree of autonomy to the interviewees in the way they choose to be represented, self-styling themselves in how they dress, how they speak, and what they say as middle class Vietnamese-American women rather than immigrants. Trinh claims that involving the participants in their own self-representation was a shift from a position of director to a collaborator.[21] This also represents a coming to voice as a collective and personal experience.

In *Self-Made*, the trope of the ventriloquist again comes to mind when identifying the filmmaker's voice. The voice of the director is not heard, almost as if the method acting coach, Sam Rumbelow, becomes an extension of the director as a stand-in to perform the traditional documentary filmmaker's role of conducting interviews. The filmmaker provides the set-up for the action to happen, a strategy that resembles the construct of reality television. The interviews with the participants, intercut throughout the film, reflect the kind of meta narration often seen in reality TV shows like *Big Brother* or *Masterchef*. These appear as commentary after the fact, and a way for the participant to reflect on themselves as experienced through the workshops and the improvised scenes. One of the participants, Lian's (therapeutic) narrative arc is built around her troubled relationship with her father. Her short film is a (metaphoric) scene from King Lear. This has the effect of Lian finding her voice, thus instigating a reconciliation with her estranged father, told through a follow-up interview after the filming period. This would seem to embody some kind of wish fulfilment of the therapy trajectory.

Non-vocal Voicing

> 'Who can represent someone else, with what intention, in what language, and in what "environment" is a conundrum which characterises the postmodern era.'[22]

The question of not only how the voice of the film is conveyed, but also how voice is constructed and exhibited in a documentary in para-vocal ways, can be explored through the use of performative elements and hybrid practices. Altman refers to the etymology of ventriloquism in Ancient Greece translated as 'belly prophets',[23] where the truth would be spoken from the body. This is also true of contemporary ventriloquism where the dummy is able to say what could not be said otherwise.

Alma Ha'rel employs a form of speaking from the body in her multi-genred *Bombay Beach* (2011). Drawing on her background as a music video director, this film also exhibits one of traditional documentary's social functions of enabling a platform for the previously unheard. Set against the backdrop of the once holiday destination for the affluent, Bombay Beach, California is now home to a small cluster of disenfranchised residents at the lower end of the socio-economic spectrum. Techniques used by Ha'rel recall the made-for-television musical documentaries of Brian Hill. In Hill's work, poet and collaborator Simon Armitage translates extensive interviews with participants into songs. These songs are subsequently taught to the subjects to perform in musical sequences, which punctuate the films. Similarly, Har'el's process involves working collaboratively with a choreographer and the participants to construct the dance sequences in her film. In this process, there is an interplay of voices between the filmmaker's aesthetic, the strong presence of the music by Beirut and Bob Dylan, the observational footage, the infrequent voice-over

HYBRID PRACTICES AND VOICE MAKING

Figure 7 *Bombay Beach* [DVD], dir. A. Har'el, Ro*co Films, 2011.

interviews and the translation of the individual narratives of some of the participants through dance.

The dance sequences in *Bombay Beach* materialise the collaborative relationship between filmmaker and participants, rethinking the idea of voice as authorship. This conflation of authorship and documentary poses some uneasy questions. Auteur theory has propelled much film criticism since the 1950s and has continued to resist the fact that most films are largely the result of collaborative ecologies. Zimmermann claims that film theory has had trouble discussing these collaborative relationships as this might undermine the belief that authorship is driven by a sole individual.[24] Jay Ruby highlights two epistemological differences in approaches to documentary filmmaking: one as the translation of the filmmaker's vision, perhaps more closely aligned with what we understand as authorship, the other being the filmmaker's attempt to replicate the perspective of the subjects of the film.[25] Both these perspectives are subjective constructions but the concept of voice might differ with each approach. These simultaneous procedures are at play in *Bombay Beach* (Figure 7) where the filmmaker's previous work and experiences have infused the film's aesthetic, while her attempts to translate the experiences of the participants are also evidenced.

In *Bombay Beach,* the dances performed by the participants speak from the body, often supplanting the vocality of experience. We are first introduced to Red, an elderly cigarette dealer, who makes his small income from buying tax-free cigarettes from an Indian Reservation and selling them on to the residents of Bombay Beach. When Red suffers a serious bout of heatstroke and has to be taken to Fresno, some 391 miles away, he is visibly displaced, wheelchair bound and unable to speak. The dance he performs in response to this unfolding narrative uses props to connect him to his home and self. This is a sequence of small and simple choreographed movements of cigarettes around a table (seen in Figure 7). With the absence of his voice, he uses these objects and movements to speak.

In *Self Made*, the technique of dramatic improvisation is used for the participants to begin to vocalise their underlying reasons for participating in the project. Forty-year-old Lesley longs for the Second World War period, believing in the fantasy that during this time, life was simple and people were polite. Early in the film, she acts out a scene in a shop where, after expressing her appreciation of a set of crockery, the shopkeeper (another participant) begins to throw the plates against the wall. Initially, Leslie shrinks away with the impact of this violent act. However, slowly she is encouraged to participate in this crockery smashing as a cathartic release of her anger towards other people. Through these actions, she begins to vocalise what makes her angry: people talking on phones while driving. Does this confession mask a less palatable response hidden beneath her placid demeanour? The vocal testimony is at odds with the physicality of Leslie's actions, undermining the sole reliance on vocality as indexical to 'truth'.

Voice in the Absence of a Body: Resurrecting the Voice

While the body may provide an avenue to access the voice, in the absence of the presence of the subject (the body), how can the voice of the participant be represented? This can be applied when making a documentary film about people no longer alive. Who can speak for the deceased, and what available tools and materials can be employed for this representation? The convergence of textures of voice (and voices) coalesce to piece together both the voice of the film and the voice of the subject in Clio Barnard's *The Arbor* (UK, 2010). Ethnographic filmmaker David McDougall claims that rather than presenting a range of voices and approaches in a film, it is the interplay between these layers that contributes to its meaning and effect.[26] *The Arbor* (Figure 8) tells the story of the tragic life and legacy of English playwright Andrea Dunbar, who died of a brain haemorrhage at the age of twenty-eight, leaving behind three children and a handful of plays.

Stylistically ambitious, the texture of this film includes interviews of family and friends lip-synced by actors, archival BBC material of Dunbar, and performances of her first play *The Arbor*, performed in situ in the housing estate in which it was set while residents look on (see Figure 8). The result is a complex and reflexive interplay between these elements, leading the viewer to question representation, truth and how biographies might be constructed. Hollinger

Figure 8   *The Arbor* [DVD], dir. Clio Barnard, Artangel, 2010.

notes two strands of feminist filmmaking emerging from the 1960s – the realist documentary turn, which aimed to give voice and visibility to women, and more experimental techniques which used theoretical premises to subvert dominant forms of filmmaking usually associated with patriarchal privilege.[27] Subversion of formal strategies enables the documentary filmmaker to work in the interstices that challenge traditional forms of filmmaking.[28] *The Arbor* both incorporates and marks a shift away from representing a neglected voice, towards what Alex Juhasz has claimed as indicative of feminist filmmaking, which is to say, towards an analysis of how voice is 'constructed, mobilised, and legislated by dominant systems'.[29]

The cutting between various modes of voice in *The Arbor* creates a kind of tripartite prism of biographical representation of Andrea Dunbar's life. The film opens with Dunbar's two daughters recalling memories from their childhoods. Later we learn how different circumstances affected the trajectory of these two lives. Though we hear the voices emanating from bodies, they are bodies of actors performing a technique similar to verbatim theatre; lip-syncing the pre-recorded words. The performances of the actors enable both a distance from the speaking body and an intimacy with the body that mimes the words. Stella Bruzzi posits that when this voice is interrupted or disassociated from the body, or when it falters, the subjective nature of that voice is called into question and we access a less objective relationship with the text.[30] The technique immediately calls into question the notion of documentary truth. This was how these two daughters remember it, but did it really happen like this? Dunbar's daughters are already telling two versions of the same event.

This point is also made by Trinh, who equates sync-sound with associations of the 'real' and 'truth', claiming that synchronous sound (differing from lip-syncing) validates our understanding of the truth, 'showing real people in real locations at real tasks'.[31] In *The Arbor*, the archival footage presents this conventional technique, yet we cannot say that this representation and interview of Dunbar is any more 'truthful' than the other strategies used in conveying voice in this film.

While physical absence is present in *The Arbor*, the weight of the absent subject becomes the central concern in Carol Morley's *Dreams of a Life* (2011). Morley positions herself, the filmmaker, as an investigative journalist in an attempt to piece together the life of Joyce Carol Vincent, whose body was found in a London bedsit, three years after her death. Unlike Andrea Dunbar, who is embodied in the archival footage, a handful of plays and family and friends to speak of, for and about her, Vincent is noticeably absent. As testimony to her circumstances, the loose strands of information and anecdotes struggle to give this person substance. This search for lost time and life give rise to comparisons to Morley's earlier film, *The Alcohol Years*.

Once again employing the strategy of the newspaper advertisement to source participants for *Dreams of a Life,* Morley posts ads on London cab doors as well as using friend-finding websites. In the interviews with those that come forward, there is a sense of distance as they recall the middle class, beautiful and intelligent enigma of Vincent. There is also an overwhelming sense of objectification from the men involved in her life and a belief that her beauty exceeded her choices in men. As the interviews proceed, they coalesce in what Bruzzi describes as a *choric* representation or 'singing from the same book'.[32] Intercut with these interviews are dramatised moments from her childhood and early twenties, as well as re-enactments of the forensic clean-up of her apartment, techniques similarly employed by Morley in *The Alcohol Years* as a way to imbue a sense of presence into the absence. However, Morley's authorial presence and voice in *The Alcohol Years* is only hinted at in *Dreams of a Life* through glimpses of post-it notes as she attempts to piece together some kind of chronology of Vincent's life. Unlike the rich textures and voices in *The Arbor*, Vincent proves to be a difficult character to bring to life. Perhaps the chorus-like voice of the interviewees erases the ability for a multi-faceted Vincent to emerge. With all the reminiscing, it amounts to something of an ungraspable chimeric presence with the material and circumstances.

The sound of the voice has been equated with the site of pleasure and the experience of the maternal. Doane writes of hearing the voice as a primal experience, with the first sound being that of the mother.[33] In what might otherwise be experienced as a bleak meditation on loneliness in contemporary urban life, Morley demonstrates the pleasure of finding a recording of Vincent's speaking voice during the filmmaking process. This short crackling memento mori gives a material quality to the film's subject. In a series of almost fetishistic moments, Morley plays this recording of Vincent speaking her own name to the interviewees, recording their responses as a kind of validating moment of existence. The human voice of the subject of this film is given substantial weight, as almost forensic evidence of her existence. In the absence of the subject and the inability of others to resurrect Vincent through recollection, the voice unearths a tangible presence.

Conclusion

'A voice without listeners might as well be silent.'[34]

This chapter has presented an alternative way of thinking about voice in contemporary female documentary practice. It is one that focuses less on the Nicholsian perspective of a unified hierarchical voice in favour of a concept that incorporates hybrid approaches to participant engagement, representation and varied formal strategies of using the voice. Additionally, as Lesage suggests, the presence of the audience adds another strand of voice making to what FitzSimons has termed the 'braided voice' of documentary. The films discussed here represent something of contemporary voice making by female documentary filmmakers. While the sample is small, the styles, concerns and approaches are representative of a wider movement towards working both within and beyond established conventions.

I have explored all display approaches to filmic voice by using strategies of vocal engagement of the participants to varying effect. Documentary voice continues to be a site for discussion not least because its very nature eludes definition. While the focus here has been contained to linear films, the potential for further explorations of voice can be seen in an expanded practice of documentary including participatory, non-linear forms and multidisciplinary practices. As the nexus between theory and practice further becomes entwined, speaking from within the practice will also enable a more reflexive addition to understanding documentary practice and the concept of voice.

Acknowledgement

The author acknowledges the support of the non/fictionLab at RMIT University.

Notes

1. Michel Chion and Claudia Gorbman, *The Voice in Cinema* (New York: Columbia University Press, 1999), p. 1.

2. Bill Nichols, 'The voice of documentary', *Film Quarterly*, 36/3, 1983, pp. 17–30.
3. Roland Barthes, *Image, Music, Text*, trans. Stephen Heath (New York: Hill and Wang, 1977), p. 188.
4. Nichols, 'The voice of documentary', p. 18.
5. Ibid. p. 18.
6. Gillian Leahy and Sarah Gibson, 'Repression and expression: the film-maker's voice in Australian documentary', *Metro Magazine: Media and Education Magazine*, 135, 2002, p. 68.
7. Trish FitzSimons, 'Braided channels: a genealogy of the voice of documentary', *Studies in Documentary Film*, 3/2, 2009, pp. 131–46.
8. Ibid. p.131.
9. Patricia R Zimmerman, 'Flaherty's midwives', in Diane Waldman and Jill Walker (eds), *Feminism and Documentary* (Minneapolis, MN: University of Minnesota Press, 1999), pp. 64–83.
10. FitzSimons, 'Braided channels', p. 30.
11. Interviewee (*The Alcohol Years*).
12. Michael Renov, *The Subject of Documentary* (Minneapolis, MN: University of Minnesota Press, 2004), p. 263.
13. Julia Lesage, 'Feminist documentaries: finding, seeing and using them', in Brian Winston (ed.), *The Documentary Film Book* (London: British Film Institute, 2013), pp. 266–72.
14. Thomas Waugh, *The Right to Play Oneself: Looking Back on Documentary Film* (Minneapolis, MN: University of Minnesota Press, 2011).
15. Darryl Hutton, *Ventriloquism* (New York: Sterling, 1974), p. 28, cited in Rick Altman, 'Moving lips: cinema as ventriloquism', *Yale French Studies*, 60, 1980, p. 77.
16. FitzSimons, 'Braided channels', p. 136.
17. Jill Daniels, 'The border crossing: experiments in the cinematic representation of memory', in Gail Pearce and Jill Daniels (eds), *Truth, Dare or Promise: Art and Documentary Revisited* (Cambridge: Cambridge Scholars Publishing, 2013), p. 31.
18. Barry Schwabsky, 'The estranged voice', in Dominic Molon and Barry Schwabsky (eds), *Gillian Wearing: Mass Observation* (Chicago, IL: Museum of Contemporay Art, 2002), pp. 28–9.
19. Ibid. p. 38.
20. bell hooks, *Talking Back: Thinking Feminist, Thinking Black* (Boston, MA: South End Press, 1989).
21. Trinh T. Minh-ha, *Framer Framed: Film Scripts and Interviews* (Routledge: London, 1992), p. 194.
22. Jay Ruby, 'Speaking for, speaking about, speaking with, or speaking alongside: an anthropological and documentary dilemma', *Journal of Film and Video,* 44/1/2, 1992, p. 42.
23. Altman, 'Moving lips: cinema as ventriloquism', p. 78.
24. Zimmermann, 'Flaherty's midwives', p. 76.
25. Ruby, 'Speaking for, speaking about', p. 43.
26. David MacDougall, *Transcultural Cinema* (Princeton, NJ: Princeton University Press, 1998), cited in Trish FitzSimons, 'Braided channels', dissertation, Faculty of Humanities and Social Sciences, University of Technology, Sydney, 2008, p. 37.
27. Karen Hollinger, *Feminist Film Studies* (London and New York: Routledge, 2012), pp. 71–2.
28. Ibid. p. 73.

29. Alexandra Juhasz, *Women of Vision: Histories in Feminist Film and Video* (Minneapolis: University of Minnesota Press, 2001), p. 24.
30. Stella Bruzzi, *New Documentary: A Critical Introduction* (London: Routledge, 2000), p 5.
31. Trinh T. Min-ha, *Framer Framed*, p. 94.
32. Bruzzi, *New Documentary*, p. 48.
33. Mary Ann Doane, 'The voice in the cinema: the articulation of body and space', *Yale French Studies*, 60, 1980, p. 43.
34. Lesage, 'Feminist documentaries', p. 266.

Filmography

The Arbor (Clio Barnard, UK, 2010).
The Alcohol Years (Carol Morley, UK, 2000).
Bombay Beach (Alma Ha'rel, USA, 2011).
Dreams of a Life (Carol Morley, UK, 2011).
Man With a Movie Camera (Dziga Vertov, Soviet Union, 1929).
Self Made (Gillian Wearing, UK, 2010).
Surname Viet Given Name Nam (Trinh T. Minh-ha, USA, 1989).

6. RECORD KEEPING: FAMILY MEMORIES ON FILM – REA TAJIRI'S *HISTORY AND MEMORY: FOR AKIKO AND TAKASHIGE* AND *WISDOM GONE WILD*

Kerreen Ely-Harper

> There are things which have happened in the world while there were cameras watching, things we have images for. There are things which have happened in the world while there were no cameras watching which we re-stage in front of cameras to have images of. These are things which have happened for which the only images that exist are in the minds of the observers present at the time. While there are things which have happened for which there are no observers, except for the spirits of the dead.
> *History and Memory: For Akiko and Takashige*,
> Rea Tajiri, 1991[1]

INTRODUCTION

Memory travels not only across time and history but within families. The legacies of one generation are passed onto the following generation, tasking them with understanding and interpreting what may have not been possible to understand at the time. This is especially true for traumatic events.

To pass on a history it needs to be told, it needs to be heard and seen, it needs to be experienced and felt in the body mind. Even unwanted histories find their way back into the body mind psyche despite the efforts to eliminate what one generation would rather forget. A parent's silence or an incoherent family story leaves room for doubt and can lead to a sense of uncertainty in a child's mind about her genealogical history and her role as a descendent and inheritor. How does transgenerational trauma affect the ability of the filmmaker who is also a family member to speak from a position of coherence as 'I'? How does transgenerational trauma complicate, even exceed, the boundaries of the notions of authorship and the possibility to document difficult histories on film?

This chapter examines these questions within the context of re-representations of trauma on film, female authorship and the documentary as a mechanism for working through traumatic events with reference to the work of Japanese American auteur filmmaker Rea Tajiri. Tajiri's filmography predominantly features hybrid works combining fiction and non-fiction elements to tell complex personal stories within the 'big' frame of human history. Her autobiographical and revisionist approach to representations of history and memory can be seen in her early seminal *History and Memory: For Akiko and Takashige* (1991) and work-in-progress essay film *Wisdom Gone Wild* (2015–). Both works are testimony to Tajiri's continuing engagement with mapping the workings of individual memory and history on film in their exploration of the absence and presence of human memory as a complex circuitry of images, voices, real and imagined histories.

Structured as a nonlinear 'experimental' hybrid, *History and Memory* incorporates the subjective voice of the filmmaker to retell a traumatic history through autobiographical and familial memories. The failure of Tajiri's mother to remember the traumatic events of being sent to an American Japanese internment camp during the Second World War is counterpointed with the filmmaker/daughter's desire to know her mother's story in order to understand her own cultural identity as a Japanese American. On and off screen Tajiri is an active participant, witness and historian in retracing and performing her lost familial history. Tajiri's reconstruction of her familial memory narrative on film is both an act of intervention against forgotten and misrepresented history and a process of 'working through' family trauma.[2]

Memory Narratives of Transgenerational Trauma

We do not know how trauma is transmitted across generations, but we do know that trauma is transgenerational.[3] Trauma within families is embodied and metabolises to be passed from and between individual family members until someone from the succeeding generation begins to ask questions about the past – 'tell me what happened'. These questions in the case of transgenerational trauma also become the starting points for the work of breaking down the metabolic structure of the original traumatic event.

Trauma embedded within familial and social networks has a way of continuing its cellular journey leaving the next generation to work through the legacy of what former generations have failed to understand. Family therapy research tells us that the facts of the original trauma cannot change but the ongoing effects can be neutralised if the appropriate therapeutic process is undertaken by family member/s to uncover and work through the original trauma. This work can occur in the present and reduce the effects of past trauma in the present.

Memory and cultural theorist Marianne Hirsch, in her studies on postmemory, argues that the second generation descendants (the 'generation after' the traumatic event) inherit the symptoms of trauma experienced by the first generation through memory transmission 'by means of the stories, images and behaviours'.[4] Within the context of Hirsch's postmemory generational structure, Rea Tajiri is a second generation 'after' filmmaker whose family trauma was transmitted to her affectively as a child: 'I could remember a time of great sadness before I was born.'[5] Postmemory theory draws attention to how these inherited memories (which are not her own) have taken form imaginatively and creatively in *History and Memory*. Motivated by a desire to bridge the gap between the forgotten events that happened in the past and their continuing effects in the present, the film is a space for Tajiri to work through and reduce the effects of her mother's trauma.

Research studies on trauma and memory formation finds that traumatic memories impact on the self-schema and are recorded in the semantic memory system (long term personal memory) where they are 'beyond reflective awareness' and remain unconscious.[6] When traumatic memories are triggered they are not recognised as memories because 'the memory system that retrieves the original episode of their occurrence cannot be accessed'.[7] This is the case for people who, like Tajiri's mother, have experienced traumatic events.

Autobiographical narratives are dependent and constructed by memory.[8] Told stories derived from memory accounts involve the selection, ordering and rearranging of lived events not always in historical order 'but to tell the most coherent story about what life felt like'.[9] The coherent life story provides a sense of continuity and well-being that is critical to the autobiographical mode of being in the world as an integrated cohesive 'I am' self. Anthropologist and filmmaker Elizabeth Provinelli defines incoherency as a state of 'non-internal non-correspondence', when the external and internal representations do not correspond and the 'pieces don't add up'.[10] Real trauma cannot be re-represented because it cannot be processed cognitively as a result of 'a damaged working self'.[11] Because the original trauma cannot be assimilated into the psyche (is 'beyond reflective awareness'), the incoherency experienced by a damaged self manifests as the incoherent 'broken' narrative. This incoherency can take form as false memories or memory loss. In a clinical setting the work of the therapist is to provide cognitive links between the non-correspondence (that which cannot be re-represented) and a re-representation of a correspondent 'match' for the patient/victim to assist in processing and breaking down the structure of the original trauma to reduce its effects.

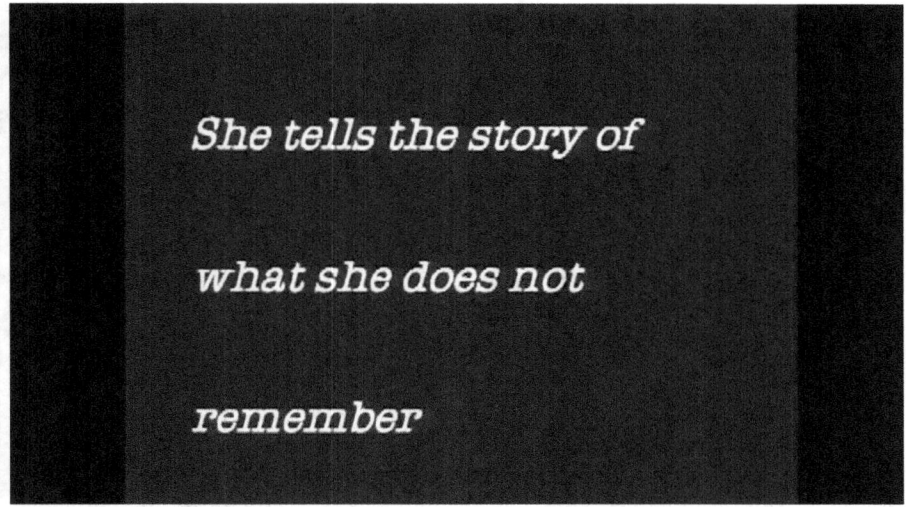

Figure 9 *History and Memory: For Akiko and Takashige* [DVD], dir. Rea Tajiri, USA, WMM, 1991.

This understanding of trauma serves as a reference point for identifying and interpreting traumatic events in Tajiri's family giving insight into how she navigates the 'working through' model to find coherence in an incoherent family narrative. I propose Tajiri moves through three stages in her filmmaking process: (1) embodiment, (2) distillation and (3) re-representation. These processes (as distinct from the commercial stages of producing a film) can be seen to parallel the narrative and trauma theory models of transformation from incoherence to coherence through Tajiri's reconstruction of her autobiographical memory narrative.

Embodiment

Tajiri's family were interned in a Japanese-American camp during the Second World War from 1941 to 1945. When the Civil Liberties Act of 1985 (Japanese American Redress Bill) was passed by the Reagan administration, entitling every Japanese American who had been interned to $20,000 in reparations, Tajiri asked her mother about their eligibility for compensation. Initially her mother could not remember being interned despite her father and other family members confirming that she, like them, had been interned. Tajiri experienced her mother's initial 'amnesia' as both disturbing and confusing (Figure 9). With the reparations Bill, previously classified files on the internment were released into the public domain. She describes her first visit to the National Archives:

> It was really like being admitted into this secret chamber ... it was strange, the archives has itself these inner rooms that you have to kind of go through ... these other passages, it was really bizarre and you went through this other separate elevator system and went into this room and they opened up this book and I was kind of trembling, you know with anticipation, because here my mother had been denying she was in camp and I felt I needed to prove to her ... I was starting to believe that she wasn't really in camp. So when I saw it I was sort of in a sense relieved and sad ... relieved with the fact that she was in camp ... but saddened that, you know, that obviously there is a trauma that she couldn't even admit to herself that she had to bury it for herself.[12]

Tajiri's visit to the archives was an embodied and affective experience. The archival evidence provided relief by validating a historical truth (yes, my mother was in the camp) but also confirmed the 'sad' truth of the extent of her mother's traumatic experience. That evening she recounts a phone conversation with her mother:

> I asked her, 'you know now I have the log book as proof ... you know this happened'. At first she was 'Oh no, no'. I said, 'No, I really have this, that says you were there, this is the date you went in, this is the date you left'. And slowly it began to dawn on her, that 'maybe ok, maybe I was there, maybe I did do this' ... she had got into this mode of forgetting and burying things, having amnesia.[13]

Her mother's absence of memory, contrasted with the visibility of evidence, raises questions about the role of personal memory in historical discourse. Tajiri's acknowledgement of the gaps that exist between the witnessed and unwitnessed events of history become creative spaces of inquiry for her in which to reimagine, embody and re-enact stories about her family's internment and her own experiences as a second generation Japanese American. Seeing images of other Japanese American people in the camps that looked the same as the people in her parents' photo album became an intriguing point, prompting Tajiri to want not only to know more about who these were people were but about her place in this archival memory. Finding a photograph of her grandmother is noted as a 'haunting' moment:

> I was going through the photographs I stumbled upon my own grandmother I was really shocked and then I realised they had had these classes in wood carving and I made this connection to that object that my mother had, 'oh my god that's where it came from, that's what this means' and

that was such a startling [moment], just haunting, a kind of wow, you know, I just had chills.¹⁴

On the back of the photograph was the inscription, 'Bird carving class. Poston, Arizona'. The recognition of the grandmother and the wooden bird, both of which have literally been framed as artefacts and inscribed by an unknown archivist, is the uncanny 'collision' moment. Tajiri's embodied experience of 'startling' and 'chills' is akin to Roland Barthes's 'punctum', where the seeing of the image 'pierces the viewer' like an arrow piercing the heart.¹⁵ The piercing affect gives her new knowledge and agency in accessing a past previously made inaccessible by her family and the American government's silences around the internment:

> They're parts of the past that kind of pierce through the present . . . somehow if we think we're not going to be affected by the past they will find a way to kind of pierce through whether it's through the idea of a haunting or a strange coincidence . . . I always feel that somehow a ghost will try to find you and point the way to you and make you see something whether we're projecting. . . [or they are] projections of our own psyche or whether it is really happening. I don't know. Maybe we actually have to resolve these things, it's a way of our subconscious projecting onto these symbols.¹⁶

Previously undisclosed information generated the interest of documentary filmmakers wanting to tell the story of the internment. Films such as *Conversations: Before the War, After the War* (Robert A. Nakamura, 1986), *Days of Waiting: The Life and Art of Estelle Ishigo* (Steven Okazaki, 1989) and *Conscience and the Constitution* (Frank Abe, 1990) were made during this period. Amateur cameraman David Tatsuno who was interned in Topaz, Utah, had hidden a camera in a shoebox and secretly filmed from 1941 to 1945. His footage became a rich archival source for filmmakers including Tajiri, who incorporated his filming of a young woman ice skating as a sequence into *History and Memory*. Within the growing body of film works around the internment (including the fiction drama *Bad Day at Black Rock*, 1955, clips of which appear in Tajiri's film) she cites a failure to represent the 'emotional impact of the internment on the generation, my generation' as a second generation child of parents who had been interned. The impact of her mother's trauma having been transmitted affectively and metabolically to her daughter ('I could remember a time of great sadness before I was born'), coupled with historical evidence that drew attention to the parts 'left out' of her family story, became motivations for wanting to make a film that would address these gaps.¹⁷ She says:

> It made me reflect how the whole notion of recording history, recording memory ... there was somehow something very precious about these firsthand accounts and ... this generation was going to move on, pass away or die ... certain things wouldn't be captured and it was like this feeling you know, 'oh god, we have to try and close in on this'. You know all these different kind of notions about memory and the role of memory, the role of firsthand accounts, all the nuances, like what role does that take up in the larger discourse, the larger narrative of history?[18]

In the absence of memory and her family's initial unwillingness (and incapacity) to engage in the process of revisiting memories of the internment, Tajiri offered herself up as one of the 'missing' bodies of history to find 'my own history.'[19] She describes her first visit to the Arizona camp:

> It was a very powerful and very emotional time and experience, it was kind of overwhelming to be thinking about the past and a particular place and then to be in that place, and you kind of feel this particular resonance, the question about what happened. So I shot there.[20]

By substituting herself and embodying 'this place that they knew about' but 'had never been there, yet I had a memory of it' she makes a transition from inhabiting to beginning to distil and make sense of her mother's lack of memory and historical truths:

> I'm trying to understand something that doesn't make sense and I'm getting the information ... the facts ... the narrative of the facts and I'm trying to also just feel it on a very kind of visceral level and a body level, like going to the camp and just feeling, what does that feel like, what does it feel like to stand in this place and I have to say it was a very odd metaphysical, strange experience, the desert is just very strange to me ... some strange things happened while I was there ... I couldn't explain them, it was a very physical and very surreal experience of that, and ... on one level very analytical, and on another very emotional and hearing voices.[21]

Distillation

Tajiri in her role as translator facilitates the communication between herself and family members in which they all play the role of speakers 'within the same cultural circuit'.[22] *History and Memory* brings together first and second generation speakers to make a bridge, a scaffold on which the first generation who have experienced trauma can begin to build upon, process and understand what they have been unable to. Tajiri as filmmaker and family member not only embodies, she must process and distil the cause and effects of the original trauma. By asking what happened and why it happened she begins to do the work of circuit breaking her mother's trauma to end it and stop it from being carried by her and onto succeeding generations.

Tajiri believed her mother's amnesia was a result of the trauma experienced in the camps. She did not in any way want to re-traumatise her by discrediting what 'she couldn't admit to herself'.[23] None of the family would agree to go on camera because there was too much shame associated with being interned. They did not want to be identified as victims, 'they just wanted to speak'.[24] Hence there are no direct camera interviews in the film, only disembodied voices. The on-screen absence of family members provided more space for Tajiri to inhabit the voices of the daughter, Japanese American citizen, historiographer and artist:

> it was always as much about me as it was about somebody, a subjectivity, a particular subjectivity that could speak for a lot of people but I knew that it had to be a subjective voice that had to drive this.[25]

Creating a multi-voiced intersubjective narrative, Tajiri begins her memory work re-enacting memories of a painful childhood 'living within a family full of ghosts', addressing questions to family members, and reworking the narratives of Japanese American history and American cinema iconography.[26] Describing her mother's memory narratives as a 'collage of stories', Tajiri's background as a conceptual video artist is reflected in her stylistic choices of montage, repeating motifs, voice-over narration, on screen text, expressionistic abstractions juxtaposed against the poetic and lyrical.[27] Free from the constraints of linear narrative conventions usually associated with traditional filmmaking training, *History and Memory* draws on filmic techniques seen in her early video works. For example, in *The Hitchcock Trilogy: Vertigo, Psycho, Torn Curtain* (1987) scrolling text without images, re-figurations of popular Hollywood film and media images and re-enactments are key features. Her approach was also intended to imitate the organic nature of memory and her experience of her mother's story as fragmented and inconsistent. She defends the poor sound quality of her recordings as an attempt to convey her feelings of dissonance: 'I was trying to capture something about the voices of my relatives ... maybe that is why I had this goofy little cassette recorder.'[28]

The film editing process was critical to the distilling process of shaping incoherency into coherent knowledge production of her 'own history'.[29] The treatment of time, such as slowing footage down in order to catch glances and responses, to 'see things you don't see when it is playing full motion', was applied to capture and narrativise her need to scrutinise and find meaning.[30] A key motif in the film is a re-enactment of her mother filling a water canteen.

It is an imagined moment that is repeated many times. The structuring of the sequence is described by Tajiri as being 'like music', the woman and the canteen is a refrain that develops through repetition to find and make coherent her mother's narrative and psychic incoherence:

> You would just see a little bit more each time, it was part of a progression that would build and you could come back and each time you would see something slightly added to that ... till finally it was a complete sequence.[31]

Making an analogy between the editing process and the act of making history Tajiri attempts to make sense of the past and make up for her mother's 'faltering' memory:

> Some things get designated as historically sanctified, the authentic version of history, 'this is history' and yet other things if they don't quite fit into that narrative they get tossed aside ... like when you are editing and you have to throw out footage [which] is not going to support this main theme. So I would have to throw it away. You know I found that to be, you know kind of interesting ... Like for instance my mother faltering or these other little anecdotal things people were saying to me, 'Well, how does that fit into this grand narrative of history? Is that going to get the rubber stamp on it? Where do you put those things? How does one carry all that stuff around and make sense of it all?[32]

Editing for the filmmaker/daughter who is also in the role of historiographer is a process of distillation, sifting through, shaping and reshaping, 'creating and dissolving' text and images to find meaning and some kind of psychic comfort through the act of structuring and making visible an absent mother on film.[33]

RE-REPRESENTATION

History and Memory is a documentary about making sense of a family legacy, of a daughter's unwillingness 'to carry all that stuff' of a past trauma, a desire to know a personal history in order to correct the 'big rubber stamp' of official histories that fail to recognise past injustices.[34] The film is made 'for' her parents; it is a gesture of recognition, an 'honourable' memory of her genealogical inheritance. From embodying their story, to distilling the bits and pieces of truth from the lies and forgettings, the filmmaker is able to move to the final stage of offering the film as visible and tangible re-representation of a family history they were unable to understand or speak about. Tajiri describes her mother's response:

> She really changed, she really changed and she was very moved by it and she started, I mean somewhere in herself, she could finally admit she [had been in camp] because she could really tell stories about the internment. She started to really tell me things ... even now in her dementia she'll start telling me stories about camp and all sorts of things. It must have shifted, must have moved some of the stuff around in there and even her sisters too became much more open and they said so. They said they were able to acknowledge it publicly and one of my aunts said they saw the film when it was broadcast on TV and they said 'Oh that was you!' They had made the connection that was her.[35]

The memory sharing between Tajiri and family members was able to facilitate an improvement in her mother's ability to remember. This observable improvement is consistent with studies in transactive memory which show that memory improves when remembering is a shared activity, and especially if people belong to intimate groups with a shared history.

Tajiri describes the film as a 'dialogue' not only with her own history, but with her generation and succeeding generations of filmmakers and audiences. The film generated a lot of discussion within her own community and second generation Japanese Americans: 'people either felt compelled to ask their parents or wanted to investigate further or felt compelled to share their story' or to make sure if they have not spoken about it, to reflect upon it.[36] She feels the film has also reached beyond speaking only for those directly affected by the internment and re-contextualises it within the broader social justice framework:

> I think also it, beyond the internment [the film] reaches across a lot of many different kinds of experiences, your own experience. It speaks to those kinds of absences, things we haven't been able to quite unfold and gather information about ... it can speak to that kind of need to bring those kinds of things to light. In terms of social justice, I think that is a constant necessity to be able to tell stories, so that as both ... as a part of healing but also to teach other people about what can happen in the world ... that we have to develop a consciousness.[37]

Referring to herself in the third person, as the 'girl who is witnessing this parent,' Tajiri is acutely aware that her family participants are also in a process of decision making of their own. Tajiri asks 'who is watching who?'[38] She regards her role as a facilitator in the process of memory transmission between herself and family members:

> It seems to be a role that I have in my family of being the annoying one who wants to ask all the questions, the annoying one who is not

> satisfied with these, the one who wants to keep all the photos, and is you know, digging and digging ... so maybe every family, every generation has to have that person the one who wants to put the album together, wants to write everything down, maybe we are ... what is that African word, the 'griot' ... I guess every culture has a name for that, the person has that role, is the record keeper ... Somebody was joking with me once. She told me I'm the shaman in the family, 'you get everyone together and you get them to talk'. Ok if that is what I'm doing, I feel Ok about it.[39]

Within the context of Bill Nichols' performative mode with its focus on knowledge through personal experience, it was from embodied knowledge that Tajiri (unlike members of her family) was able to move from the subjective and affective to the representational and intersubjective, which in turn enabled her family members to finally recognise and 'see' themselves.[40] The act of filmmaking was a process that required Tajiri to endure a catharsis her family was unable to enter into:

> It was very cathartic definitely. I think I was grieving for my entire family. When I look back it was really catharting what my family could not sum up or feel, and I was hoping that the film could in some way gather all this stuff up and say, 'these are all the things we need to say and think about and grieve and question and ask,' and at the same time I didn't want to indulge ... you could definitely go down this other path like sobbing into the camera but I didn't want to make one of those kind of films either.[41]

Keeping her eye on history, Tajiri avoids self-dramatisation and keeps her audience's attention on what she refers to as the 'metaphysical question' of what it is to be in the world. By 'her efforts to learn the story of her family's internment' she shows us how we might come to better know and re-imagine our place in history.[42]

Wisdom Gone Wild (2015–): A Memory Post-script

In 2015, Tajiri returns as an on-screen presence in her documentary project *Wisdom Gone Wild*. In a short trailer sequence titled 'November 2015 – LACMA' she wheels her mother through an interactive installation at the Los Angeles Museum of Art (Figure 10).[43] In amongst a cascade of plastic yellow hoses children play and interact with Rose, now ninety-three years old. No longer disembodied voices of *History and Memory*, mother and daughter engage in playful conversation. Rose asks 'How come they are looking for

Figure 10 *Wisdom Gone Wild* – Trailer 2:39 – 'November 2015 – LACMA on Vimeo', dir. Rea Tajiri, USA (https://vimeo.com/144466477).

their mothers?' Rea replies 'They're not. They're not looking for their mothers they are having fun.'[44]

In the accompanying synopsis a mother's loss of memory is reframed as a daughter's personal journey 'toward an understanding of aging as an evolution, rather than simply a decline'.[45] Describing her mother as 'a time-traveller', Tajiri offers audiences a new paradigm for representing and understanding dementia on film.[46]

The yet-to-be completed work demonstrates glimpses of key stages identified in *History and Memory* beginning with embodiment. The choice to have an unseen camera operator enables Tajiri to be fully present and responsive to her mother. The images are sequenced chronologically, shifting points of view from observational to subjective accompanied by first person voice-over:

> Over the next three years I decided to try things to engage Rose's crazy wisdom . . . our small outings became forays into adventure . . . I entered her house as a guest and time and space expanded.[47]

A visitor into her mother's psyche, Tajiri casts herself in a multiplicity of roles as 'I' daughter, film subject, filmmaker and storyteller. Representational images are contrasted with moments of pondering and stillness. Continuity editing choices maintain clarity and narrative cohesion. The sequence is a distillation of Tajiri as filmmaker and author of her own story and surrogate author for her mother's story. 'November 2015 – LACMA' is a re-representation of a daughter caring for her mother. It is an act of caregiving on film.

In *History and Memory* and *Wisdom Gone Wild* we witness not only an evolution of a woman's life but a filmmaker's deep engagement with her maternal legacy. Lifetimes of remembering and forgetting pass between and across both film texts. With each film Tajiri renews her commitment to meet her ancestral obligations, to bear witness, understand and seek out new knowledge beyond perceived physiological boundaries. A mother's loss of coherence becomes an 'adventure' and the confusion symptomatic of her vascular dementia is lovingly described as 'Rose's crazy wisdom'.[48] Tajiri's reframing of her mother's condition points to what Endel Tulving so aptly noted in his study of episodic memory and trauma, although something once known maybe forgotten it does not mean the memory is lost, 'only inaccessible'.[49]

Just as she challenged the authorship and authority of a history based only on visible evidence in *History and Memory*, Tajiri in *Wisdom Gone Wild* works toward a re-representation of maternity, memory loss and ageing that speaks from the subjective. As a record keeper she remains invested in her own genealogy in a bid to stay connected to the mother she is simultaneously losing and re-discovering. Memory loss potentially brings with it new knowledge and an understanding that we all share discontinuous histories.[50]

Conclusion

In the absence of images from the past, the voices of those who were witnesses at the time also go missing from history. But things not memorialised on public record are not necessarily lost forever in living personal and social memory.

Tajiri's work demonstrates that the documentary film format can be a space for working through transgenerational trauma, difficult and forgotten histories. Film as a form of memory transmission can reconstruct and retrieve lost memory traces, commemorate and acknowledge the memories and experiences of others for the purposes of commemoration, memorialisation, reconciliation and caregiving. Film can assist you to understand the memories of things you do not remember, or things that did not happen to you.

Film can be a mechanism for achieving historical justice for victim communities and documenting the legacies of past sufferings for interrogation, discussion and reflection in the present and future. For those of us who, like Tajiri, were not there and do not remember, the film that tells history through personal memory can be a form of witnessing 'as if' we had been there. Even when there are no memories it is possible to feel their loss.

Lost histories that are recovered and re-told on film take on an afterlife that is intended to outlive the filmmakers and their subjects. Film as a mimetic act of memory making also becomes a memorial strategy, retelling known stories and capturing living moments, and thus creating opportunities for new legacies and the re-imagining of our national and familial histories, ourselves.

Acknowledgement

The author wishes to thank Rea Tajiri for the opportunity to have this interview with her.

Notes

1. *History and Memory: For Akiko and Takashige* [DVD], dir. Rea Tajiri, USA, WMM, 1991.
2. Dominick LaCapra, *Writing History, Writing Trauma* (Baltimore, MD: Johns Hopkins University Press, 2001), p. 148.
3. See studies on transgenerational trauma: Yael Daieli, *International Handbook of Multigenerational Legacies of Trauma*, 2 (New York: Plenum Press, 1998); Yana N. Feodorova and Victoria S. Sarafian, 'Psychological stress – cellular and molecular mechanisms', *Folia Medica*, 54/3, 2010, pp. 5–13; Tamara B. Franklin, Holger Russig, Isabelle C. Weiss, Johannes Gräff, Natacha Linder, Aubin Michalon, Sandor Vizi and Isabelle M. Mansuy, 'Epigenetic transmission of the impact of early stress across generations', *Biological Psychiatry*, 68/5, 2010, pp. 408–15; Johannes Bohacek, Katharina Gapp, Bechara J. Saab and Isabelle M. Mansuy, 'Transgenerational epigenetic effects on brain functions', *Biological Psychiatry*, 73/4, 2013, pp. 313–20.
4. Marianne Hirsch, 'Generation of postmemory: writing and visual culture after the Holocaust', University of Columbia, 2012. Available at <https://cup.columbia.edu/book/the-generation-of-postmemory/9780231156523> (last accessed 2016).
5. *History and Memory: For Akiko and Takashige* [DVD], dir. Rea Tajiri, USA, WMM, 1991.
6. Russell Meares, 'The conversational model: an outline', *American Journal of Psychotherapy*, 58/1, 2004, p. 61.
7. Ibid. p. 60.
8. Itay Sapir, 'Narrative, memory and the crisis of mimesis: the case of Adama Elsheimer and Giordano Bruno', in Matti Hyvärinen, Anu Korhonen and Juri Mykkänen (eds), COLLeGIUM: Studies across Disciplines in the Humanities and Social Sciences, vol. 1, *The Traveling Concept of Narrative* (Helsinki: Helsinki College for Advanced Studies, 2006).
9. Daniel N. Stern, *The Present Moment in Psychotherapy and Everyday Life* (New York: W. W. Norton, 2004), p. 6.
10. Elizabeth Povinelli, 'New Media/Other Worlds? ICI Berlin, 2011'. Available at <http://www.youtube.com/watch?v=IKEJcMnRENA> (last accessed 2016).
11. Martin A. Conway, 'Sensory–perceptual episodic memory and its context: autobiographical memory', *Philosophical Transactions of the Royal Society B*, 356/1413, 2001, p. 1377.
12. Rea Tajiri, interviewed by Kerreen Ely-Harper, July 2011, New York.
13. Ibid.
14. Ibid.
15. Roland Barthes, *Camera Lucida: Reflections on Photography* (New York: Hill and Wang, 1981).
16. Rea Tajiri interview, 2011.
17. Ibid.
18. Ibid.
19. *History and Memory: For Akiko and Takashige* [DVD], dir. Rea Tajiri, USA, WMM, 1991.

20. Rea Tajiri interview, 2011.
21. Ibid.
22. Stuart Hall, *Representation: Cultural Representations and Signifying Practices* (London: Sage, 1997), p. 11.
23. Rea Tajiri interview, 2011.
24. Ibid.
25. Ibid.
26. *History and Memory: For Akiko and Takashige* [DVD], dir. Rea Tajiri, USA, WMM, 1991.
27. Ibid.
28. Rea Tajiri interview, 2011.
29. *History and Memory: For Akiko and Takashige* [DVD], dir. Rea Tajiri, USA, WMM, 1991.
30. Rea Tajiri interview, 2011.
31. Ibid.
32. Ibid.
33. See Gilles Deleuze and Félix Guattari on their classifications of the refrain in music as a process of 'deterrorialisation and reterritorilisation' in *A Thousand Plateaus: Capitalism and Schizophrenia* (Minneapolis, MN: University of Minnesota Press, 1987). Tajiri's use of repetition can be likened to Stuart Tait's reference to Deleuze and Guattari's 'creating and dissolving existential territories that help us to make sense of chaotic situations and environments'. 'Schizo-productive Performance Fictions', conference paper presented at 'A Make Believe World' symposium, Chelsea Theatre, London, 13 November, 2011. Available at <http://stuarttait.com/writing/schizoproductive/> (last accessed 2016).
34. Rea Tajiri interview, 2011.
35. Ibid.
36. Ibid.
37. Ibid.
38. Ibid.
39. Ibid.
40. Bill Nichols, *Introduction to Documentary*, 2nd edn (Bloomington, IN: Indiana University Press, 2010), pp. 130–2. Bill Nichols regards *History and Memory* as a 'performative' documentary which 'sets out to demonstrate how embodied knowledge provides entry into an understanding of the more general processes at work in society'.
41. Rea Tajiri interview, 2011.
42. Nichols, *Introduction to Documentary*, p. 202.
43. *Wisdom Gone Wild* – Trailer 2:39 – 'November 2015 – LACMA on Vimeo', dir. Rea Tajiri, USA. Available at <https://vimeo.com/144466477> (last accessed 2016).
44. Ibid.
45. Ibid.
46. Ibid.
47. Ibid.
48. Ibid.
49. Endel Tulving, 'Cue-dependent forgetting: when we forget something we once knew, it does not necessarily mean that the memory trace has been lost; it may only be inaccessible', *American Scientist*, 62/1, 1974, pp. 74–82.
50. Ann Curthoys and John Docker (eds), *Is History Fiction?* (Sydney: University of NSW Press, 2010), p. 184.

FILMOGRAPHY

All We Could Carry (S. Okazaki, USA, Farallon Films, 2010).
Aloha (R. Tajiri, USA, 1999).
Bad Day At Black Rock (Sturges, USA, J. Metro-Goldwyn-Mayer, 1955).
Bridge (R. Tajiri, USA, 2009).
Conscience and the Constitution (F. Abe, USA, PBS Film, 1990).
Conversations: Before the War, After the War (R. A. Nakamura, USA, CAAM Films, 1986).
Days of Waiting: The Life and Art of Estelle Ishigo (S. Okazaki, USA, Farallon Films, 1989).
Family Gathering (L. Yasui and A. Tegnell, USA, PBS Video, 1990).
History and Memory: For Akiko And Takashige (R. Tajiri, USA, MWW, 1991).
Little Murders (R. Tajiri, USA, 1998).
Manzahar (R. A. Nakamura, USA, 1972).
Something Strong Within (R. A. Nakamura, USA, 1955).
Strawberry Fields (R. Tajiri, Vanguard Films, USA, 1998).
The Hitchcock Trilogy: Vertigo, Psycho, Torn Curtain (R. Tajiri, USA, Electronic Arts Intermix, 1987).
Topaz (D. Tatsuno, USA, National Film Registry, 1945).
Wisdom Gone Wild, – Trailer 2:39 – 'November 2015 – LACMA on Vimeo' (Rea Tajiri, USA [online video https://vimeo.com/144466477 (last accessed 2016)], 2015–ongoing).
Yuri Kochiyama Passion For Justice (R. Tajiri, USA, 1993).

7. 'NOT BECAUSE MY HEART IS GONE; SIMPLY THE OTHER SIDE': FRANCESCA WOODMAN'S RELATIONAL AND EPHEMERAL SUBJECTIVITY AT THE LIMIT OF THE IMAGE

Anna Backman Rogers

It is that life as lived by me now is a series of exceptions . . . I was (am?) not unique but special. This is why I was an artist . . . I was inventing a language for people to see the everyday things that I also see . . . nothing to do with not being able to 'take it' in the big city, or with self-doubt or because my heart is gone . . . and not to teach people a lesson. Simply the other side.

Francesca Woodman's last diary entry[1]

the opacity of the subject may be a consequence of its being conceived as a relational being, one whose early and primary relations are not always available to conscious knowledge. Moments of unknowingness about oneself tend to emerge in the context of relations to others, suggesting that these relations call upon primary forms of relationality that are not always available to explicit and reflective thematization. If we are formed in the context of relations that become partially irrecoverable to us, then that opacity seems built into our formation and follows from our status as beings who are formed in relations of dependency.

Judith Butler[2]

INTRODUCTION

Francesca Woodman's personal history, more specifically her suicide at the age of only twenty-two years old, is often used as an heuristic framework through which her highly intricate and complex photographic work is read retroactively. Peggy Phelan,[3] for instance, in an essay that despite beautiful elucidation of her work elides Woodman's fascination with photography as the commemorative medium of the twentieth century (a century that paid witness to death and genocide on an astronomic scale) and the tragic facts of her own biography, has asserted that Woodman's work is a kind of ritualised rehearsal for an act of disappearance;[4] Isabella Pedicini has noted further that there is a marked tendency amongst scholars and critics to equate her photographs with a suicidal psyche. Indeed, Pedicini remarks that such readings eschew Woodman's fascination with liminality and states of transition precisely in order to contain her fundamentally ambiguous images within a generic narrative that serves to cast her in the role of a tragic, female artist; she writes that her work is read: 'not in relation to her own investigation of an identity poised inevitably between life and death, but out of a determination to find endless tropes within her work of anguish, restlessness, and female depression'.[5] Moreover, accounts of Woodman that portray her as an intense, passionate and prodigiously talented young artist loom large over, and at times obscure, the considerable archive of images she left behind her – some 800 photographs, many of which are self-portraits. While the facts of Woodman's biography may enrich our reading of her work, they are certainly not imperative for drawing out the multifaceted and fundamentally philosophical nature of her images. I contend, alongside scholars such as Chris Townsend[6] and Pedicini,[7] that Woodman's persistent self-documentation evinces a will that radically fights against erasure. Her images are not biographical, but the presence of the artist is always insistently and subversively there. Yet what her fleshy manifestation within these images reveals is the limitation, if not the impossibility, of capturing subjectivity as presence; as such, Woodman's work, I argue, dramatises and complicates the moment in which we come into being for someone or something else – a process which is always beset by ideology. Woodman's images precipitate the question of what is at stake when one is both the subject and object of the gaze, and whether the stakes are raised when the central focus of the image is the female body.

Woodman's performance of selfhood – for Woodman is, above all else, a performative artist – renders clear the vulnerability, mutability and ephemerality of subjectivity. Woodman's self-portraits trouble and question the notion of persistent and exhaustive identity – and by extension the possibility of self-authorship – since they capture the moment in which an ability to 'give an account of oneself'[8] radically fails. I would suggest, then, that Woodman's work is far more complex than any biographical reading of her work can allow for precisely because her photographs insistently question central tenets that form the basis of what it means to provide a personal and descriptive account of oneself. To read her work as the externalisation of psychic pain or as a self-destructive iteration is to miss the fact that her work centres on the very mechanics of photography as the medium that brings absence and presence into disquieting proximity. As Amy Sherlock notes: 'ultimately, this is what Woodman's self-portraits so powerfully articulate: the fleetingness of presence always touching the limit of absence. Woodman is never there where she is.'[9] In other words, her work professes an awareness of what will always remain radically out of reach, however much she may try to grasp it artistically; what is made manifest in a number of Woodman's pictures is something akin to Barthes' notion of the *punctum*,[10] that unintended, ambiguous, and fundamentally unreadable aspect of the image which conjures up, by making the past forcefully present, an ineffable sense of not only what is already lost to the past, but also a queasy and disquieting sense of one's own mortality. That one cannot lay claim to or explain this sense of what is already lost in the photograph only compounds its fundamentally odd and decentring nature: as Barthes writes: '(t)he incapacity to name is a good symptom of disturbance'.[11] Woodman, in a sense, presents herself as always already missing since her identity never coincides with her photographic likeness and that likeness, in turn, is presented in such a way to obfuscate and complicate any notion of a consistent and abiding sense of self.

This is not a tragic impulse (a misreading which the details of her own biography have been deployed to promulgate), but rather a concerted and intelligent engagement with what it might mean to be captured and frozen precisely as an image at the moment in which one comes into being for an other – whether that other is an observer or the apparatus. Woodman's work is undoubtedly concerned with the elision of photography with commemoration, mortality and mourning, but it would be erroneous to conclude that this is based in self-destructive tendencies rather than a keen fascination with the tension between stillness and movement, mortality and immortality implicit within the photographic form itself and what happens when one abandons oneself to the photographic apparatus: that is, the violence of stasis that is wrought on the body as a result. What Woodman gestures towards in her work are the in-between, obscure and ambiguous moments that elude and refuse capture and exhaustive understanding. It is not her own death, then, with which she is fascinated, but on the contrary the small dose of death that the moment of photographic capture delivers on the human form; as Susan Sontag has noted astutely: 'all photographs are memento mori. To take a photograph is to participate in another person's . . . mortality, vulnerability, mutability. Precisely by slicing out this moment and freezing it, all photographs testify to time's relentless melt.'[12] It is this essential vulnerability that is felt in the face of exposure to a world outside of oneself that Woodman's work so sensitively dramatises. In short, however much one may try to control the making of one's own image, there will nearly always be an infinitesimal detail that precludes the possibility of sovereignty over oneself and one's representation – life always essentially escapes capture.

It is not my intention here to discredit autobiographical readings of Woodman's work, but rather to set aside the facts of her biography in order to examine the manifold ways in which her work throws into crisis the ontological stability of the image through a determined engagement with space, time and reflexivity. As such, the Francesca Woodman I am writing of is an embodied, fleshy, and inquisitive artist who is more invested in presenting her corporeal interaction with the world and other people than she is in externalising her inner world and sense of self – which, by necessity, remains highly elusive. Woodman may have focused her camera on her own body, but the images she produced are revelatory of a kind of phenomenological and feminine being-in-the-world in which the human body is rendered deeply imbricate with its environment – an environment that always precedes and exceeds it; as Pedicini argues: 'Woodman's work celebrates the contiguity of all types of matter and establishes a connection between the body of the artist and the objects with which she becomes entangled to the point of complete synthesis.'[13] For what she asks us to do insistently is to look again, to look askance, at this world that we inhabit communally with and through our bodies. Woodman's work is far from being narcissistic, then, since it expands outwards in order to posit the very condition for the possibility of existence as relationality to other people and to the world. As such, what Woodman dramatises in her images is the excessive nature of existence and the impossibility of its summation or capture in isolation because human existence is always contaminated by its inter-relationality. Additionally, her work reframes or recasts this process of trying to capture as a form of death: a death which Woodman herself eludes by making herself persist and endure as movement *within* the confinement of an image that, by its very nature, extrapolates and freezes life.

Untitled: Subjectivity at the Limits of the Photographic Frame

It is perhaps somewhat pedestrian to note that we live in an image-saturated culture in which, according to Google statistics, over ninety-three million self-portraits are uploaded daily to social media platforms such as Facebook, Twitter and Instagram,[14] but as an overwhelmingly popular – and therefore important – current iteration in the history of self-portraiture it provides a fecund reference point, by way of contrast, with Woodman's work. This wave of socially sanctioned narcissism invokes tendencies amongst people – the overwhelming majority of whom are female young adults and teenagers – to dissect, choreograph, distort, re-frame, package, airbrush and filter their own image in order to shore up a virtual, online identity; moreover the prevailing norms of beauty that govern this form of image making ensure that these images recuperate and appropriate visual tropes that play to the male gaze. Indeed, Samsung has recently launched a model of mobile telephone camera that claims to enhance the human face by automatically slimming it down, enlarging the eyes and mouth and removing natural blemishes and pores via a free application known as 'Beauty Face'; perhaps it will be of interest to readers to note that the primary demographic this 'app' is aimed at is the young female market and, more disturbingly, that the image being propagated and sold as beautiful is one that resembles the face of a small doll (an aesthetic which the pornographic industry draws upon readily). The implication of this automatic amelioration of appearance is that one should always unhesitatingly comply with the impossible and therefore arguably pernicious norms of the beauty industry.[15]

As such, the 'selfie' is, at its very worst, a malign tool for prompting young women to hail their position as normative female subjects by making them complicit with an oppressive form of patriarchal, regressive politics.[16] What is at stake in this painstaking and laborious process is not merely approbation by one's peer group – although this has surely intensified within such a hermetic and false environment – but one's very sense of self. For what this perpetual cycle of obsessive and compulsive behaviour reveals is that if one is not constantly seen, one ceases to exist altogether. As Guy Debord[17] and Jean Baudrillard[18] already predicted with the rise of spectacular and digital cultures, the virtual image has now lost its representative function and has come to stand in for the actuality of the person. This perverse reversal demands, therefore, that a person's validity depends on her ability to approximate her own virtual and highly artificial image – a dilemma which feminist scholars from Naomi Wolf[19] to Angela McRobbie[20] have noted affects women acutely. Young women, especially, seem unwittingly able to acquiesce to a form of mediation that ensures internalisation of the deleterious norms of the ideology that governs this process of mediation in the first place. It is my contention that female virtual identity – as it is currently manifest – is characterised by an obsession with one's own image *as it may be seen* by an (implicitly male) observer; indeed, sociologist Ben Agger has claimed that: 'the selfie is the male gaze gone viral'.[21] The forms of identity it creates are repetitive (by which I mean the ubiquity of certain gestures, repeated framings, and hashtags), homogenous and static. The selfie functions as a clichéd image precisely by evacuating the human subject of her complexity and irreducibility in favour of singularity and superficiality. However disposable and spurious it may be, it fixes and reduces identity so that alterity – oddness, if you will – is eradicated.

I am not invoking or offsetting this comparison between Woodman's work and the contemporary culture of the selfie to be facetious, but rather to elaborate in what follows on what sets Woodman's concerns and artistry apart from more flagrantly narcissistic and unthinking forms of image making and meaning. Indeed, Woodman's penetrating self-examination works to evacuate rather than affirm her sense of identity and to challenge and complicate her relationship with her observer; as Pedicini argues: 'Woodman was not motivated by narcissism . . . She manifests her *self* in a body which screams and dissimulates, forever blurring and disappearing in the space of the photographic narrative.'[22] If the selfie is a catalyst to bring into being a form of, albeit shallow, false and superficial, identity, Woodman's self-portraiture throws into crisis any notion of a persistent and abiding self that can be captured or framed. Woodman, as a photographic subject, is determinedly and defiantly evasive. I would suggest that it is Woodman's preoccupation with time and movement and her engagement with the photographic apparatus as an already ideologically loaded medium, especially when turned on her own naked likeness, that precisely gestures towards the impossibility of laying claim to any definitive subjectivity. Woodman's images visually translate the existential problem of *I is another* by presenting the photographic body precisely as a liminal body *in movement* that is always on the cusp of becoming other; her work continually foregrounds processes of change and metamorphosis. This is particularly evident in a series such as *Space* (Figure 11), in which the human form is refracted and dispersed through space via the use of a slow shutter release. What we see here is evidently not a statement of identity on the part of the artist, but rather a representation of her body under the conditions of time, space, light and movement. The focal point of this image is *movement* in and of itself. If one were to extend this movement out as visual metaphor, this image functions as a translation of the processes of metamorphosis and change that are intrinsic to any object and being that exists in duration. As such, what we have is a statement on the impossibility of rendering *being as change* as a static entity – this image is both, very deliberately so, an attempt and a failure to essay capture of the human body. This is the radical point of failure, which I wrote of earlier, which is incorporated into the very form of her images and constitutes the ambiguous and tentative 'meaning' at the heart of her work. It is this determination to get at the 'truth' of the image, a truth which lies in the contradiction implicit in repeatedly failed attempts to assert *here I am,* that marks her work out as deeply existential. Her *On Being An Angel* (1977) and *Angel* (1977) series recast the human body as a liminal entity within a profane environment (perhaps symbolised by the detachment of her wings from her body). Here, the body is suspended in movement and duration as an entity that comes into being through a momentary, fleeting and fragile (im)possibility: the defiance of gravity. The point of capture – the height of Woodman's ascension – delineates visually the moment in which she both rises and begins to fall. The indistinct, blurred contortions of her body register a state of ambiguity and resolute in-betweeness that can be said to be characteristic of much of her work.

Figure 11 *Space, Providence, Rhode Island, 1975–8.*

Judith Butler, in her work on subjectivity, community and ethics,[23] identifies this tension in any attempt to gain purchase on or lay claim to a coherent, self-same identity; she writes: 'if the identity we say we are cannot possibly capture us and marks immediately an excess and opacity that falls outside the categories of identity, then any effort "to give an account of oneself" will have to fail in order to approach being true'.[24] Moreover, she suggests that in questioning the manifold ways in which meaning is made – that is, the processes by which someone or something comes to be recognised as part of a cultural narrative that precedes its being – and the forms of mediation that make an object collectively apprehensible as *something*, we are also examining the terms under which our own subjectivity becomes meaningful and personhood is produced; she writes: 'to call into question a regime of truth, where that regime of truth governs subjectivation, is to call into question the truth of myself and, indeed, to question my ability to tell the truth about myself, to give an account of myself.'[25] It is my contention that Woodman sets herself the artistic task of questioning how one comes to be seen and what this tells us about the nature of human identity at the centre of her work.

By interrogating identity, her work undercuts the possibility of authorship by foregrounding the ways in which we are never fully in control of ourselves because that self is inextricably caught up in processes that already shape and delimit our subjectivity. Her work also reveals the extent to which our sense of self is dependent on and constituted incontrovertibly by and for another and that this relationship contains an implicit violence in its reduction of our complexity. What Woodman's work both stages and fights against is this dynamic in which we wrestle with our identity *through* the gaze of another. However suffocating this relation is, it is also fundamental to our very existence as a human subject because we often make sense of our lives through collective cultural narratives (of which the self-portrait is but one example), and while it is possible (and right) to contest the boundaries of those narratives, trying to lead a life outside of narrative altogether results in obscurity as a form of death –nobody can survive a radically non-narratable life.[26] As Butler notes:

> I am not, as it were, an interior subject, closed upon myself, solipsistic, posing questions of myself alone. I exist in an important sense for you, and by virtue of you. If I have lost the conditions of address, if I have no 'you' to address, then I have lost 'myself' . . . one can tell an autobiography only to another . . . without the 'you', my own story becomes impossible.[27]

Woodman's work does not *reveal* a consistent and abiding self, but rather the ways in which the photographic apparatus works to evacuate that self whilst foregrounding the photographic apparatus itself. Woodman is supremely aware that in exposing herself for the camera, she is also performing for another. In their refusal of stasis and fixity, her photographs are attuned to the precarity and fundamental unpredictability of the moment in which they are made – a moment that is contextualised and subsists within duration. The self, as presented here, is vitally decentred and destabilised. As Harriet Riches notes:

> within a body of work in which her own body is a recurring subject, Woodman returned again and again to the ways in which her camera worked to displace any 'essence' of identity. Manipulating light to achieve effects of blurring and deep fragmentation and taking advantage of the camera's ability to crop and frame the body, Woodman exploits a photographic language of violence, as she explores the medium's proclivity for excising subjectivity from the world.[28]

Implicit within Woodman's work is the fact that she knows her attempts to create her own image, to author her own identity, are shot through with impossibility and failure. Her agency is always compromised by her imbrication with the other, for whom she performs. As Amy Sherlock argues: 'even in the case of the self-portrait one exposes oneself to the camera for another, to appear to another or . . . to see oneself from the side of the other'[29] and this duality in the image not only makes visible the violence implicit in the gaze (that I present myself as an image to be dissected and consumed), but also renders prevalent how Woodman is concerned with presenting and understanding herself as a *seeing subject*. Woodman places herself outside in order to gaze at her own image: as such, she sees herself as that 'other' for whom she presupposes and creates her likeness. Yet if Woodman somehow manages to 'capture' or hold herself as image as seen by another, her work also clarifies that this is by nature ephemeral and fleeting since one's self is always, as Chris Townsend argues, 'outside one's own representation'.[30] Woodman's project is one of excess in terms of the multiple ways in which her own subjectivity exceeds all interpretive, textual and ideological boundaries: she is defiant in her refusal to accede to any attempt at capture, even her own.

A Woman is a Mirror for a Man: Confronting the Male Gaze

Implied within Woodman's reflexive approach to making her self-image is a meditation on what it means to photograph the naked female form. She confronts phallocentricity via overt reference to violence (often wrought on the female body) and by exploring the implicit power dynamics of the gaze (that is coded as male). Woodman responds directly to the camera as an apparatus of ideology. As Claire Raymond notes: 'legible in Woodman's self-portraits . . . is the traumatic violence of being made into an image, violence that Woodman's self-portraits . . . signify as implicitly linked to her body's femaleness'.[31] Woodman is, in other words, both outside of and inside her own gaze – a discrepancy which opens up her image making to possibilities of divergence and subversion. This duality, which can be harnessed and channelled as a form of politics, is a dynamic that John Berger has identified as intrinsic to, and deeply rooted within, female experience; he writes:

> she comes to consider the surveyor and the surveyed within her as the two constituent yet always distinct elements of her identity as a woman . . . Her own sense of being in herself is supplanted by a sense of being appreciated as herself by another . . . one might simplify this by saying: men act and women appear. Men look at women. Women watch themselves being looked at. This determines not only most relations between men and women but also the relation of women to themselves. The surveyor

Figure 12 *Untitled, Providence, Rhode Island, 1976.*

of woman in herself is male: the surveyed female. Thus she turns herself into an object – and most particularly an object of vision: a sight.[32]

It is precisely the political implications of the gaze, which Berger appropriately identifies, and the subversive sites of contestation that are opened up within the disjuncture of being inside and outside of that gaze with which Woodman is concerned; and as Elisabeth Bronfen notes: '(a)ny female artist must engage with this double gaze of herself, always aware of the effect she has for the implied viewer'.[33] Indeed, images, such as *Untitled* from 1976 (Figure 12), seem to allude to this directly via a complex order of the gaze: the gaze of the photographer/artist (who is not consistent with Woodman as she appears within the photographic frame), that of the anonymous and mechanical eye of the photographic apparatus, and that of Woodman herself as she sits aside her own form from within the confinement of the image. She is *both* active and passive in this image since it bifurcates her body into an adumbration of her own naked form, whilst offering her body precisely as 'nude, seated female' to an anonymous observer (whose own gaze is filtered and directed through Woodman's choreography of this scene). It is Woodman's intense physical presence in the photograph and her gaze as an artist that compounds and complicates this image. Moreover, the deliberate placement of her arms serves to section off and draw attention, through partial concealment, to her nakedness and those parts of her body that tie her to essential (and therefore highly problematic) forms of identity politics that fuse 'femaleness' with 'femininity'. However controlled this image of her likeness is though, it also elicits a palpable sense of her own vulnerability as a body that is there to be looked at and the simplicity with which her 'shadow' is rendered speaks to the highly reductive and superficial nature of how the female body is often read within images (that she is reduced to her anatomical parts or to her body). Here, the collision of two presences within the frame – that of the fleshy embodied artist and the dark silhouette or outline of that body as it is inscribed on the floor's surface – disrupts and ruptures the surface of the image to reveal depth. Once again, Woodman signals towards the complexity of human subjectivity and the violence implicit in its reduction to a cliché (the French etymology of which precisely designates a photograph). As such, this image is as much a comment on Woodman's own process of self-documentation as it is an implicit indictment of patriarchal forms of visual culture at large that render the female body purely as a specious form of spectacle.

In *I Could No Longer Play, I Could Not Play By Instinct*, Woodman explicitly poses for the camera and her placement within the frame is rigorously choreographed and purposeful; by exposing and presenting herself as a body, once again, that is placed there to be gazed upon, she integrates herself within an artistic tradition that is already codified within Western aesthetics. In this photograph, which draws explicitly on a Surrealist and somewhat misogynist visual history, Woodman displays to the viewer her seemingly mutilated and naked breast from which the photographic negative of her own image 'bleeds'. This is an image which makes manifest the inherent violence of objectification: that is, one is transformed into an object *by* and *for* an other; yet if Woodman places herself as the subject of her own gaze – and by extension, that of the viewer – it is her subjectivity (or its imaginary equivalent) that leaks out of her here as if to assert that her own mastery over this image is illusory – a form of violence is still visited upon her. However, our own sense of mastery over the female form is trumped or undermined by Woodman who offers herself up knowingly as an object to be consumed primarily by her own gaze – as if to say defiantly, 'go ahead then, try to objectify me if you can'. Both her mastery over her own image and our visual pleasure are always already precluded.

Here, Woodman stages once again a scene of doubling: she is at once both the subject and object of her own gaze; again, Raymond notes that: 'Woodman's self-portraits picture the heuristic project of trying to see: the ... moment when you see yourself seeing'.[34] If the photograph comes to be read as a moment of capture and stasis, Woodman stages an event in which her body is not only made imminent within its environment, but also is cast as liminal, unfixed and in-between. Caught between looking and being to-be-looked-at, this body gives nothing away in terms of its own history. For what we see is not biographical – much as many of the titles of her images seem to intimate personal motivation – but a subjectivity that comes into being as it is created, in a sense, via the photographic apparatus and its coterminous ideology and norms. As such, Woodman's work functions not as an auteurist statement, but investigates the always already ideologically laden ways in which a being becomes something rather than nothing for someone else. In *I Could No Longer Play, I Could Not Play by Instinct*, it is striking, for instance, that Woodman's head is severed from her body – indeed, for someone who made so many self-portraits, her face is often (d)effaced or left out of the frame altogether.[35] Initially, this seems a statement about how objectification divests us or evacuates us of our essential humanity, but closer inspection also reveals a violence that subsists within this moment: the repetition of the artist's face and the disarming and gleaming presence of the knife foreground the power of that subjectivity which, at first, seems to be dispossessed yet is renewed via the image's very construction. Moreover, the nature of the long exposure technique gives time back to the image: this is an entity that endures and refuses capture.

In Woodman's work the surface of the image is anything but fixed and lifeless; rather, it is the surface upon which the crisis of subjectivity is played out. Her reintroduction of time (as that which throws into crisis the notion of abiding identity) into the image is a form of radical resistance against not only exhaustive readings of her work and her own identity as an artist, but also against the affective death the medium itself delivers upon her body. For what is revealed in Woodman's images is the impossibility of capture, of summation, of finality. By examining what it means to be rendered as an image for another, Woodman herself becomes altogether more complex and elusive. Her defiant presence as an artist, in all its vulnerability and ambiguity, endures in its fight against erasure. Rather than staging an act of disappearance, it seems to me, as I have argued here, that Woodman's work is marked by an elusive yet insistent manifestation that taunts both the viewer and the camera: *here I am (not); you may try, but you cannot take my existence from me.*

Notes

1. Jillian Steinhauer, <http://www.theparisreview.org/blog/2012/05/23/finding-francesca-woodman/2012> (last accessed 28 November 2016).
2. Judith Butler, *Giving an Account of Oneself* (New York: Fordham University Press, 2005), p. 20.
3. Peggy Phelan, 'Francesca Woodman's photography: death and the image one more time', *Signs*, 27/4, Summer 2002, pp. 979–1004.
4. Phelan suggests that we should acknowledge: 'the possibility that suicide might be the result of a well-considered logic and that Woodman's photography was a way to help her, and us, survive her disappearance from the surface of the visible world . . . And perhaps it was impossible to propose in 1986, when Woodman's suicide was still recent and her work was largely unknown. But now, with some of the benefits of afterwardness, we can return more directly to the insights Woodman offered us about art and death' (ibid. p. 991); and that: 'Woodman invites us to see her suicide, like her art, as a gift. Perhaps not the one we might have wished for, but the one she gave us when she did not have anything to give' (ibid. p. 1002). In short, she posits, not un-controversially, Woodman's suicide as an inextricable part of her artistic achievement.
5. Isabella Pedicini, *Francesca Woodman: The Roman Years: Between Flesh and The Film* (Rome: Contrasto, 2012), p. 37.
6. Chris Townsend, *Francesca Woodman* (London: Phaidon, 2007).
7. Pedicini, *Francesca Woodman*.
8. Butler, *Giving an Account of Oneself*.
9. Amy Sherlock, 'Multiple expeausures: identity and alterity in the "self-portraits" of Francesca Woodman', *Paragraph*, 36/3, 2013, p. 388.
10. Roland Barthes, *Camera Lucida* (London: Vintage Books, 2000), pp. 40–9.
11. Ibid. p. 51.
12. Susan Sontag, *On Photography* (London: Penguin, 1979), p. 15.
13. Pedicini, *Francesca Woodman*, p. 98.
14. See Nicholas Mirzoeff, *How To See The World* (London: Penguin, 2015), p. 65.
15. See <http://www.samsung.com/uk/consumer/flagship/SM-C1010ZWABTU/tutorial/tutorial/beauty_face_correct_facial.html> (last accessed 9 May 2016).
16. Rosalind Gill has written on this disturbing phenomenon at length across a series of articles. See in particular, Rosalind Gill, 'Beauty surveillance: the digital self-monitoring cultures of neoliberalism', forthcoming in *European Journal of Cultural Studies*, 2017.
17. Guy Debord, *Society of the Spectacle* (London: Rebel Press, 1992).
18. Jean Baudrillard, *Simulacra and Simulation* (Ann Arbor, MI: University of Michigan Press, 1994).
19. Naomi Wolf, *The Beauty Myth* (London: Vintage Books, 1991).
20. Angela McRobbie, 'Notes on the perfect', *Australian Feminist Studies*, 30, 2015, p. 83.
21. In Mirzoeff, *How To See The World*, p. 64.
22. Pedicini, *Francesca Woodman*, p. 22
23. Although Butler is writing of autobiographical narratives and the ethical implications or (im)possibility of being able to claim sovereignty over one's own actions, I read the self-portrait as a form of self-narration, implicit within which is the possibility of being able to say 'I': to be both the subject and object of one's own narrative.
24. Butler, *Giving an Account of Oneself*, p. 42.
25. Ibid. p. 23.

26. Ibid. p. 60.
27. Ibid. p. 32.
28. Harriet Riches, 'A disappearing act: Francesca Woodman's portrait of a reputation'. *Oxford Art Journal*, 27/1, 2004, p. 99.
29. Sherlock, 'Multiple expeausures', p. 380.
30. Townsend, *Francesca Woodman*, p. 57.
31. Claire Raymond, *Francesca Woodman and the Kantian Sublime* (London: Ashgate, 2010), p. 32.
32. John Berger, *Ways of Seeing* (London: Penguin Books, 2008), p. 46.
33. Elisabeth Bronfen and Gabriele Schor (eds), *Francesca Woodman: Works from the Sammlung Verbund* (Cologne: Walther König, 2014), p. 19.
34. Raymond, *Francesca Woodman and the Kantian Sublime*, p. 82.
35. In fact, Elisabeth notes that even when Woodman's face is clearly recognisable across a series of images, she never looks consistently the same. See Bronfen and Schor, *Francesca Woodman*, p. 18.

8. OTHER WOMEN: THINKING CLASS AND GENDER IN CONTEMPORARY BRAZILIAN DOCUMENTARY FILM

Carla Maia

Brazilian society is among the most unequal in the world, and the cinema *métier* in Brazil reproduces its social and economic asymmetries. The majority of Brazilian film directors are male, white and middle or upper class. The country's few female film directors are also white, well educated and from middle or upper class backgrounds, which seems to influence their low engagement with feminist issues. The feminist agenda may not apply to privileged Brazilian women in the same way that it applies to the majority of the nation's women, who are systematically oppressed not only for their gender positions, but also for their class and race.

It is thus interesting to note that, when looking at contemporary Brazilian documentaries, several films directed by women emerge, focused on 'Other' women. I say 'other' because, in most cases, these films' characters are lower class women who live in the slums and outskirts of large cities. This is the case for the films *Girls* (*Meninas*, Sandra Werneck, 2006), *Abortion of Others* (*O aborto dos outros*, Carla Gallo, 2008), *Milk and Iron* (*Leite e ferro*, Claudia Priscilla, 2010), and *Like Water Through Stone* (*A falta que me faz*, Marília Rocha, 2009), all of which are focused on female characters in socially perilous situations. How each filmmaker approaches her subjects varies, but the films all share a stark contrast between the women recording and the women that are recorded.

This article seeks to compare these films' representational and narrative strategies in order to understand how issues of gender and class intersect when women from different backgrounds encounter each other with cinema as a mediator. I therefore organise the films into two groups. The first includes films with a more sociological focus – *Girls*, *Abortion of Others*, and *Milk and Iron* – while the second contains a single – and singular – film, *Like Water Through Stone*, with a more performative approach, in which elements from the experience and subjective perceptions of both director and subjects are called into focus. I examine the relational dimension of each work and propose to consider my subject matter as films *with* women rather than films *about* or *by* women. My main effort lies in understanding something that takes place within *in-between spaces* – the space before and in front of the camera, but also between viewer and film – and in critically reflecting on the aesthetic, ethical, and political potentials that a cinema marked by different women's perspectives can bring into light.

WOMEN UNDER SCRUTINY

In *Girls*, *Abortion of Others* and *Milk and Iron*, female experiences, especially pregnancy and motherhood, are addressed in symptomatic and problematic fashion. *Girls* is a film about adolescent pregnancy among *favela* inhabitants in Rio de Janeiro; *Abortion of Others*, as its title suggests, explores the universe of abortion by visiting São Paulo clinics and presenting interviews with women who have had abortions; and *Milk and Iron* portrays a group of female prisoners temporarily living in a breastfeeding detention centre in the southernmost Brazilian state of Rio Grande do Sul. The central characters in all three films are impoverished women with a heavy burden to carry – that of an unexpected child. While their responses to this burden may differ – having the baby in *Girls*, not having the baby in *Abortion of Others*, giving the baby up for adoption after four months of breastfeeding in *Milk and Iron* – the issue is one that many women have to deal with, regardless of class or social position: motherhood.

The narrative structures of *Girls* and *Abortion of Others* have some points in common. Both films consist of several parallel stories involving people that do not know each other and are brought together by a cinematic premise. The main focus in these works is subject matter related to women, more so than specific women, who figure on-screen as illustrative sociological types rather than as complex and diverse individuals. Particular stories point towards more general pictures: the high occurrence of pregnant teenagers among Brazilian favela inhabitants in *Girls*, and in *Abortion of Others*, the perilous conditions that impoverished women who decide to interrupt unwanted pregnancies face in a country where abortion is still criminal except in cases of rape and risk to the mother's life.

The four teenagers in *Girls* and the six women in *Abortion of Others* therefore become a sampling of gloomy statistics. In Brazil, approximately 20 percent of children are born to women under eighteen years old. In the slums of Rio de Janeiro, where *Girls* take place, the fertility rate of women is five times higher than in other locations in Brazil due to early pregnancy. While there exists a lack of official figures, unofficial statistics regarding abortion in Brazil indicate that one in five women under the age of twenty have had one. Class impacts these numbers; early pregnancy tends to occur less often among middle- and upper class girls than among lower class girls, but when it does occur, abortion is a common solution for these individuals who, with family support, can afford the high cost of private medical assistance. For impoverished young women whose pregnancies are not carried to term (with child delivery in fact seeming to be the most common outcome), risking their lives through violent abortion methods is the only option, since it is not possible for them or their families to afford safer procedures. This is the context that both films, with their different foci, explore and represent.

However, it is important to bear in mind that if the films succeed in doing so, it is only because some women on-screen have agreed to open and reveal their lives, fears, and sorrows to the filmmakers. These women are more than just a sampling of a complex social problem – they are complex themselves. Unfortunately, the documentaries fail to make their complexities visible and audible, leaving them aside in order to compose a larger, more general picture of the women's situation. The four characters in *Girls* all have very similar dramas, with little to no space for subtle differences among them. The first character that we see, for example – a young woman named Luana – declares that her pregnancy was 'planned and desired'. She is fifteen, in love and with dreams, but in order for the film to prove its argument, her dreams, love and desires are silenced by narrative. Luana's mother plays an important antagonist who characterises her daughter's ideas and feelings as naive, irresponsible and inconsequential. It is easy for any reasonable adult to understand the mother's position as she speaks – but what happens, then, to Luana? Who is really listening to the teenager's voice? 'If she only knew better', we responsible adults in the film's audience might think, easily identifying with the girl's mother while she lectures her daughter. Due to the way that *Girls* is edited and organised, Luana's own words only echo blindness and ignorance of the facts of life.

Characters in *Girls* are passive and stable. They submit their images to the filmmaker's desires and storytelling intentions, but do not seem to build their stories along with her. In fact, their stories appear to have been built a priori, before the encounters; pregnancy and its coterminous difficulties were all part of a script and come into scene only to fill or occupy gaps by giving faces and names to previously defined characters. No dissonant word or gesture from any of the girls emerges to undermine the stability of their stereotyped representations.

In a similar way, the complexity and density of the subject matter in *Abortion of Others* does not leave space for any character's subjectivity to appear, to the point that the women's names and faces are even often concealed. Extreme close-ups cut their bodies off from view so that we only see one eye, finger or thigh at a time, in a formal procedure that resonates with the violence of the film's theme. Although the choice of keeping the characters anonymous could be a way to protect their privacy given their uneasy situation, the nature of the framing is also analogous to the different kinds of violence against women that are presented in the characters' speech.

The women discuss violence committed against them by strangers on the street and by their own husbands and neighbors, as well as from within institutions such as medicine, law and religion. One woman, after experiencing the considerable pain and suffering caused by a 'homemade' abortion, was denounced by her neighbour and arrested in the hospital before she could recover completely; another became pregnant after being blackmailed by her husband, who promised to give her a divorce if she agreed to have sex with him each day for one month. The film's main character – whose storyline, intercut with *Abortion of Others*' five other episodes, is explored in 'vertical', in-depth fashion compared to the more 'horizontal' tangential approach taken with the others – is a hospitalised thirteen-year-old rape victim watching all the steps of her abortion procedure. We never see her face, nor that of her mother, who is always by her side in the claustrophobic hospital room. The few things that we know about her are relayed during an interview with the social security agent who welcomes her at the hospital in the beginning of the film: such as the fact that she was on her way to school when a stranger took her by force.

It becomes obvious how this film in particular is moved by a strong need to denounce the violence and injustice suffered by Brazilian women. For years prior to this writing, Brazil has been facing social campaigns to legalise abortion that have met with little success, primarily because of the strong role played by religion in the Brazilian public's moral and political formation. Religious leaders insist that motherhood – whether it is desired or not – is a destiny for women, who should never interfere in God's plan by murdering a child in their belly. A merit of this film is that it makes visible such a relevant matter. However, in following the path of denunciation, *Abortion of Others* forgets that it is important not only to think about what we say or see, but also to consider *how* we say or see it. Just before it comes to a close – when we see the teenager finally leaving the hospital – the film includes a talking-head sequence containing interviews with doctors, lawyers and other male public figures who legitimise the work's basic premise; abortion is a matter of public health rather than of public security, and should therefore be legal.

In contrast with the film's other interviewees – the abortion victims with their cropped, fragmented, 'failed' bodies – the men here appear with their names, social positions and faces all framed in well-composed medium-shots. Their testimonies, however, are not only redundant, but also unnecessary since they ultimately expound on something that the experiences of the interviewed women have already made clear. The women's reality should be enough to prove the film's argument, but the filmmakers seem to believe that their shared inner cry is not audible enough (in the same way that the women themselves are not visible enough): 'If we want to make it more visible, audible, and relevant, we need men to say it, explain it, and endorse it', the film seems to say. Its discourse finds synthesis with this final sequence of interviews by allowing us to think that the white, upper middle class, well-positioned men's speeches both offer closure to the story and identify with the director's position. Although Gallo is a woman filming other women, it becomes clear that she identifies her filmic discourse with the men's words, and consequently class identification becomes stronger than gender identification. It should also be noted that the film presents not a single case of a woman that chooses abortion simply because she does not want a child and has the right over her own body, without dire extenuating circumstances. Women are consistently portrayed as victims, and never as active subjects in control of their own lives (as the men who speak are, as the director herself is). The abortion is, no doubt, that of others.

Both in *Girls* and in *Abortion of Others*, motherhood is portrayed as a tragic destiny. Differently, in *Milk and Iron*, women frequently speak about how blessed they are to have children about whom they can care. Prisoners of a special detention centre for breastfeeding women, isolated from society, find bonds and relief in being mothers. Also present in the film, however, are the tensions and problems of their situation. Babies can make the present seem softer and brighter, but it becomes clear how the future is unpromising both for mother and for child, who will be separated by the justice system as soon as the first four months of breastfeeding ends. Some children will be given up for adoption while others will grow up in orphanages, with only a few taken in to be raised by their mother or father's family. The detention centre's prisoners are usually themselves orphans, and rarely do the fathers of their babies appear to help raise the infants.

The narrative structure of *Milk and Iron* (Figure 13) is grounded in interviews with one main character – the veteran prisoner Daluana – and scenes of the group of prisoners in cells as they talk with each other and care for their babies. The women talk a great deal and overlap with each other's voices as they share their common backgrounds of poverty, addiction and crime. It becomes quite evident that they want and need to talk. The camera never seems to make them shy or uncomfortable. On the contrary, it even instigates and incites situations. As it faces multiple voices and characters talking at the same time, the camera's behaviour becomes somehow erratic. The result

Figure 13 *Milk and Iron* (*Leite e ferro*), Claudia Priscilla, Brazil, 2010.

is a film that is not particularly clear about its formal decisions, though very much engaged in giving the women a chance to speak for themselves. In short, the interest of *Milk and Iron* lies in what is registered and not in how it is registered. Once more, the subject matter is more relevant than the cinematic experience.

This time, however, the characters are not as archetypal as in the previously discussed films. When filming the prisoners amongst themselves or focusing on their affective moments with their babies, *Milk and Iron* avoids sociological determinations in favour of subjective instances: The women are not only 'prisoners,' but are also friends, mothers, and human beings with dreams, regrets and fears. Nevertheless, the fact that most of the time they are talking loudly and overlapping makes it difficult to hear each one of them. This difficulty might represent the main problem facing films that try to compose a critical discourse about socially perilous situations by filming specific and singular cases: how to make the passage between the general and the particular? Or perhaps: how to create bonds between them, with the understanding that 'the personal is political', as the famous feminist slogan claims?

The documentaries discussed so far have approached common subjects for women by framing those subjects within a universe of poverty and marginality. Nothing is really shared among the ones that film and the ones that are filmed, not even their feminine condition. Strictly speaking, class discrepancies seem to speak louder than gender identity in these cases. The filmmakers 'speak about' (determine, scrutinise) rather then 'speak nearby',[1] which would give the Others a chance to help build the filmic discourse and relations as well as take part in the relationship themselves. The work would become more personal through abandoning the supposed neutrality of a safe, distant, and objective approach in favour of a more subjective and unstable, and therefore riskier, one.

LIKE WATER THROUGH STONE

So far we have discussed films that remain faithful to their country's sociological matrix by creating a common repertoire of experiences among their characters in accordance with certain characteristics and specific contexts. In order to make such structural aspects more visible, the filmmakers keep a safe distance from their human subjects. The critic Jean-Claude Bernardet has previously identified such a tendency: According to him, since the 1970s Brazilian films have tended to portray 'the Brazilian people', who are understood to comprise mainly low-income individuals. He points out that, in most cases, filmmakers act as spokespeople or representatives of the population by expressing what he calls a 'national consciousness'.

What is not questioned, says Bernardet, is the representational limits of the process through which 'the people' are always determined or represented by the ruling classes with access to media production, including cinema. I discussed some consequences of this unequal distribution of creative resources, especially in consideration of how differences between women in front and behind the camera are not explicitly present in filmic discourse. When addressed, the films still avoid discussing the power relations implied in overall process of 'making visible' by way of hiding or disguising differences. As a result, the impoverished, black, and socially marginalised women remain in the margins of speech and representation. Even if they talk about themselves, they are not protagonists in their own stories. Instead, the protagonist is the director's own discourse, so that what he or she thinks of people, usually even before meeting them, proves to be more definitive and determining for the *mise en scène* than anything that they could say or do. This previous knowledge, based on social studies and statistics, determines the filmic discourse and the characters' locus within it.

Like Water Through Stone offers a strong contrast to such a sociological matrix, especially because, in this film, the director's presence is not disguised. In fact, the distances between the ones that film and the ones that are filmed are at stake and seem to be determinant to the *mise en scène*. When something from the experience and subjective perception of the director is called into the scene, gender and class issues tend to be presented in a more sensible and complex, less determined manner than in the other three films. This is a film that creates a kind of self-awareness through constantly questioning its own possibilities and limits – quite different from the other group of films, in which the 'limits of the representable' are not questioned.

The director Marília Rocha and her crew closely follow a group of five female friends who are leaving childhood and adolescence to become adult women. Two of them become pregnant during the period of shooting between summer and winter. Their children's fathers are to remain physically absent, although constantly evoked by the girls in chats and recollections. In fact, boys prove to hold a strong presence in their romantic imaginary. Differently from *Girls*, love, desires and dreams are not suppressed or underestimated here, but rather form the very basis of the narrative. These things create a common repertoire for the women in front of and behind the camera to share: After all, we are all beings of desire and dreams, regardless of our gender or class. With its observational strategies, the film tries to speak nearby rather than speak about – in this sense, it is remarkable how intimate moments are filmed in a very naturalistic, direct manner. The director's interventions – we hear her voice from offscreen, she never appears in front of the camera – are minimal, discreet, but decisive, in order to build a film not about the girls, but rather about Rocha's encounter with them.

This is a film made of quotidian, almost insignificant experiences: regardless of whether they are working, cleaning, going out for a dance or playing together, the girls are portrayed with no special subject matter or defined frame. It might be a demanding task for the viewer to understand or even enjoy such an unpretentious proposal, in which what is seen and heard is a sequence of ordinary events with no teleological function. There is some sort of latent absence expressed through scattered, non-progressive actions that lack dramatic outcomes. Banal situations such as trading fake diamond rings and discussing nail polish colours are sufficient unto themselves. They create less of a *telos* than a *pathos*. Affects matter and are materialised in different situations that the film brings to light while searching for a quality of presence of the images themselves.

In this sense, we observe a subtle but decisive passage from *social inquiries* to *forms of affects* when we move from the first group of films to *Like Water Through Stone*. While focusing on minor gestures and insignificant details, the film also proves to invest not only in the forms of affects but in the affects of form: With an observational camera attitude and a non-dramatic montage structure, *Like Water Through Stone* does not sacrifice form in favour of subject matter or theme. Therefore, the duration of shots and exploration of space seem to be guided by principles other than contextualising ones. The usages of time and space are significantly different from the first examples, as they are not operated in function of thematic principles to create a coherent discourse. They find significance in themselves, allowing the viewer to have an experience based primarily upon sensations and feelings, rather than on narrative progression.

It is interesting to note another difference between *Like Water Through Stone* (Figure 14) and the first group of films: the filmic space here is not a

Figure 14 *Like Water Through Stone* (*A falta que me faz*), Marília Rocha, Brazil, 2009.

confined one (a favela shack, a prison cell, or a hospital room), but a wide-open and vast one – the landscape of a mountainous region in the state of Minas Gerais called Serra do Espinhaço ('Saw Ridge'). The scenery formally expresses a liberty that the film itself grants its characters, in contrast to the claustrophobic spaces that translate the representational prisons in which the characters from the other films are kept. Form and content here mutually affect themselves.

When addressing her characters, Rocha does not seem to be following any narrative interest or predetermined theme. She instead seems to be experimenting with forms of approaching the Other. Such forms, however, do not function as means of creating a fictional, unrealistic intimacy between director and character. On the contrary, they make all the more visible how far apart the two worlds are – the one of a filmmaker who lives in a metropolis and the one of a group of female countryside inhabitants. The proximity that the film creates between these people does not search to 'include' the Other. It is instead built upon the sharp differences between their realities. As a result, the film questions the very possibility of creating proximity.

Marília Rocha does not hide the distance between her universe and that of her characters. This distance, however, is not one that would allow a director to create a totalising meaning for filmed events by offering information or proposing interpretations of what is seen and heard. She approaches and retreats, sometimes observing, sometimes discreetly intervening. In other words, her behaviour as a filmmaker is that of assuming her hesitations and inscribing her experiences not just as a woman, but as a middle class, liberal, professional woman living in an urban centre. At one point, she is stunned when she realises that one of the young women, even while pregnant, continues to drink and smoke. In another, she remains silent when one of the girls asks her to be godmother to her unborn child. As Claudia Mesquita remarks, 'a "yes" might sound demagogic, a "no" might rigidly mark the differences between life and film, world and scene, blocking empathy'.[2] The space behind the camera thus becomes a 'place of passage and limit between what belongs to the world and what belongs to the scene: limit or passage, the director hesitates'.[3] As she swings between yes and no – and the film does not reveal her ultimate answer – the difficulties of approaching the relationship that Rocha has with the girls becomes visible and sensitive and motivates the film. It is not despite the distances, but rather with the distances, that their encounter can happen.

We can say that it is not only for what it shows (what is on-screen) but mostly for what it does not show or say, what it lacks, what it exceeds (an offscreen space) that this film is significantly distinct from the previously discussed ones. Thematically, it is still a film that approaches 'feminine' matters such as love, marriage, motherhood, family and intimacy, but the manner in which those issues are approached underlines a non-correspondence between women in front of and behind the camera. As a consequence, the two kinds of women remain very different within their similarities. For instance, marriage: One girl declares that she never wants to get married, as it can result in a lack of freedom and even risk of violence, to which Rocha replies, 'But marriage is a good thing, girl!' Could it be that the filmmaker can say that only because, in her universe, feminist achievements make a difference and marriage arrangements follow other parameters? In making such differences visible, the documentary complicates any 'natural' attribution related to gender positions, destabilising them not as reality but as a process that depends on many variable factors. Gender is not produced by a discourse that gives it form and content, but it is put in perspective and is therefore at stake.

Anything that could exceed the representation of women to make their images more unstable and complex is lacking in the other films, whose directors never hesitate to determine a specific locus and a universe of senses for registered experiences. Additionally, these filmmakers never really share something of their own experiences marked by gender and class positions. *Like Water Through Stone* offers a counter-discourse built upon ambiguity, not only of its characters, but also of the relation between filmmaker and filmed subject. Differences – including class differences, so determinant to the other films although clearly left out of their discourse – are now exposed, and any fixed places for those who are filmed are now avoided. Gender matters in this case, and maybe more so than in the others, precisely for being at the same time an element of union and of fissure, proximity and distance, recognition and de-identification, creating what Teresa de Lauretis has called 'discontinuous but intersected spaces'.[4]

No longer defined – or confined – by a problematic field (abortion, early motherhood, or the harshness of prison life), the female experience can be reinvented by the strength of its indeterminacy, its destabilising power. By preserving an offscreen space that leaks into the on-screen space and contaminates the *mise en scène*, Rocha's film creates a broader gap to shelter the characters' own indeterminacy. The affects that take form in the girls' relationships – among themselves and with the director – make image a dwelling-place for something that can never be defined in rigid terms but only caught in movement, while escaping through this very same movement: 'Like water through stone'.

It is not accidental that, in the film's last scene, a motorcycle appears on the road with an embracing couple, while the landscape rapidly shifts and a French song plays on the soundtrack about the dream of another (*'Je rêve de toi'*). An inconclusive scene, a conclusion that does not want to finish but to continue, this final sequence insinuates that everything, right now, might be about to begin.

Acknowledgement

The author would like to thank Aaron Cutler for his contribution in reviewing this text.

Notes

1. This is a reference to the director Trinh T. Minh-ha, in her first film, *Reassemblage* (1982), which begins with a comment in voice-off: 'I do not want to speak about, just speak nearby'.
2. Mesquita, 'Os nossos silêncios: sobre alguns filmes da Teia', in André Brasil, Marília Rocha and Sérgio Borges (eds), *Teia 2002–2012* (Belo Horizonte: Teia, 2012). p. 41.
3. André Brasil, 'Formas do antecampo: performatividade no documentário brasileiro contemporâneo', *Revista FAMECOS*, 20/3, September–December 2013, p. 588.
4. Teresa de Lauretis, *Figures of Resistance: Essays in Feminist Theory* (Urbana and Chicago, IL: University of Illinois Press Chicago, 2007).

Filmography

Abortion of Others (*O aborto dos outros*) (Carla Gallo, Brazil, 2008, 72 min.).
Girls (*Meninas*) (Sandra Werneck, Brazil, 2006, 71 min.).
Like Water through Stone (*A falta que me faz*) (Marília Rocha, Brazil, 2009, 85 min.).
Milk and Iron (*Leite e ferro*) (Claudia Priscilla, Brazil, 2010, 73 min.).

INTERVIEW: 'VISUALISING OUR VOICES' – HONG KONG SCHOLAR AND FILM DIRECTOR VIVIAN WENLI LIN IN CONVERSATION WITH BOEL ULFSDOTTER

Who is Vivian Wenli Lin? I shall let the following statement, found on the website for Reel Women Hong Kong, serve as introduction:

> Vivian Wenli Lin is a Taiwanese-American video artist, documentary filmmaker, and media educator who was born and raised in San Francisco, California. In 2007, she founded Voices of Women Media – a non-profit organization that offers multimedia workshops to marginalized communities of women – including teenage girls, asylum seekers, victims of human trafficking, and sex workers in Amsterdam's Red Light District. Vivian also facilitates One Minute Junior workshops and Training for Trainers workshops for UNICEF and The One Minutes Foundation throughout Europe, Asia, Africa, and America.[1]

In her capacity as a scholar, Lin's research explores how using participatory arts-based methods can encourage the empowerment of marginalised communities of women – sex workers, marriage migrants, and workers in the emotional labour or informal labour sectors. Although the term 'empowerment' is often criticised for its uncritical celebratory nature and is often used as a buzzword that dismisses third world feminism, Vivian Wenli Lin's exploration of women's empowerment begins with the identification of the process as such, and then develops into an evaluation of the result of that process. She works with women in target areas, teaching them to gain the tools and resources to take control of their voices, self-representation and stories. The result of this process is what Claire Johnston calls a 'counter cinema' that challenges negative portrayals of marginalised women in the mainstream media, particularly those that contribute to social stigmatisation, through the expressive potential of alternative voices.[2]

The topic of this book is female authorship and the documentary image. How would you position your own work within these remits?
For roughly the past decade, my work has primarily focused on the importance of female self-authorship by using participatory arts-based methodology to engage communities of women in the emotional and informal labour industries to actively create their own images and self-portraits. I have a background in documentary film, psychology and video art and started to become frustrated behind the lens. I felt burdened by the responsibility of conveying my subject's image in a manner that would not betray their trust in me. I found that by having an exchange in our relationship, by teaching and providing new forms of technology and skills, I was able to still participate in the media making process but alongside and with the so-called 'subjects'.

What is the meaning of 'female authorship' to you?
The concept of 'female authorship' is how one can be responsible for her own representation. It is a response to how we may be wrongly perceived and counteracting the negative portrayals that may exist. This resonates deeply to me, as an Asian American woman who grew up in the USA, lived in Europe and then in Asia. I have witnessed and experienced different forms of discrimination in each locale. In 2003, I co-directed a short video titled, *Hello Kitty is Dead* that addresses the overly sexualised role of the Asian woman using found footage from both historical and contemporary Hollywood films. In my documentary *Loving Work* (2008) my subject is a Chinese-British fetish model who arranges her own photo and video shoots, edits her videos and updates her website. I was curious about how she was responsible for her own image, considering she was in the fetish porn industry. She took part in being objectified by others but also possessed her own power in controlling this objectification of her image.

In your opinion, what characterises the documentary image today, and what is its function?
I believe that the documentary image today is important to uphold, especially considering how media can manipulate or effect bias. Although, I am not implying that the documentary image will always represent a pure truth either. Choosing when and where to push record can always be considered biased. With technology becoming more affordable, accessible, and more portable, the evolution of cameras allows anyone to be an imagemaker. The camera has

become a witness, especially considering the Black Lives Matter movement and documenting police violence. What comes with these technological advances are newfound ethical and moral responsibilities to both the subject and the intended audience when recording and exhibiting our images.

You recently made a film entitled Voices of Women Media *(2015), which reflects on your work in the organisation with the same name. Tell us about the organisation, your film, and how it can be said to represent a notion of female authorship.*

To create a space for migrant women in the emotional labour industry to challenge experiences and narratives of marginalisation, risk and isolation, I co-founded a media and women's rights organisation, Voices of Women (VOW) Media in the Netherlands in 2007 with Pooja Pant. Our motivation was to fill a gap of representation that we witnessed as new arrivals to the Netherlands. We noticed several communities being talked about in the media and the news, yet failed to hear their own voices and opinions on the matter. For example, the call to shut down Amsterdam's Red Light District because of 'gang' activity or the ban on the hijab. By working with women directly affected by such issues, we were able to provide a personal perspective and alternative viewpoint.

VOW Media has conducted projects with migrant sex workers in Amsterdam's Red Light District, daughters of migrants growing up Dutch, undocumented migrants and asylum seekers, and victims of human trafficking. Since 2010, we were able to set up as an official women's organisation thanks to Mama Cash International Fund for Women and the Global Fund for Women, in addition to support from many others. We grew and added key staff members, Minouk Konstapel and Maria Şerban-Temişan, who were imperative as we were able to conduct more projects with different groups each year.

Since 2012, VOW Media has expanded their work to Hong Kong, Indonesia, Nepal and India (Figure 15). Communities in these countries utilised participatory arts-based methodologies in order to produce audiovisual media works grounded in life stories. The objective was to encourage migrant women workers to participate fully in the storytelling process both creatively and technically, resulting in what I refer to as a 'counter cinema'. Voices of Women Media will be celebrating its ten-year anniversary in 2017.

The idea of female authorship as a form of 'counter cinema' is interesting and pertinent. In your view, is this notion applicable to all your work? Was it one of the leading prerogatives when you set up VOW Media?

When we set up VOW Media back in 2007, we were responding to what we saw as a lack of representation of minority voices. In making my own transition from documentary film to participatory media, along with Nepalese

Figure 15 Behind the scenes VOW Media and IWE collaboration in Yogyakarta, Indonesia (2015).

media activist Pooja Pant, we started Voices of Women (VOW) Media, because we were curious about the women and girls around us, considered *allochtoon*,[3] a Dutch word used to refer to immigrants and their descendants, non-ethnic Dutch. Large communities of Turkish, Moroccan, Surinamese, Indonesian and Chinese immigrants have long settled in the Netherlands, and we wanted to know about their experience in our new country. We had both moved the same year (2006) and became friends over discussions on our status as women of colour living in a homogenous Dutch society. This was our primary motivation for starting Voices of Women (VOW) Media and by partnering with organisations we were able to engage several communities – daughters of migrant workers in Osdorp with Studio West, a cultural centre for teens; with Huize Agnes, a transitory housing shelter for refugees and asylum seekers; with victims of human trafficking at BLINN (Bonded Labour in Nederland); with sex workers and trans sex workers at the *Prostitutie & Gezondheidcentrum,* Prostitution and Health Centre (P&G 292), and at Fier Fryslân a shelter for girls and young women (ages eleven to twenty-three) who have fallen victim to *loverboys*, a Dutch term for pimps. During these seven years, we worked closely with women who are invisible in society but visible to the public – often being discussed by other people, such as politicians, the media or policy makers but not being included in the discussion. An element that was lacking for both Pooja and I was our inability to work more with women from our own ancestral regions of East and South Asia. We felt a personal desire to expand our work to Nepal and Taiwan to establish connections to the countries of our parents. Moving to Hong Kong in 2012 to start my doctoral research was the first time in my life I became part of the racial majority and walked freely without self-consciousness of my hypervisibility. While in Hong Kong, I also found the opportunity to live and work for some time in my parents' home country of Taiwan.

With my experience in documentary video production and Pooja's experience as an activist, our complementary skill sets contributed to the success of our young organisation. Pooja spent several years in the late 1990s and early 2000s working with at-risk youth and victims of domestic violence in San Francisco and later in London. She is comfortable in various social situations, essential in establishing trust and relationships with new target groups. We started noticing the increasing trend of the feminisation of migration and began to consciously explore topics regarding sex work and trafficking. We wanted to understand the larger picture of how women move from one place to another, from one community to another, and among groups of women who are alienated in the community they live in due to their professions or immigration status. The women we worked with since 2007 were able to navigate opportunity through the informal labour industry as sex workers, domestic helpers, caregivers, migrant workers, women porters or marriage migrants. These women filled the demand for emotional labour from more developed countries. These women are connected through shared experiences of movement, migration and labour in the face of globalisation and transnationalism. Using media engagement as a tool to access one's voice is necessary in a world where both one's existence, body and labour as a woman of colour is objectified, devalued and dehumanised.

In researching and relating the lives of women among diverse communities of migrant women and female labourers, their self-made media reflecting their life experiences offer various perspectives that are not represented by mainstream media. Even though Pooja and I were not aware of the term 'cine-feminism' when initiating our first Voice of Women (VOW) Media projects, we have been developing methodologies with a 'cine-feminist' framework, that in ways extend feminist film studies, since the resulting visual and/or narrative works offer rare materials of women's self-representations that are not recognised by women's groups and feminist scholars, let alone society at large.

You have written in your biography that you 'use the lens as a means to deconstruct the feminine myth'. Is this deconstruction best performed in a fictional or documentary sense? Which is the 'female myth' you refer to? Please elaborate.
The female myth I refer to is the perceptions, misconceptions and stigmas experienced by my participants, who are often involved in the emotional or informal labour industries. Burdened with societal stigmas from their choice of profession, for example, sex workers most often have to work in anonymity, these groups may be viewed by others as second class citizens or unfairly portrayed by mainstream media. I want the camera to serve as a means for these women to reconstruct these portrayals and to create alternative narratives. In the *A Day In Her Life* project, sex workers in Amsterdam and

Hong Kong were able to answer to the myths behind their profession by offering their own voice to counter assumptions of sex workers that are held by society. There are multi-faceted viewpoints, from each video in the series, there are different reasons for entering sex work, different opinions about the profession, but more so, the videos were trying to bring a personal and human voice to the dialogue, instead of being talked about by politicians or policy makers.

Your work seems to be motivated by social issues in that it involves collaborative components and is performed within groups that are not automatically included in the current notion of authorial work in documentary cinema. Does this make your work political in character? Does your work also have an activist side to it? And if so, in what way?
I would definitely consider the collaborative work both political and activist. We partner with local women's organisations and human rights organisations who work directly to support women from these communities. For example, in Amsterdam we partnered with P&G292 (Prostitution and Health Center) and in Hong Kong we partnered with Zi Teng, an organisation dedicated to supporting and advocating for sex workers. A huge part of this work is about women's rights – besides raising awareness of their right to work (especially in the case of sex workers) or the validity of their work (women in the emotional labor industry) – by asking the women to actively participate, the projects make them aware of their rights to education, media literacy and also self-expression. A focus for Voices of Women Media is to work with younger women. In the regions of Nepal and India this has proved quite successful as we have partnered with Feminist Approach to Technology, to raise new generations of young female feminists who are familiar and adept with technology.

Why are these social and collaborative points of view important to include?
These viewpoints are important to include because they are rarely told from this perspective. In documentary filmmaking, we are often pointing our cameras at our subjects, in the participatory process we work alongside the 'subjects' to make them the directors and to be completely involved in the media making process – from idea, storyboard, shoot, to the final edit. I think a key aspect of this work is that we try our best to convey in a strong visual image what is the essence of their story.

How do these societal/activist/political implications affect the documentary image you are working with?
It becomes more so about the process rather than the end product. Of course, I am still concerned about the resulting quality and the content of

the media, and do have to think about a potential audience. I've found that the process for the participant is overall the most important aspect of this work; this results in a diverse and wide variety of works that really address personal stories, raising multiple perspectives and viewpoints about migrant women workers.

You use participatory art-based methods to create feminist leadership – could you elaborate on that?
Voices of Women Media collaborated with the Institute for Women's Empowerment (IWE) to run a five-day video workshop to teach informal women workers who were leaders in their individual labour unions how to use media as a tool for activism and feminist leadership. In five days, informal women workers from all around Indonesia came to Yogyakarta to participate in this training. In one example, Endah wanted to show her strength in carrying 70 kg crates of produce for 0.02 USD per load. She described a strong visual of how she would hoist a large wooden crate filled to the brim with produce. Endah and her fellow porters were able to create a storyboard and shoot by themselves as they were familiar with the experience. As a woman porter, she is part of the informal labour industry, which is essentially unregulated and without any benefits or social security. Many of these women porters have banded together to form labour unions to organise for break rooms, a decent pay wage and breaks. By learning the possibilities of making videos, they were able to represent their fellow workers and to also raise issues of their working rights and demands.

What is the exact nature of the art-based methods you use in your work?
The methods vary – but consist primarily of using old and new forms of technology to facilitate storytelling. It really depends on the group we are working with. For example, with daughters of migrant workers in the Netherlands – taking polaroids and learning how to use Photoshop to manipulate photos was particularly successful. They were delighted by the analogue technology and also furious about the ease with which photos could be manipulated. If time allows, incorporating a radio session can really encourage participants to open up to us and more so to each other, creating an additional sense of cohesiveness and sense of closeness.

What would a 'radio session' entail here? Do you mean a radio documentary? Why do you think this particular media form has become so popular in the Asian region?
Typically our radio sessions are the second phase of the overall media workshop where participants learn about using one's voice. In preparation for a live show, there is training on maintaining equal voice levels, interview techniques,

Figure 16 Learning the video camera. *Displaced Daughters* (2011).

and monitoring the live sound feed. A practice run, with handheld sound recorders and headphones, is used to create the simulation of being on-air. The initial reaction to hearing one's voice is embarrassment, self-consciousness and anxiousness. After the training, participants conceptualise a radio show together and select one or two of the participants as hosts, interviewing each guest about an agreed upon topic.

In *Displaced Daughters* (2011) (Figure 16), the young women split into two teams to debate the proposed ban on the hijab/burqa in Europe. Initially, they wanted to discuss the Dutch politician Geert Wilders and the effects of his anti-Islam views on their local Muslim communities. After much heated discussion in preparation for their radio show, they realised that they did not want to give Wilders any more unnecessary attention. The participants decided to address Wilders' burqa *verbode*, the ban on hijab/burqa, and decided that this was the issue that they were not being consulted on, or having their thoughts or voices heard on this subject. The resulting radio show, 'Real Life', presents the debate from the voices of young Muslim women themselves. Out of the seventeen participants, around five of them wore the hijab daily. All of them felt that the ban was a restriction on their religious rights and outright discrimination. In *A Day In Her Life* (2012), current and former sex workers created 'Where is your rainbow?', a show about what it means to leave home and start new lives in the Netherlands. This simple act of speaking to an unseen audience with the safety of remaining faceless is usually a turning point in this project. The experience of having live listeners sparks a vitality and strong feeling to express themselves and get their opinions heard.

Applying the radio session within the Asian region is also quite successful as participants appreciate the level of anonymity and that it allows them to discuss taboo subjects such as difficulties at home in regards to demands from parents or physical and domestic abuse from family members, as we learned from our teenaged participants in *Apna Haq: Our Right* (2013). In the radio session in *With Love From Taiwan!*, foreign spouses discuss with each other aspects of their homeland that they miss and share their experiences of attempting to assimilate and belong to a new country.

You recently received your PhD degree. What was the subject of your thesis?
My doctoral dissertation and subsequent book project, *Visualizing Our Voices: Self-made Audiovisual Media by Women from Social, Economic and Cultural Margins in the Era of Global Migration*, is an analysis of this 'counter cinema', that demonstrates how participatory action research within a cine-feminist approach can unveil hidden experiences of women's migration. In the dissertation, each chapter analyses the participatory media making experience with a specific community: migrant sex workers in Amsterdam and Hong Kong, marriage migrants to Taiwan, domestic migrant workers in Hong Kong from Indonesia and informal workers based in Indonesia. Key research questions were: How can participatory media making contribute to the self-empowerment of communities of migrant women? Can self-made media dispel myths, stereotypes or misrepresentation? What are the harmful consequences to the communities it effects? The research findings and outcomes demonstrate that women in the informal and emotional labour industries can use their videos for advocacy, affirm identity, reduce associated stigmas, and as a tool for political and economic empowerment. In addition, marriage migrants, refugees and asylum seekers can use their media works to connect to home, and foster transnational familial ties. In summary, self-made audiovisual media contributes to an affirmation of identity, artistic expression and empowerment of migrant women and their communities.

Please tell us a little about your future plans, and upcoming projects.
In 2017, in collaboration with Dr Julie Ham at the University of Hong Kong's Department of Sociology, we will produce a series of public programmes: panels, workshops, and exhibition. Titled *Visualizing the Voices of Migrant Women Workers*, this project will aim to reach a wider audience of communities in Hong Kong of migrant women workers, women and human rights organisations, academic and arts-based institutions about the results and potential of how participatory media can directly benefit.

Concurrently, VOW Media co-founder Pooja Pant is conducting a series of projects for Voices of Women Media in Nepal called 'She is the Story', using photography and texts of women's experiences to document and account for the various unsung female heroes in and around the region. VOW Media Nepal is also running a series of feminist film screenings for communities in and around Kathmandu to create more open dialogues about the issues of gender and its role in media.

Notes

1. <http://www.reelwomenhongkong.org/ms--vivian-wenli-lin-bio> (last accessed 23 October 2016).
2. Clare Johnston, 'Women's cinema as counter-cinema', in Philip Simpson, Andrew Utterson and K. J. Shepherdson (eds), *Film Theory: Critical Concepts in Media and Cultural Studies*, vol. 3. (New York: Routledge, 2004), pp. 183–92.
3. *Allochtoon* is an official word used by the government, but used negatively within society, creating further displacement between ethnic Dutch and 'the other'.

PART THREE

IDENTITY POLITICS OF DOCUMENTARY

9. FROM VISCERAL STYLE TO DISCOURSE OF RESISTANCE: READING ALKA SADAT'S AFGHAN DOCUMENTARIES ON VIOLENCE AGAINST WOMEN

Anna Misiak

AN AFGHAN AUTEUR?

Since the fall of the Taliban numerous Afghan women from different professional backgrounds have actively engaged in making documentaries.[1] Very few of them, however, have managed to turn their filmmaking activity into effective international careers. This is why Alka Sadat (Figures 17 and 18), a self-taught documentarian from Herat, stands out as one of the most dynamic Afghan female directors of factual films. At first glance, Sadat's output does not differ from other documentary footage coming from Afghanistan. Just like her contemporaries, her camera focuses on social problems and human rights in the war-torn country. Yet, she enjoys a strong reputation as an influential activist who in her short documentary films has skilfully unveiled, if not shrewdly analysed, the dark side of gender inequality in the Islamic Republic of Afghanistan. Sadat's dedication to victims of violence against women – for whose legal defence she has openly campaigned – has formed the staple of her documentary method. Several festival trophies, which the filmmaker has collected since her debut in 2005, have helped her achieve an eminent position on the international festival circuit. Cutting across social divisions and speaking with, rather than for, her filmed subjects, Sadat resists international audiences' impressions, which tend to essentialise gender dynamics in her country. Her half-observational, half-analytical storytelling strategies constitute the quintessence of her documentary method.

Figure 17 Alka Sadat.

Given the relative consistency of Sadat's style and her global visibility, it may be tempting for Western critics to discuss her output as that of an emerging world cinema auteur. In Western film scholarship, dating back to the mid-twentieth-century publications in *L'Écran français*[2] and *Cahiers du cinéma*,[3] authorship has played a significant role in critical recognition of filmmakers, including many non-Western directors. Auteur theories, which have undergone several shifts from emphasising creative agency to textual approaches,[4] evolved into what Timothy Corrigan labelled 'the commerce of authorship',[5] a tactic of promoting individual directors. When feminist film scholars – including, among others, Claire Johnston,[6] Kaja Silverman[7] and Judith Mayne[8] – joined authorship debates, they observed that, however varying, auteur criticism typically favoured male directors. The thought-provoking feminist push to recognise women filmmakers as auteurs was born out of political necessity to acknowledge marginalised gendered perspectives and to give the original messages and styles of female directors an equal status in male dominated film history.[9]

In her documentaries, Sadat offers a unique view from inside her country, serving as a catalyst for her filmed subjects' voices, which in some respects qualifies her as a female auteur. However, aware of reaching international viewers she develops a specific oppositional discourse, which unlike many feminist films in the West, is not orientated at challenging the male-dominated film culture. Sadat's key shorts about violence against women frequently provide viewers with visceral documentation of current outcomes of the gender situation in Afghanistan, paying attention to multiple markers of social difference and exposing plurality of female identities and experiences. With her anti-essentialist stance the director resists Eurocentric[10] categorisations of the Islamic female other. Her films are intended for non-gender-specific audiences, implicitly defying simplistic Western assumptions about Afghan society, including victimisation, romanticisation and Islamophobia.

When for the first time approached from a critical perspective, Sadat's work needs to be placed in contexts from which she originates, as well as those she addresses. Considering the director's messages, authorial analyses of her films seem counterproductive, if not inappropriate. In her seminal article 'Can the subaltern speak?', Gayatri Spivak advises against discursive assimilation of cultural products from outside Europe and America.[11] She suggests that to engage with non-Western voices, critics and audiences must first acknowledge global power structures with their ensuing symbolic hierarchies. Spivak also warns that reception of 'the subaltern' is often clouded by schematic ideological surface judgements. With their Eurocentric background, theories of authorship can hardly open critical exploration of Sadat's documentaries. Their routine application to her work would result in superficial commodification of non-Western subject to fit Eurocentric ideologies.

However, in her book *Women's Cinema, World Cinema: Projecting Contemporary Feminisms*, Patricia White demonstrates the analytical potential of looking at world cinema directors through the prism of authorship. Her study focuses on female directors of narrative productions and aims at examining as well as publicising their outputs in Western film culture. Following Catherine Grant's suggestion that authorship 'help[s] organise the fantasies, activities and pleasures of those who consume cultural products',[12] White examines both production and reception of female filmmakers to interrogate their visibility, agency and power.[13] Her questions could perhaps also illuminate Sadat's output once solid lines of critical engagement with her documentary messages were established. At this stage, however, it seems more productive to situate Sadat's films in local, national and transnational contexts to initiate a dialogue with her on-screen realities. Authorial analysis of her yet critically unexplored films would subject her work to the parameters of Western discourse, which she herself resists. It would increase her visibility and satisfy Western audiences' appetite for the next big thing, an object for the spectator to consume, but not a speaking subject worth interrogation.

Sadat's Success

To please English-speaking viewers, Sadat's biography could open like a traditional fairy tale: once upon a time there lived a talented Afghan girl, Alka Sadat. Under the Taliban regime she was secretly schooled by her mother. When democracy returned to Afghanistan, in 2005 she attended two weeks of film workshops that were organised in Kabul by the Goethe Institute.[14] Shot that year, her debut documentary, *First Number* (2005)[15] – in which close-ups of calm faces are crosscut with images of battlefields – received the Peace Prize from the Afghan Civil Society Organisation.[16] Soon Sadat was offered a scholarship to participate in a 2006 video course at Fabrica in Treviso,[17] where she completed her first narrative short, *We are Postmodern* (2006).[18] With its slow pace, this meditative story of human kindness in the barren Afghan mountains challenges the Western media imagery of manic crisis in Sadat's country, evoking a fairy-tale atmosphere for the location.

Upon her return to Afghanistan, Sadat worked at her sister's studio, writing and directing *1,2,3?* (2006), her first documentary on violence against women.[19] Over the following years the director completed a few more films dedicated to women's rights, including the award-winning *Half Value Life* (2009),[20] which chronicles the career of Maria Bashir, a public prosecutor from Herat. For her commitment to improving the position of the female in Afghanistan, Sadat was noticed by both domestic and international women's rights organisations. Her next film, *After 35 Years* (2012)[21] – an account of the arduous Kabul campaign for ratifying the Family Law – was funded by the Afghanistan Human Rights and Democracy Organisation.[22] Owing to the quality of all her previous work, Sadat received her next, even more substantial commission from the UN Assistance Mission in Afghanistan, to produce a series of films summarising social developments since the fall of the Taliban. In separate shorts, her ensuing trilogy, *Afghanistan: 10 Years On* (2012–13)[23] examined violence against women, children and police.

Sadat has worked hard to promote her documentaries on the international stage. With no long-term support from Western distributors, her shorts have been screened at several international festivals, including the Women's Voices Now Film Festival in Los Angeles, the Al Jazeera International Documentary Film Festival, the Bilder von Film Festival and the International Trevignano Film Festival, to mention just a few.[24] Nearly every festival screening has left the filmmaker with an award in hand. Her relatively high professional standing also earned Sadat invitations to join juries for the 2013 Afghan Contemporary Art Prize and the 2013 Asiatica Filmmediale.[25]

It is worth noting that the Internet has played a vital role in Sadat's professional growth. She uses YouTube, Vimeo and Culture Unplugged, posting English-subtitled copies of complete shorts and trailers for new projects. Not

FROM VISCERAL STYLE TO DISCOURSE OF RESISTANCE

Figure 18   Alka Sadat.

only are the latter displayed online to reach viewers, but also to attract funding, as was the case with *Afghanistan Night Stories* (2015),[26] her recent film about Afghan soldiers fighting Taliban commandos. Its production was supported by volunteers from Bpeace – an organisation for developing entrepreneurship among violence-torn populations[27] – and a grant of €17,500 from the IDFA Bertha Fund in Amsterdam.

Entering a Dialogue with Sadat's Films

If described as above, Sadat is a self-made woman, a talent that was fulfilled against all odds. Her biography becomes the journey of a heroine climbing up from a background with little privilege to higher levels of professional hierarchy – yet another sought-for inspirational fable set in an exotic remote location. Although it is an attractive story, there are at least a few reasons not to chronicle Sadat's achievements in such a sensational way. With the emphasis on her successes, the director's biography reads as a prototypical Eurocentric narrative of a non-Western achiever who, despite her origins, has managed to meet Western capitalist measures of individual progress, much like the character Jamal Malik from the Academy Award winning film *Slumdog Millionaire* (2008). Even without any such intention, similar practices of narrating non-Western creative biographies by accentuating one's result in terms of popularity or critical acclaim in the West, tend to emphasise otherness and thus always verge on discursive colonisation of the non-Western subject and her cultural production.

Framing Sadat as a successful director or an auteur instead of entering a dialogue with her on-screen realities would mimic what Mark Graham describes as 'the rhetoric of the empire'.[28] Having analysed a range of available narrative titles including, among others, *Rambo III* (1988), *Kandahar* (2001), *In this World* (2002), *Osama* (2003) and *The Kite Runner* (2007), Graham concludes that to date, Western appreciation of Afghan film stories has often been marked by a Eurocentric mindset. Most popular films from and about Afghanistan include those that English language viewers find exotic, shocking or ideologically accessible. Told in narrative frames that appear familiar to Western audiences, such productions either promote values which comply with a Western symbolic order, or justify Western politics towards the distant nation. Graham demonstrates that such readings of on-screen Afghanistan are often rooted in superficial judgements lacking in-depth contextualisation. At the end of his book, he advocates a change in critical perspective: 'To look at Afghanistan in film, one must be prepared for Afghanistan to look back . . . in an exchange based not on domination, but on reciprocity.'[29]

To enter a dialogue with Alka Sadat, Western viewers need to discard their measures of success and failure, as well as preconceptions regarding social dynamics in Afghanistan. Only by straying away from subjugating Sadat's shorts to the rhetoric of the empire, can her Western audience emotionally and discursively 'engage with reality'[30] of her documentary subjects. Although incomparable in terms of analytical depth, in some respects Sadat's film practice is reminiscent of arguments coming from globally renowned scholars and cultural critics.

Revealing the then-existing practices of patronising and fictionalising non-Western cultures to fit Western ideologies, in his 1978 seminal work *Orientalism* Edward Said called for informed and multidimensional portrayals of 'the other' to contest inaccuracy of the dominant white gaze.[31] Thirty-five years later, Spivak's book *An Aesthetic Education in the Era of Globalization* points to 'the contamination of the subject' with sociocultural and political ideologies, which still impede Western ethical and epistemological engagement with multicultural or non-Western works.[32] When discussing Sadat's output, to overcome this contamination, we need to pay close attention to the subtle dynamic between her seemingly effortless gaze at Afghan women and her documentaries' power of engaging the viewer in critical dialogue.

Since her debut, not only has Sadat acquired stronger directing skills, but also more substantial budgets and crews. Her latest productions strike one as much more polished than those from the past. Yet, she has always consistently highlighted the complexity of contexts behind the social issues she chooses to explore. This pattern of providing a multi-layered insider perspective best manifests in Sadat's three productions on violence against women. The earliest of these titles, *1,2,3?* interrogates circumstances of domestic violence victims in her province. Sadat patiently listens to her on-screen subjects reproducing the frame of mind of the disempowered, impoverished female, whose wellbeing is ignored by the law. In *Half Value Life* the filmmaker again focuses on the fate of the female victim, but this time her camera follows the Chief Prosecutor from Herat. This broadens the outlook and introduces the figure of the male oppressor, allowing for multidimensional analysis of the Afghan gender situation.

In *Afghanistan: 10 Years On: Elimination of Violence Against Women*, Sadat continues to employ some of her tested discursive strategies, even if this film appears formally different from her two earlier shorts. Observational shots now only feature as a background for interviews with Afghan officials, scholars, and activists. Sadat's commentators discuss factors contributing to cruelty toward women, showing that its causes go deeper than religion or tradition. This film is symptomatic of Sadat's creative progression. Shifting from the local to the national, she started to cut across Afghan social classes. Her style also evolved. Now with more reliance on logically constructed arguments, she is much less confident in the power of visceral imagery. To examine Sadat's discursive and stylistic trajectory, it is best to start with a detailed look at her first film on violence against women.

As Complex as *1,2,3?*

1,2,3? examines the harsh realities of Afghan women who have experienced domestic violence. The short is divided into three parts. Each centres on wretched lives, marked by constant fear and an absence of hope. Subsequent digits from the title serve as headings for these sections, signifying that no words can describe the traumas of the victims. Sadat first dwells on the desperation of several young women, who found self-immolation to be their only available route to freedom. The following two segments of the film respectively explore underage marriage and runaway wives who seek legal help. The physical agony of suicidal women from the first part later turns into anguish that is competently communicated by the filmmaker toward the end of the third section. In a few long shots we watch some of the abused wives – who entrusted representatives of the law to protect them – being escorted by men. Seeing them returned to the control of their abusers forms a harrowing conclusion. Absence of legal sanctions enslaves and dehumanises many among the Afghan female population. It is a situation without resolution or end.

At the beginning of the film, Sadat pays a visit to a hospital in Herat. Her hand-held camera pauses on wounds and faces that are matched in visceral duality. As the director talks to the patients, she exposes burns all over their bodies. Interviews reveal that men caused many of these grave injuries. Some patients, however, admit to self-inflicted harm. In a shocking open declaration that is interrupted by heavy breathing, one young girl says that she burnt herself to get away from her abusive older husband, whom she had been forced to marry before her puberty. Numerous tracking shots amplify the aura of omnipresent violence. There is no privacy in this setting. Accompanied by their children, the patients share overcrowded rooms and corridors. The uncomfortable condition of the ward and the appearance of many prematurely aged women make the viewer aware that the majority of these female victims come from impoverished backgrounds.

By persuasively editing words of her interviewees, Sadat emphasises that financial dependency on men often becomes a significant factor contributing to social acceptance of violence against women, as well as to helplessness of its victims, whose fear stops them from pointing fingers at their abusers, or from speaking about their experience. This is implied in the first ten minutes of the film, where to the director's off-screen question, 'Who burnt her?' close female relatives of convalescent teenage girls reply, 'Jinns' or 'Lantern fuel'. As the narrator in the film states, these women spend their whole lives under the roof of their fathers and husbands. Their abusers convince them of their low status. Besides death, they see no escape from domestic violence.

Later the director moves to a police station and a prosecutor's office, where the fate of other abused women is being decided. Quite a few say to the camera that they had to run away from home, because they were afraid of further torture. One mother and her daughter declare, 'We'd rather be killed than be returned to our fathers.' Some women present their scars from wires and ropes on their necks and shoulders, showing the scale of cruelty they experienced. When Sadat grants these victims space to voice their fear, she provides emotionally charging evidence for statistics that at the time were often publicly cited in support for the implementation of the Elimination of Violence Against Women Law. Withheld for a while in the Afghan parliament, this legal act was eventually enacted by President Hamid Karzai in 2009. A part of the campaign for this law, *1.2.3?* is illustrative of the director's emerging style, which cuts deeper than the alarming statistical data.

The filmmaker offers visceral imagery in support of frightening facts from female experience in her country that have been confirmed by both domestic and international research. According to the UN Assistance Mission in Afghanistan, women's life expectancy in the country is forty-four years, much shorter than that of the male population. Next to poor health care and war, the contributing factors that influence such a short female life span include forced marriages that constitute between 60 per cent and 80 per cent of all marriages, poor education, with 90 per cent female illiteracy in rural areas, as well as the fact that about 57 per cent of girls get married before the age of 16.[33] Pushed by their families to become mothers and wives before they reach puberty, without any education, Afghan women frequently become totally dependent on their husbands. Maria Bashir – the Chief Prosecutor of Herat Province, who briefly appears in the third segment of *1,2,3?* and later becomes the main character in *Half Value Life* – confirms, 'The top issues facing women in Afghanistan are weak economy and limited access to income. Women are mainly suffering from illiteracy, joblessness, and lack of knowledge about their rights.'[34]

Informed by these facts, Sadat transports her viewer to a real life setting, where violence is experienced first hand. The careful display of local details with all underlying emotions awards her short with an unusual appeal. The oppressed female gains her own identity. Facial close-ups often engender intimacy between the viewer and the on-screen women, whose eyes meet those of the audience, as though, in Graham's words, 'Afghanistan look[ed] back at us',[35] not asking for help, but for understanding. According to Ib Bondebjerg, documentaries in the globalised world are 'powerful human and emotional stories with characters which we can identify strongly with or distance ourselves from'.[36] *1,2,3?* provokes an emotional response thanks to its balance between unsettling proximity to the abused women, which builds on physical closeness of the camera to the filmed subjects and distancing tactics, such as voice-over, brief excerpts from interviews with doctors, prosecutors and activists, as well as long/medium observational shots.

Formally imperfect because of its abrupt cutting, *1,2,3?* emits an aura of chaos mimicking the disorderly social and legal situation that contributes to the oppression of women. English subtitles on the YouTube copy of the film are at times difficult to read due to unusual phrasing. Elsewhere they appear totally missing, as if the words of the women defied any translation and could only echo with sounds of their original native tongue or with uncomfortable silence. Intentional or not, these unpolished formal aspects of Sadat's film match her subject matter. The viewer is trapped between close engagement with the stories of the women and the inconsistent mixture of documentary styles, from interactive, through observational, to authoritative. The latter is yet another distancing technique, with voice-over that speaks for 'you and me' and our disempowerment to assist the on-screen victims.

The authoritative tone of the filmmaker's commentary and the calm off-screen music complement the rough naturalistic nature of the rest of the film with a meditative mood. Rather than calling for intervention, Sadat invites her viewer to ponder over Afghan reality. *1,2,3?* starts and ends with shots of a woman covered in a traditional burqa who wanders around ancient-looking walls. These frames are accompanied by a female narrator, who asks rhetorical questions about the violence. At the end, the anonymous woman disappears in a tunnel. We only hear her last words: 'You and I can't answer this. The law can ... but it is silent.' The tranquillity of the opening and closing sequences is contrasted with fast-speaking, distressed women in the main three sections of the film. This is how Sadat highlights the difference between her own privileged social position that offers space for critical thoughts on the position of disenfranchised and that of uneducated lower class women.

As the last line of *1,2,3?* implies, responsibility for the gender situation in the post-Taliban society does not rest with individual men or with Islam. To free Afghan women from violence would require a long-term legal, economic and educational reform, developed by the government in collaboration with Western organisations and politicians. The UN Women Country Representative in Afghanistan, Elzira Sagynbaeva admits, 'There needs to be effective implementation of the laws ... women and girls [must] feel safe and ... provided with an opportunity for development'.[37] This is what Sadat continues to inspect in her following films on violence against women.

HALF VALUE LIFE OF THE AFGHAN FEMALE

The core story of *Half Value Life* consists of an edited record of Maria Bashir's daily routines. More than once we see her at home with three children and then in her prosecutor's office, where she conducts interviews with female clients and their abusers. Here, for the first time in Sadat's documentaries, the viewer meets the violent male. In an uncomfortable arrangement, three female victims are sat next to their oppressive husbands. The scruffy appearance of the couples quickly contrasts with that of the well-groomed female lawyer. This visual juxtaposition provides the first characteristic of the abusive men, who tend to come from impoverished backgrounds. What further contributes to their descriptions are the stories anxiously told by their wives, one of whom is underage.

The prospects of gradual erosion of traditional Afghan gender structure, as advocated by international activists, may play a role in the prevalence of violence against women in lower class families. Lina Abirafeh reminds us that, 'While [some-AM] women may benefit from increased emphasis placed on them by aid agencies, men tend to feel emasculated as a result'.[38] In failing to provide for their families in difficult economic circumstances, men may become psychologically disturbed; just like one of Bashir's interviewees who is a drug addict forcing his wife to collect opium for him and his companions. Another woman in the film mentions that her abuser is aged and disabled, whereas yet another, who was severely beaten by her husband while pregnant, admits that her family has no financial means to survive.

In all these cases, the female victims are scapegoats, blamed for what is the result of the poor economic situation. Where traditional gender roles cannot be met, women whose needs and ambitions are denied by customary practices pay the highest price; violence becomes part of a struggle for social authority. Bashir also mentions that many demoralised men, some of them husbands of her clients, join Taliban forces to escape from justice, indicating the post-Taliban heritage that reinforces violence against women. Sadat comments, 'We have two problems that stand in our way ... the Taliban and family pressures from people who believe their daughters should stay at home until they marry. We have a lot of underage marriages and we have girls who are out working on the street to earn income for their families.'[39] Although *Half Value Life* was released in the year when the Elimination of Violence Against Women Law was passed, the film clearly suggests that Afghanistan is still characterised by insufficient means to prevent violence and to protect its victims. Bashir's office seems overloaded with work, a lot of which is wasted due to lack of justice codes to prosecute abusers, who tend to be manipulative: using threats, they manage to discourage their victims from further testimonies.

Sadat shows that no woman can feel safe in Afghanistan, even if her domestic setting is free from abuse. Several times in the film Bashir speaks to the camera, disclosing that her family lives in constant fear of revenge from those whom she prosecuted. Her children are schooled at home, so as not to invite any potential attackers. Incidentally, towards the end of the film we witness an explosion in Bashir's home. Although there are no casualties, this act of terror intensifies the dark aura surrounding the female in the country. However, subsequent shots reveal that the social position of the prosecutor allows her to hire guards that escort her from home to the office – means of protection that are unavailable to lower class women.

Sadat openly contrasts the educated professional woman and the impoverished victim of domestic violence. The distinction is formally reinforced by the compositional frame of *Half Value Life*, which similarly to *1,2,3?* starts with shots of a woman in a desert-like setting, a place reminiscent of an old citadel. This time her face is fully visible. The viewer quickly recognises the director. Sadat is first filmed in an empty claustrophobic room putting on her make-up and then walking outside in high heels. Although the shoes perhaps symbolise Western-like female empowerment, the lyrics of the traditional song that plays from an old radio recall women's problems in Afghanistan: 'It's spring and I am still a cloud. Oh, Lord ... I am full of anxiety and pain.' With this blend of Western and non-Western signifiers, Sadat points to the displacement of women in Afghanistan, where Western activists call for mobilisation of women, while traditional forces oppose them.

The shots of the director in her desert reclusion are later intercut with factual material. Sadat's character, separated from the city, can only listen to its sounds played on her radio, which, by the way, was often the only means of communicating with the world for women forced to stay at home during the Taliban era. When Sadat returns to her isolated chamber and gazes through bars in the window, she again listens to the radio that is now hanging from the ceiling on a piece of barbed wire. The chamber becomes this woman's prison and the metaphor for her helplessness. The sequence reaches its climax with Sadat shedding tears over the news of the explosion in Bashir's house. At the end of the film she walks away from the camera through a tunnel, with only little sparkle of hope in the form of a proverbial light at its end. We hear the last verses of the traditional song, this time playing off-screen, as a reminder of the forced silence of Afghan victims of violence, 'Grow mother to daughter generation . . . Where is your voice?'

The reflective mood of this staged sequence re-positions the progressive Afghan female by transporting her to the traditional dwelling. When intercut with images of the attack on Bashir's house, this de-contextualisation serves as a chilling reminder of the potential danger of returning to conservative gender roles. It is also an allegorical commentary pointing out that Afghan women are often forced to negotiate between two ideological standpoints: the Western calls for their social advancement and the conservative voices pushing them back to their domestic settings. What adds to their despair, Sadat seems to suggest, is the potentially temporary character of any of their emancipation. With all these interpretative contexts, Sadat produces a discourse resisting simplifications of female identity that often circulate in the West, where Afghan women are seen either as victims of their social settings or their individual success stories shroud issues that the rest of the female population faces on a day-to-day basis.

The first approach has been most often visible in Western news, as well as in some documentaries, including *Beneath the Veil* (2001) and *Lifting the Veil* (2007), *Burqas behind Bars* (2013) and *Love Crimes of Kabul* (2011). The latter is symptomatic of a number of factual films that highlight the resilience of Afghan women, such as *The Boxing Girls of Kabul* (2012), *The Afghan Star* (2009) and *I am a Girl* (2013). The tendency to find optimism in Afghan female experience has also been a guiding light for several Western photographers, most notably for Katherine Kiviat and Scott Heidler, who published their collection of portraits of strong female figures in *Women of Courage: Intimate Stories from Afghanistan*.[40] Showing Afghan women as high flyers, such publications provide an inspiration for social workers, politicians and activists, without necessarily disagreeing with Sadat's vision.

Indeed, the director declares that focusing solely on victimised women is one, but not the only way to explore female experience in Afghanistan: 'I was tired of only showing poor women in Afghanistan and making a film about Maria was my chance to show a powerful Afghan woman to the world.'[41] Despite her intention, Sadat hints that the lawyer's resilience exposes her to potential mistreatment. Although Bashir's biography matches all standards of a high achiever's journey, even her life is of half value when faced with violent male abusers.

Crosscutting factual footage with staged shots in *Half Value Life*, Sadat indicates that identities of Afghan females are fragmented and always context-specific. But she also suggests that some women's existence verges on enslavement, which cannot be resolved without government action. Inspirational stories in the country have their limits. Female identity, as well as her individual experience, depends on a variety of other markers of difference including tribal/regional belonging, economic status, levels of education, and even her family history. Such factors are also central when it comes to potential margins of personal freedom and respect that individual women can receive. This is the underlying critical idea behind Sadat's third documentary on violence against women.

What has Changed *After 10 Years*?

Even though in *After 10 Years* Sadat slightly changes her documentary style – shifting her formal focus away from staged shots and observational footage to talking heads – the film still starts and ends with her signature images of a traditionally dressed Afghan female. This time the woman stands on a hill above metropolitan landscape. Turned backwards to the camera, with a street megaphone as her only companion and a visual reminder of conservative gender propaganda in the country, in the first shot she gazes towards the distant city. Her isolation from the vibe of the metropolis is highlighted in the following point of view shot, which is obscured by shadows that bring to mind the barred windows of a prison cell. This symbolic visualisation foreshadows the main theme of the documentary, which next to analysing the current gender situation in the country debates the impact of tradition on the slow process of delegalising violence against women. Sadat punctuates her series of interviews with statistics. More than once, written numbers appear on the screen and are read out by a female voice-over. This inclusion of shockingly high figures of rapes, immolations, and murders committed on women by their close male relatives adds to the tension of the debate.

Carefully selecting her interviewees, Sadat again shows social differentiation among Afghan women. She speaks to female members of Afghan parliament and women scholars. They are contrasted with shelter-seeking victims of domestic violence and women beaten by their beggar husbands who also momentarily appear on the screen. The director's previously subjective perspective on the link between social status and violence against women finds validation in the words of several experts, who confirm that the latter is more common in rural, uneducated communities than in metropolitan provincial capitals, where women are overall more emancipated.

To cover the full picture, Sadat invites conservative religious scholars to debate potential solutions to gender-based oppression. Although open to defend women, one of the traditionalist scholars refers the issue of protection back to the family, which as the narrator of the film informs, is symptomatic among opponents to the reinforcement of legislation. Numerous shots from courts, however, reveal that prosecuted male oppressors tend to be as uneducated and helpless as their victims. The problems some of them face with articulating simple sentences may indicate that violence is the only outlet for their emotions and they use physical strength to control women whom the fundamentalist propaganda reduces to their reproductive and sexual functions. It is made clear a few times in the film that the post-Taliban legacy takes its toll where even religious education in rural environment is at it lowest level. Sadat observes, 'the Taliban . . . is present in the shadows and their brutal practices and policies towards women, especially in the countryside, are still profoundly visible.'[42] This legacy finds its most fertile ground among the impoverished and the uneducated.

Overall, in this short Sadat implies that post-Taliban Afghanistan has seen significant improvements in terms of emancipation of women from privileged backgrounds. However, because of little government action, often hindered by conservative opposition, lower class women still pay the price for Taliban demoralisation of the Afghan male. In the film's pessimistic conclusion, Sadat returns to the traditionally veiled female figure on the hill, who stands still, separated from the potentially liberating city. Waiting in vain for the government to protect her, she becomes a symbolic representation of the rural female's condition.

Sadat's Discourse of Resistance

Ultimately, Sadat demonstrates that unlike in Western democracies, in rural and lower class post-Taliban settings, gender identities are perceived not as negotiated,[42] but as imposed:[44] this is the main reason for the overbearing helplessness of many domestic violence victims. From the earliest days of their socialisation, poor women are being convinced of their traditional role. It is naturalised by reference to biological reproduction that reduces their choice and agency to the domestic setting, whose walls are often the container of their entire lives. Brick and stone fences around Afghan households on one hand can offer comforting safety, on the other they reinforce the confinement of the female, become her prison and her chamber of torture. With unusually thin legal protection and the separation of women from any immediate channels to report potential maltreatment, even basic human rights of lower class Afghan females rest in the hands of men in their families.

Although to break their silence Sadat offers her on-screen women lots of opportunities to speak for themselves, she always serves as a catalyst for their voices. Her narrative voice-over is marked by an authoritative and educative tone helping those who lack the means to articulate their experience. Sadat's work may thus be compared to that of Western feminists, who promote female rights and empowerment. Yet, as Fabienne Darling-Wolf warns, historically, Western feminists' efforts to empower non-Western women to self-represent have been problematic, because they 'frequently resulted in reductionist and essentialising notions of identity'.[45] Naturally distanced from the cultural baggage of whiteness, Sadat demonstrates that she is mindful of the potential dangers of limiting and homogenising identities of women, who appear in her documentaries. Yet, in her films she clearly shows that despite otherwise important social divisions, there exists cross-class female solidarity to improve the gender dynamic in Afghanistan and to end violence against women. Even if her films only reach privileged women, their social mobilisation is still worth the effort, because it strengthens the overall position of the Afghan female.

To engage with Sadat's complex analysis of Afghanistan's gender dynamics, not only do we need to acknowledge that she successfully makes and promotes her films, but also that she is a speaking subject situated in national and global power structures – a subject who in both these contexts is heavily engaged in the discourse of resistance. Aware of Western preconceptions about Afghanistan, Sadat constructs her documentaries to challenge Western audiences. Her shorts force the viewer to suspend the rhetoric of the empire. To avoid reductionist traps, she capitalises sensitively on her privileged status by presenting the experience of Afghan women as heterogeneous. Her gaze is always context-driven. In accordance with Graham's assertion, 'The real Afghanistan cannot be reduced to a few ... points of view. Rather, it may be grasped ... only by listening to plethora of different voices.'[46] Sadat gives her viewer access to a range of male and female voices to sample the complexity of the gender situation in her country. Opposing the oppression of women, she also resists Eurocentric approaches that essentialise Afghan culture.

Notes

1. The most often mentioned Afghan female documentary filmmakers include: one of the winners of International Afghan Documentary Film Festival (ADFF) in Sweden, Mona Haidari, <https://vimeo.com/16867644> (last accessed 20 January 2015), <http://afghandocumentaryfilmfestival.com/2015/12/17/from-frame-by-frame-to-death-to-camera-3rd-afghan-documentary-film-festival-in-sweden/> (last accessed

20 January 2015); Kabul-based artist Mariam Nabil Kamal, <http://www.dazeddigital.com/artsandculture/article/10576/1/venice-biennale-2011-denmarks-lilibeth-cuenca-rasmussen> (last accessed 20 January 2015); the founder of Afghanistan Documentary House, Sahra Mosawi, <https://vimeo.com/user14450289> (last accessed 20 January 2015); the well-known actress from Samira Makhmalbaf's *At Five in the Afternoon* (2003), Aqeela Rezai <http://csfilm.org/films/fruit-of-our-labor/> (last accessed 20 January 2015), and many others who have participated in international film projects and festivals.
2. Alexandre Astruc, 'The birth of a new avant-garde: le camera stylo', in Ginette Vincendeau and Peter Graham (eds), *The New Wave: Critical Landmarks* (London: BFI Books, Palgrave Macmillan, 2009), pp. 31–6, translated from *L'Écran français*, 144, 30 March 1948.
3. François Truffaut, 'A certain tendency in French cinema', *Cahiers du cinéma*, 31, 1954, pp. 15–29, reprinted in Scott MacKenzie (ed.), *Film Manifestos and Global Film Cultures* (Berkeley, CA: University of California Press, 2014), pp. 133–44.
4. See: Andrew Sarris, 'Notes on auteur theory in 1962', in Gerald Mast, Marshall Cohen and Leo Braudy (eds), *Film Theory and Criticism* (Oxford: Oxford University Press, 1992), pp. 585–8; Roland Barthes [1968], 'The death of the author', in *Image-Music-Text* (London: Fontana, 1977), pp. 142–8; John Caugie (ed.), *Theories of Authorship* (London: Routledge/BFI, 1981).
5. Timothy Corrigan, 'The commerce of auteurism: a voice without authority', *New German Critique*, 49, Winter 1990, pp. 43–58.
6. Claire Johnston, 'Women's cinema as counter-cinema', in Claire Johnston (ed.), *Notes on Women's Cinema* (London: Society for Education in Film and Television, 1975). Reprinted in: Sue Thornham (ed.), *Feminist Film Theory: A Reader* (Edinburgh: Edinburgh University Press 1999), pp. 31–40; Claire Johnston (ed.), *The Work of Dorothy Arzner* (London: BFI, 1975).
7. Kaja Silverman, *The Acoustic Mirror: The Female Voice in Psychoanalysis and Cinema* (Bloomington, IN: Indiana University Press, 1988).
8. Judith Mayne, *The Woman at the Keyhole: Feminism and Women's Cinema* (Bloomington, IN: Indiana University Press, 1991).
9. See: Catherine Grant, 'Secret agents: feminist theories of women's film authorship', *Feminist Theory*, 2/1, April 2001, pp. 113–30; Anneke Smelik, *And the Mirror Cracked: Feminist Cinema and Film Theory* (London: Macmillan Press, 1991).
10. See: Ella Shohat and Robert Stam, *Unthinking Eurocentrism: Multiculturalism and the Media* (London : Routledge, 1994).
11. Gayatri Spivak, 'Can the subaltern speak', in Cary Nelson and Lawrence Grossberg (eds), *Marxism and the Interpretation of Culture* (Chicago, IL: University of Illinois Press, 1988), pp. 271–313.
12. Catherine Grant, 'www.auteur.com?', *Screen*, 41/1, 2000, p. 107.
13. Patricia White, *Women's Cinema, World Cinema: Projecting Contemporary Feminisms* (Durham, NC: Duke University Press, 2015).
14. Doniphan Blair, 'Afghan filmmaking on the edge: interview with Alka Sadat', Women's Voices Now: Advocating Gender Equality Through Film, <http://www.womensvoicesnow.org/interview-with-alka-sadat> (last accessed 5 January 2016).
15. *First Number*, dir. Alka Sadat, Afghanistan, Roya Film House, 2005, <https://vimeo.com/53772511> (last accessed 10 January 2016).
16. 'Alka Sadat: biography', Roya Film House, <http://royafilmhouse.org/staff/alka-sadat> (last accessed 30 December 2015).
17. This date is cited after 'Alka Sadat: biography', Roya Film House, <http://royafilmhouse.org/staff/alka-sadat> (last accessed 30 December 2015). However, Fabrica website states that Alka Sadat was awarded their scholarship in 2008 and that the

film was completed in 2009: 'We are postmodern', Fabrica: The Benetton Group Research Communication Center, <http://2009to2012.fabrica.it/project/we-are-postmodern> (last accessed 2 January 2016).
18. *We are Postmodern*, dir. Alka Sadat, Italy/Afghanistan, 2005. Available at <https://www.youtube.com/watch?v=bWnnuAZaZWc> (last accessed 10 January 2016).
19. *1,2,3?*, dir. Alka Sadat, Afghanistan, Roya Film House, 2006, <https://vimeo.com/81100047> (last accessed 10 January 2016).
20. *Half Value Life*, dir. Alka Sadat, Afghanistan, Roya Film House, 2009. Available at <https://www.youtube.com/watch?v=UwY-BDYoOk8> (last accessed 9 January 2016).
21. *After 35 Years*, dir. Alka Sadat, Afghanistan, Roya Film House, 2012. Available at <http://www.cultureunplugged.com/documentary/watch-online/play/10438/After-35-Years> (last accessed 19 January 2016).
22. Afghanistan Human Rights and Democracy Organization (AHRDO), 'Insight on Conflict', <http://www.insightonconflict.org/conflicts/afghanistan/peacebuilding-organisations/ahrdo/> (last accessed 10 January 2016).
23. *Afghanistan: 10 Years On: Elimination of Violence Against Women*, dir. Alka Sadat, Afghanistan, Roya Film House, 2012. Available at <https://www.youtube.com/watch?v=juVweKPjNdk> (last accessed 20 January 2016). *Afghanistan: 10 Years On: Children Rights in Afghanistan,* dir. Alka Sadat, Afghanistan, Roya Film House, 2013. Available at <https://www.youtube.com/watch?v=cQB_I-iAuOw> (last accessed 20 January 2016). The third film of the series has not been made available online.
24. For a full detailed list of Alka Sadat's international festival awards see: 'Alka Sadat: Biography', Roya Film House. Available at <http://royafilmhouse.org/staff/alka-sadat> (last accessed 30 December 2015).
25. 'Encounters with Asian cinema', Asiatica Filmmediale, 20–28 November 2013. Available at <http://www.asiaticafilmmediale.it/?lang=en> (last accessed 20 January 2016).
26. *Afghanistan Night Stories* (Official trailer), dir. Alka Sadat, Afghanistan, Roya Film House, YouTube, 26 February 2014. Available at <https://www.youtube.com/watch?v=9UOHdg3FCnw> (last accessed 10 December 2015).
27. 'Welcome to Bpeace', Bpeace, <http://www.bpeace.org/> (last accessed 10 January 2015).
28. Mark Graham, *Afghanistan in the Cinema* (Urbana, IL: University of Illinois Press, 2010), p. 8.
29. Ibid. p. 167.
30. Ib Bondebjerg, *Engaging with Reality: Documentary and Globalisation* (Bristol: Intellect, 2014).
31. Edward Said, *Orientalism* (London: Penguin, 1977).
32. Gayatri Spivak, *An Aesthetic Education in the Era of Globalization* (Cambridge, MA: Harvard University Press, 2012).
33. 'UNAMA Factsheet on the situation of women and girls in Afghanistan United Nations Assistance Mission in Afghanistan', UNAMA 2009, <https://unama.unmissions.org/sites/default/files/UNAMAfactsheet%20VAW-Nov%202009.pdf> (last accessed 10 December 2015).
34. '*Half Value Life: A Documentary on Afghanistan's Only Female Prosecutor*', Muslima: Muslim Women's Art and Voices, 2001, <http://muslima.globalfundforwomen.org/content/half-value-life> (last accessed 26 January 2016).
35. Graham, *Afghanistan in the Cinema*, p. 167.
36. Bondebjerg, *Engaging with Reality*, p. 9.

37. 'UN Press Release on The International Day for Elimination of Violence Against Women', UN Assistance Mission in Afghanistan, 25 November 2015, <https://unama.unmissions.org/un-press-release-international-day-elimination-violence-against-women> (last accessed 5 January 2016).
38. Lina Abirafeh, quoted in Rosemarie Skaine, *Women of Afghanistan in the Post-Taliban Era: How Lives Have Changed and Where They Stand Today* (Jefferson, NC: McFarland and Co., 2008), p. 3.
39. '*Half Value Life*: A Documentary on Afghanistan's Only Female Prosecutor', Muslima: Muslim Women's Art and Voices, 2001, <http://muslima.globalfundforwomen.org/content/half-value-life> (last accessed 26 January 2016).
40. Katherine Kiviat and Scott Heidler, *Women of Courage: Intimate Stories from Afghanistan* (Salt Lake City, UT: Gibbs Smith Publisher, 2007).
41. Yma de Almeida, 'Interview with *Half Value Life* Alka Sadat', London Feminist Film Festival, 22 November 2013, <http://londonfeministfilmfestival.com/2013/11/22/interview-with-half-value-life-director-alka-sadat/> (last accessed 26 January 2016).
42. Quoted in Nupur Basu, 'Light at the end of the tunnel', *The Hindu*, 24 March 2013, <http://www.thehindu.com/todays-paper/tp-features/tp-sundaymagazine/light-at-the-end-of-the-tunnel/article4543063.ece> (last accessed 20 January 2016).
43. For more theoretical background on negotiated gender identities in the West see: Gail Hawkes, *A Sociology of Sex and Sexuality* (Maidenhead: Open University Press, 1996); Judith Butler, *Gender Trouble: Feminism and the Subversion of Identity* (London: Routledge, 1990).
44. For more theoretical background on imposed gender identities see: Mira Marody and Anna Giza-Poleszczuk, 'Changing images of identity in Poland: from the self-sacrificing to the self-investing woman', in Susan Gal and Gail Kligman (eds), *Reproducing Gender: Politics, Publics and Everyday Life After Socialism* (Chichester: Princeton University Press, 2000), pp. 151–75; Simone Beauvoir, *The Second Sex,* translated by Constance Borde and Sheila Malovany-Chevallier (London: Vintage, 2010 [1949]).
45. Fabienne Darling-Wolf, 'Negotiation and position: on the need of developing thicker descriptions', in P. D. Murphy and M. Kraidy (eds), *Global Media Studies: Ethnographic Perspectives* (New York: Routledge, 2003), p. 109.
46. Graham, *Afghanistan in the Cinema*, p.166.

Filmography

1,2,3? (Alka Sadat, Afghanistan, 2006).
Afghanistan Night Stories (Alka Sadat, Afghanistan, 2015).
*Afghanistan: 10 Years On: Children Rights in Afghanistan (*Alka Sadat, Afghanistan, 2013).
Afghanistan: 10 Years On: Elimination of Violence Against Women (Alka Sadat, Afghanistan, 2012).
*The Afghan Star (*Havana Marking, UK, 2009).
After 35 Years (Alka Sadat, Afghanistan, 2012).
Beneath the Veil (Cassian Harrison, UK, 2001).
The Boxing Girls of Kabul (Ariel Nasr, Canada, 2012).
Burqas behind Bars (Maryam Ebrahimi and Nima Sarvestani, Sweden/Afghanistan, 2013).
First Number (Alka Sadat, Afghanistan, 2005).
Half Value Life (Alka Sadat, Afghanistan, 2009).

I am a Girl (Rebecca Barry, Australia/USA/Papua New Guinea/Cambodia/Cameroon/ Afghanistan, 2013).
In this World (Michael Winterbottom, UK, 2002).
Kandahar (Mohsen Makhmalbaf, Iran, 2001).
The Kite Runner (Marc Foster, USA/China, 2007).
Lifting the Veil (Sharmeen Obaid, USA, 2007).
Love Crimes of Kabul (Tanaz Eshaghian, USA, 2011).
Osama (Siddiq Barmak, Afghanistan, 2003).
Rambo III (Peter MacDonald, USA, 1988).
Slumdog Millionaire (Danny Boyle and Loveleen Tandan, UK/France/USA, 2008).
We are Postmodern (Alka Sadat, Italy/Afghanistan, 2005).

10. DOCUMENTING GEORGIA IN TRANSITION: THE FILMS OF SALOMÉ JASHI AND NINO KIRTADZE

John A. Riley

Since the break-up of the Soviet Union, Georgia has been caught between its communist past and capitalist future, between its ancient traditions and its desire to modernise, between the sphere of influence of Russia and of European/ American interests, and perhaps most crucially for visual culture, between the nebulous and ill-defined notions of East and West.[1] It has frequently fallen to women to document and comment upon Georgia's state of liminality and transition. This chapter focuses on the films of Nino Kirtadze and Salomé Jashi, as two standout examples of a tendency in Georgian cinema towards transitional documentary, a form that arises at times of protracted socio-political transition and which mixes more conventional forms of reportage with subjective and impressionistic commentary. Women have been in an ideal position to document the changes in Georgian society due to their status as outsiders in a traditionally highly patriarchal society. As a result, women directors such as Kirtadze and Jashi, along with a slew of prominent female fiction film directors (Rusudan Chkonia, Nana Ekvtimishvili and Tinatin Gurchian are amongst the most prominent of the current wave) have risen to prominence in Georgia.

A 2013 project called 'Who's Afraid of Feminism in Georgia?' aimed to highlight the contributions of women to Georgian culture and society, raising awareness of feminist ideology in the process. Lela Gaprindashvili, discussing part of the project, a collection of annotated postcards depicting fifty famous or influential Georgian women, stated that despite these women's names being familiar to many in Georgian society, people 'don't connect them to the idea of feminism or women's rights, to the right to education, the right to vote, political rights'.[2] Gaprindashvili also notes that 'in the Post-Soviet period, society always questioned whether the idea of [gender] equality was a Georgian idea'.[3] Suspicions that this was an imported, inauthentic idea abounded, and still do. Furthermore, as Keti Khidasheli of the project points out, in Georgia it is particularly important to make a distinction between urban and rural feminism.[4] In cities, women may have greater access to social mobility with its attendant freedoms, while in villages women are busy with farm labour and family duties. Meanwhile unemployment and lack of access to education and modern amenities contribute to chronic social problems in rural areas. Consequently, the project's organisers made a point of not confining their lectures and workshops to Tbilisi and other main urban areas, but visited provinces and villages as well. As we can see, Georgia has a long history of active women, but not a specifically Georgian tradition of feminism to underpin these individual personalities, or to theorise the stark distinctions between Georgia's urban and rural class of women.

Thus, Georgian women involved in intellectual and creative pursuits are creating a Georgian feminist tradition as they go. Furthermore, they are doing so in a country widely perceived as undergoing a long transition period. Of course, societies are always in a state of flux, but for reasons mentioned earlier, Georgia has particular reason to feel itself in a state of transition. Furthermore, for creative and artistic pursuits such as film, what matters is less an exact definition and more a lived experience and its documentation.

Where states of transition have been felt as particularly protracted, as in the Soviet collapse, transitional documentary film has arisen to comment on and document this state. In film studies, examination of this transition in documentary and fiction film has tended towards the centre rather than the periphery. For example, Nancy Condee's *The Imperial Trace* shows how several Russian directors moved from the Soviet to the Post-Soviet era and the ways in which their films present shifting conceptions of the Russian empire and Soviet Union.[5] Meanwhile, away from the Soviet Union, Jessica Stites Mor has invoked the importance of transition for Argentina's film culture, arguing that Argentina's long transition from military regime to democracy was debated and documented by a long line of political filmmakers who used film's capacity for documentary and montage to play with and sometimes contest collective memories and norms, complicating official and counter-narratives by questioning the complicity of ordinary people with the regime. Elsewhere, Ruby Cheung has examined fiction film in relation to Hong Kong's lengthy transition from British colony to become part of China's 'one country, two systems' principle.[6] Cheung shows how Hong Kong cinema portrays the complexity of Hong Kong identity against the cultural dominance of mainland China.

It is worth comparing the notion of transitional film with Hamid Naficy's notion of accented cinema, where a dominant cinema (without accent) recounts closed stories within an official narrative; accented cinema usually derives from exilic, diasporic and other minority groups, and runs counter to mainstream narratives, contrasting them with memories, impressions and dreams, posing open questions and displaying the multifaceted nature of taken for granted certainties such as gender roles and national/ethnic identity.[7] Kirtadze and Jashi are not exiles, but studied in Western Europe and often live and work away from Georgia, returning for their documentaries. In summary, although transition film and documentary can only be loosely defined, as any definition will depend on the details of a necessarily specific and shifting transition, it should be clear that transitional documentary responds to political and social change with personal, idiosyncratic films.

Tourist guidebooks and other related material often introduce Georgia to outsiders as a country 'at the crossroads' between East and West. This cliché, like many clichés, contains an element of truth. This crossroads is not only geographic but a matter of temporal and ideological perception. Since gaining independence Georgia has been attempting to reinvent its image from barely visible Soviet periphery to modern European country. To that end it has been seeking NATO membership since 2002, along with other modernising projects such as the Baku-Tbilisi-Ceyhan project (the subject of one of Kirtadze's documentaries; discussed in detail here) which all further an aim to link Georgia with the West, thus threatening its status as one of Russia's 'zones of privileged interest'. A brief precis of recent Georgian history will help to explain how this transitional, liminal state of affairs has come about.

It may seem disingenuous to describe Georgia as still in transition, some 25 years after the Soviet collapse. That time span already covers approximately a third of the time Georgia spent as a Soviet republic. As I noted earlier, the objection can be raised that all countries are always in some sort of transition. However, Georgia's trajectory since gaining independence has been anything but straightforward, involving time spent as a failed state and a redrawing of the country's borders. In the late 1980s protests against Soviet rule were violently put down by the army, resulting in the deaths of twenty protesters.[8] The violent and indifferent handling of this incident was a significant factor in the Soviet Union's break-up, Georgia's independence, and the rise to power of Zviad Gamsakhurdia, a charismatic nationalist who clashed with the Abkhazians and Ossetians, distinct ethnic groups within Georgia who wanted their own form of independence. Eventually Georgia became locked into a violent conflict with the two regions, and then in a civil war between supporters of Gamsakhurdia and of Edward Shevardnadze, the former leader of Soviet Georgia, brought in to replace Gamsakhurdia. After a decade of rule by Shevardnadze, The Rose Revolution toppled Shevardnadze in favour of the Western-educated Mikhail Sakashvili, who was determined to give Georgia a PR makeover as a modern European country. Clashes over South Ossetia resulted in the 2008 war and the final cessation of both Abkhazia and South Ossetia. In 2012 a prison abuse scandal seriously damaged the credibility of the Sakashvili administration, and in 2013 power was peacefully and democratically transferred to the Georgian Dream Party, who pursue a more moderate stance towards Russia while continuing to seek closer relations with Euro-Atlantic countries. Despite gaining independence in 1991, Georgia spent much of the 1990s being described by outsiders as a 'failed state'. It has endured several devastating wars and only recently democratically transferred power from one political party to another. For these reasons Georgia can be considered a country experiencing a long and complex socio-political transition.

Compared to other national European cinemas, Georgian film is not widely known outside specialised film festivals, despite a ringing endorsement from celebrated Italian auteur Federico Fellini that 'Georgian film is a strange phenomenon – special, philosophically light, sophisticated and, at the same time, childishly pure and innocent.'[9] Fellini was presumably thinking of Otar Iosseliani and Mikhail Kobakhidze who, along with Tengiz Abuladze and the aesthetically singular Sergei Paradzhanov, defined the Georgian auteur cinema during the Soviet era. As director and critic Zaza Rusadze has noted, even during the Cold War era Georgian cinema was often programmed separately from other Soviet cinema, as the distinctive formal and cultural qualities championed by Fellini made for a different type of programming.[10] After the Soviet collapse, this filmmaking tradition temporarily dwindled while the country lapsed into fighting and economic chaos.

Since the Rose Revolution, and more recently, following the peaceful transfer of power between the NMD and Georgian Dream parties, Georgian film and documentary have seen an international renaissance in critical and curatorial interest. Fiction films such as *Tangerines* (Zaza Urushadze, 2013) and *Corn Island* (Giorgi Ovashvili, 2014) have received, respectively, an Academy Award nomination and the grand prize at the Karlovy Vary film festival. Across 2014–15, the Museum of Modern Art in New York (MOMA) programmed a retrospective sampling the whole of Georgian cinema from its first moments to the present day.[11] The 2014 Busan International Film Festival programmed a showcase of fiction films by female directors from Georgia. The fourth edition of the London Georgian film festival was held in October 2015, including a personal appearance from Kirtadze herself promoting her docudrama *Don't Breathe*.[12] In the spring of 2015, the Swiss festival Visions du Réel focused specifically on Georgian documentary and screened the work of seven female directors, including two films by Jashi and one by Kirtadze.[13]

This slew of new films from Georgia, from arthouse fiction to experimental documentary, all capture, whether deliberately or inadvertently, the complexities of a country in transition. Female practitioners have always been central to Georgian filmmaking. An early example was *Their Kingdom* (1928), a documentary collaboration between Georgia's first female filmmaker, Nutsa Gogoberidze, and Mikhail Kalatozov, the latter of whom would go on to become a Palme d'Or winning Soviet filmmaker. Gogoberidze's daughter and granddaughter have both gone on to become filmmakers, joining female fiction filmmakers such as Nana Jorjadze, Nana Janelidze and the subjects of the present chapter, Jashi and Kirtadze.[14]

Nino Kirtadze was born in 1968 in Tbilisi. She studied medieval literature and worked as a journalist during the first Chechen war. Moving to Paris after her experience in Chechnya, she began acting in fiction films, most notably in Nana Jorjadze's work. She has subsequently returned to Georgia for a number of documentaries, parsing the country's rituals of death and mourning (*Tell My Friends That I'm Dead*, 2004), documenting the impact of the BTC pipeline's construction on Georgia's rural communities (*The Pipeline Next Door*, 2005), the 2008 war and re-election of President Sakashvili, (*Something About Georgia*, 2009), and most recently, focusing her attention on a single Georgian family (*Don't Breathe*, 2014).[15] Taken together, these films form a portrait of post-Soviet Georgia that seems to alternate between the point of view of an authorial insider and outsider.

A generation younger than Kirtadze, Salomé Jashi was born in Tbilisi in 1981. She began working as a TV journalist for the channel Rustavi-2, but was dissatisfied with the restrictive format of television. She abandoned television to study documentary filmmaking at Royal Holloway University in London, where her tutor was Gideon Koppel.[16] *Their Helicopter*, her graduation film, was made in Georgia in 2006. *A Mr Minister* and *Speechless*, both short subjects like her graduation film, followed in 2008 and 2009. Subsequently, longer-form pieces such as *The Leader Is Always Right* (2010) and *Bakhmaro* (2011) followed. *A Mr Minister* is a byproduct of Jashi's career in journalism, while her other films are impressionistic vignettes of contemporary Georgian life that use stillness and quiet to convey something of the unique atmosphere of Georgian life. In addition to her work as a director, Jashi also runs Sakdoc Film with her business partner Anna Dziapshipa, a production company which produces her own films and the work of others. Sakdoc aims to foster a collective of filmmakers working on documentary, such as the fiction filmmaker Tato Kotetishvili (*Ogasavara*, 2015) and co-producing (*Altzaney*, 2009) with Nino Orjonikidze and Vano Arsenishvili from Artefact Productions. In addition to production activities it organises screenings, workshops and other activities to promote and sustain documentary in Georgia. Sakdoc Film states its mission on its website:

> The aim of Sakdoc Film is to depict the transitional period that Georgia is now undergoing from being a Soviet state to becoming a modern country. We believe that there are a number of topics, places and people that will

not exist in Georgia in a few years and which are worth and even essential to film before the opportunity fades away.[17]

Jashi's organisation thus consciously forefronts the notion of transition, framing it in terms of a Soviet past and a modern future.

Georgia's transition is proclaimed by politicians as well as artists and media practitioners. Rhetoric from the political elite has positioned Georgia as seeking its rightful place in modern Europe. For example, Georgia's 2011 National Security Concept claimed: '[Georgia is] part of Europe geographically, politically and culturally; yet it was cut off from its natural course of development by historical cataclysms.'[18] More recently, Georgian President Giorgi Margvelashvili 'explicitly linked Georgia's "Europeanness" with state-building and thus modernity'.[19] The official narrative posits a time out of joint that will be set right when Georgia becomes European or perhaps when it regains its lost separatist territories. Three questions arise. First, can Georgia shift itself from the periphery to the centre, as its mainstream politicians hope? Second, will doing so mean sacrificing its traditional culture and way of life? The desire to modernise and 'Westernize' clashes with traditional religious and cultural values. Third, what will be the role of filmmaking, whether documentary or fiction, in this transition? On the one hand, there are purely propagandistic films, such as the Renny Harlin directed *Five Days of War* (2011), which depicts American characters in solidarity with the Georgians as Russia attacks in 2008. On the other hand film, and particularly documentary cinema, provides opportunities for sustained reflection on modern Georgia and its place in the world.

Writing about Argentina, Jessica Stites Mor comments:

> transition film as an event wielded a tremendous mimetic capacity for representing competing narratives of the cold war era. Filmmakers of the transition reproduced coded encounters among images, testimonies, narratives and sound that could simultaneously resonate with and challenge subjective experiences of the past. In a general sense, these films situated the individual viewer within a past only partially accessible but from which new collective memories could be cobbled together.[20]

Although Argentina is a markedly different country, with its own culture and history, both countries endured a long transition period and emergence from a troubled past. Further, certain similarities in their respective cinemas of transition can be easily noted. Kirtadze's *The Pipeline Next Door* strikingly juxtaposes two competing narratives or worldviews, while Jashi's films in particular, along with many others, demonstrate individual experiences that both resonate and challenge.

Zaza Rusadze notes that 'Most Georgian documentaries are historical and ethnographic films. They are far from the so-called "observational-creative" documentaries.'[21] However, with the long transition period, questions about the present and future have become more pressing, and perhaps the influence of studying and working abroad (Jashi at Royal Holloway in London, Kirtadze in Paris) have encouraged a markedly non-Soviet approach to documentary.

Asked about the future of documentary, Kirtadze responded:

> Well, I think that there will be a reinvention. There is a big debate at the moment in France, about what is allowed and what is not allowed in documentary. You have documentaries with actors; you have documentaries with [re-enactments]. It's like a child that is born, and starts to grow and grow and grow. You cannot just put him in a box and say, 'Now you stop growing.' It's a living thing. So I think that many things are going to change.[22]

Kirtadze implies that the medium of documentary is in transition as much as Georgia itself is: that is, as a medium in transition documenting a country in transition. Documentary filmmaking then, could play a major part in how Georgia sees itself (at the Tbilisi documentary film festival, Jashi and Kirtadze's films play to packed cinemas) and how Europe sees Georgia (Jashi and Kirtadze have had commissions from German and French television stations respectively).

The competing narrative of East and West is nowhere better illustrated than in Kirtadze's *The Pipeline Next Door*. The pipeline in question is the Baku-Tbilisi-Ceyhan oil pipeline which, as its name suggests, passes through Georgia. Conceived in the 1990s, in the wake of the Soviet collapse and the first Gulf War, it was an ambitious multibillion-dollar construction project with enormous geostrategic and security implications.[23] In addition to the pipe physically connecting 'East' and 'West', it provides an opportunity for dialogue between the two.

Kirtadze's documentary, however, transports viewers to the villages of Tadzrisi and Sakire, where residents maintain a traditional agrarian way of life, and through which the pipeline is due to be driven. The film contrasts the BTC executives and their modern, globalised way of doing business, with the traditional community of villagers, anxious about the possibility of landslides affecting their village and getting a fair price for their land. The competing narratives are starkly juxtaposed, and the pipeline itself is a noisy, material intrusion making a greater impression than either the villagers or the cosmopolitan BTC workers. At the end of the film, Kirtadze shows the villagers ceremoniously commemorating their dead (a link to her earlier film *Tell*

A Friend I'm Dead) and then playing music; dancing joyously with the BTC construction site visible in the background. Slowly, as a truck bringing more sections of pipeline arrives, the camera drifts away from the villagers, and the truck's sounds rise on the soundtrack, drowning out the music. At the very last moment we hear birdsong. It is unclear who will benefit in the future, or even what the village will look like in a few years' time.

Another place where narratives and ideas compete is the arena of politics. As mentioned earlier, the Rose Revolution led to a more Western-friendly government that was in many ways out of touch with traditional Georgians, and yet still keen on the nationalism of the Gamsakhurdia era.

Two short films by Jashi illustrate this dichotomy, *A Mr Minister* (co-directed with Giorgi Tsiqarishvili), a portrait of politician Bakur Kvezereli, and *The Leader is Always Right*, a forty-minute piece about a youth patriot camp on the outskirts of Kutaisi. *A Mr Minister* is a shorter and more modest affair than Kirtadze's portrait of Sakashvili, but just as telling about his era's politics. Commissioned by Dutch TV to make a film about what it means to be young in Georgia, Jashi thought immediately of politics, and of Kvezereli, the then minister of agriculture, who was the same age as Jashi at the time.[24]

In the space of sixteen minutes we see Kvezereli go-karting, residing in a Soviet era tower block with a grey run-down exterior, planning a festival of Georgian wine in California, meeting farmers, scutinising his own press interviews with his heavily pregnant wife, bringing his own party and the opposition together in a televised event harvesting grapes, meeting his newborn baby and finally speculating about the future. The overriding theme is Kvezereli's pragmatism. In voice-over he contrasts an aim with a dream, concluding that 'an aim should be achievable within a time limit'. In a meeting, he is asked why he chose the USA over Europe (which is assumed to be culturally and geographically closer) as a venue for his wine promoting activities. He points out that currently the US–Georgia relationship is closer, citing 'CNN and NBC' coverage of Georgia as examples. His modest tower block apartment and constituency of rural farmers seem at odds with his plans for global exposure and success.

Meanwhile, *The Leader is Always Right* shows the rise of nationalist 'patriot' camps across Georgia, and follows activities in one such camp as the teenage attendees do team building activities, chant patriotic chants and prepare for and eventually perform a patriotic play.

These camps existed during the Sakashvili era, during which the Georgian government tried to project an image of transformation into a modern liberal democracy with much in common with Western European nations. However, the wish 'may we meet in a patriot camp in Sukhumi' expressed by one of the camp counsellors (once during a one-on-one with an unruly camper, and again in front of a massed audience), has a threatening undertone that sounds anything but peaceful. This aggressive form of nationalism, funded by the Georgian government and lain bare by Jashi, is at odds with the official narrative.

The students struggle with the kitsch material ('Why are you so sad, my country?' is one stand-out line of dialogue) and receive rapturous applause from their audience. After the performance, however, the leader of the camp chastises the teens for their 'many gaps', his back to the camera sharply in focus while the teenagers blur into an unfocused mass. Close-ups show their pained expressions. The angle changes and we are right behind the leader's ear, the teens he is talking to out of focus. 'Any questions? None? Good.' Statistics appear on-screen listing the number of camps and their participants.

Commenting on the harsh regime within the camp, Jashi said:

> It's really a hierarchy, and they try to please their leaders, completely losing their individuality in the process. That was really the model for me: the young leaders that worked there were trying to punish their team members, to show their leaders that they are good leaders.[25]

Even without Jashi's given opinions, the final moments of the film, along with the statistic that the camps had admitted 100,000 teenage participants, make her critique pronounced.

Kirtadze began making a film about the then-current president Mikhail Sakashvili, which would soon transform into *Something About Georgia*. She had previously made a film about the previous president Edward Shevardnadze, and this time wanted to focus on Sakashvili seeking re-election four years after taking power in the Rose Revolution. However, halfway through Sakashvili's campaign, fighting began in South Ossettia. Consequently Kirtadze edited the film backwards.[26] It begins as a war narrative, with harrowing footage of bombed Ossetian Georgians, before taking the viewers back eight months to focus on Sakashvili's campaign for the remaining hour of the film. Consequently Sakashvili's meetings and confidently delivered press conferences take on an air of menace as they are viewed in the context of the coming violence, which viewers have paradoxically already seen. In doing so, Kirtadze highlights the difficulties (as mentioned earlier, Georgia had already experienced war with breakaway Abkhazia and an overlapping civil war by this point) of transitioning from a post-Soviet state, but also contrasts a polished official narrative with an unpredictable, violent and unofficial one.

In *Speechless*, Jashi trains her camera on the immediate aftermath of the 2008 war. While working as a fixer for the BBC during the conflict, she visited the military hospital in Gori. Impressed by the stoic facial expressions of the doctors and other hospital staff in the face of their difficult tasks, she decided to return to the war zone and film audiovisual portraits of people in the hospital, and in nearby villages and hastily constructed IDP camps. As per the title, the subjects of the film are speechless; the unmoving camera records their portrait for a minute or so at a time, while birdsong and traffic are heard on the soundtrack. While *Something About Georgia* contrasts two differing narratives of transition-era Georgia, *Speechless* uses the documentary form to suggest inner states: something unspoken, unspeakable, beyond official narratives, and at the same time to insist upon the unpalatable faces that are testament to the war that threatened to throw Georgia's narrative of progress off course.

Their Helicopter is an impressionistic piece that shows children playing in an abandoned helicopter that crashed in the remote northern region of Khevsureti. The helicopter had crashed while exporting cheese from the Khevsureti region of Georgia to neighbouring Chechnya. Shorn of this context (which is not revealed until an intertitle at the end of the film), the helicopter seems like a relic of one of Georgia's wars. Voices talk while the camera looks out from within the husk of the helicopter. 'At first I thought of opening a library in it', says the children's father as a cow inspects the wreckage. Throughout the film, the insides of the helicopter form a secondary frame, framing but partially obscuring the activities of the family.

In one remarkable shot, the camera looks out, framed by part of the helicopter, at a dog emerging from a kennel; yet another frame made from the disused helicopter. In the background the family, their conversation audible on the soundtrack, load their donkey with firewood.

The helicopter frame seems to influence the rest of the film, so that we always see partial people; children disappearing into long grass, or sitting in a space between shadows that form another frame within a frame. The repeated imagery is far away from that of modern, Western Europe. The participants are framed extremely closely, almost claustrophobically, to the landscape, or else they are in extreme long shot; small figures in the distance, though the viewer can hear every word.

Across Jashi's films, this temporality is explored in different ways; there is a calm ritual to *Their Helicopter*, while *Bakhmaro* shows the empty time of waiting. *Speechless*, though, turns that waiting into an emotionally stark experience. On the outside we can only guess what these people are thinking; perhaps a harrowing memory, a nostalgic longing or a quotidian thought. *Bakhmaro*, Jashi's most sustained look at Georgian society yet in some ways narrowest in focus, deals with a building that was once a hotel. Situated in Chokhatauri, Western Georgia, close to the Nabeglavi health resort, this once grand Soviet building is now multi-purpose and is home to a restaurant, around which much of the film revolves, and additionally a Chinese shop, a betting shop, a dentist and other businesses. The building even houses refugees from Abkhazia though these people are not seen in the film.

As with *Speechless*, the film focuses on the passing of time as recorded by a stationary camera, rather than seeking moments of activity or intrigue. While *The Pipeline Next Door* sets up a clear distinction between the BTC executives and the villagers, *Bakhmaro* leaves viewers wondering as to the precise location, purpose and nature of the scenes unfolding. In doing so, it allows us to feel the duration of waiting, of having nothing to do, few distractions, only the ability or inclination to look.

Commenting on how far Jashi has moved away from her roots in journalism and television reporting, the critic Teo Khatiashvili notes:

> Despite showing a concrete authentic environment, there is no representation of one locality (the title of the film, Bakhmaro, is symptomatic: the name of a famous resort in Georgia, which in this case is not a toponym but the name of a former restaurant). It does not matter whether the action takes place inside the capital or beyond; in any other region or suburb the situation is similar. The social problems of Bakhmaro turn into existential problems; despair, helplessness, the so-called 'sadness and unfairness of the unbearable weight of reality' are felt in the silence of the characters.[27]

Jashi frequently empties her films of cluttering contexts in order to reveal these deeper problems, and in *Bakhmaro* this technique reaches its apex.

Don't Breathe, Kirtadze's most recent film, is a docudrama featuring a Georgian couple playing themselves, and also aims to reveal a deeper predicament than the one inherent in the film's immediate story. When Levan is diagnosed with bursitis he and his wife Irma seek a second opinion, and then another, as hypochondria takes over. After Levan's MRI scan, we see various relatives and friends surrounding Levan, some leaning out of the window into the downstairs courtyard where this scene takes place. Everybody has their own opinion about Levan's predicament, and some predict gangrene and amputation.

In publicity surrounding the film, Kirtadze has hinted that the film is about much more than Levan and Irma's predicament. 'What does it mean to face an uncertain future?',[28] she asks, citing wars and global unrest. Although these topics were covered in previous Kirtadze films, here they are not to be found on the surface of the film. With their most recent works, Jashi and Kirtadze allow new collective memories to be forged, either through a collaborative docudrama assembled with the family who act as the film's principal actors, or by emptying a place and a situation of context so that waiting and looking themselves are foregrounded.

As I have shown in this chapter, Jashi and Kirtadze have trained their cameras upon the competing narratives of post-Soviet Georgia, depicting the forces of globalisation clashing with a traditional village, and a rural family salvaging the wreckage of a destroyed helicopter. They have engaged with the major events of post-Soviet Georgia's recent past; the optimism of the Rose Revolution era and subsequent decline into propaganda, the 2008 war and its aftermath. Jashi and Kirtadze have examined landmarks in recent Georgian history, adding their own subjective commentary to the events. Finally they have both moved away from traditional documentary methods into more experimental territory, allowing viewers a greater ability to interpret for themselves the experiences projected on screen.

If visual culture is central in not only creating, but maintaining the imagined community of a nation, what happens when the community is newly emerged, and a collective imagination has not yet solidified? Georgia becomes a blank screen on which can be projected the futuristic skyline of Batumi, or the ultra-modern architecture of the Sakashvili era, or the static waiting of *Bakhmaro*, or the mixture of fact and fiction found in *Don't Breathe*.

NOTES

1. For a discussion of the constructed nature of the concepts of Western and Eastern Europe, see Larry Wolf, *Inventing Eastern Europe: The Map of Civilisation on the Mind of the Englightenment* (Stanford, CA: Stanford University Press, 1994).
2. *Who's Afraid of Feminism in Georgia?* [online video], 2015. Available at <https://www.youtube.com/watch?v=vXtgHhVd2T0> (last accessed 9 September 2016).
3. Ibid.
4. Ibid.
5. Nancy Condee, *The Imperial Trace: Recent Russian Cinema* (Oxford: Oxford University Press, 2009).
6. Ruby Cheung, *New Hong Kong Cinema: Transitions to Becoming Chinese in 21st-Century East Asia* (New York: Berghahn, 2015).
7. Hamid Naficy, *An Accented Cinema: Exilic and Diasporic Filmmaking* (Princeton, NJ: Princeton University Press, 2001).
8. Spyros Demetriou, 'Rising from the ashes? The difficult (re)birth of the Georgian state', *Development and Change*, 33/5, 2002, p. 868.
9. Zaza Rusadze. 'Georgian film in emigration', *Kinokultura*, Special Issue 12. Available at <http://www.kinokultura.com/specials/12/rusadze-emigration.shtml> (last accessed 10 January 2016).
10. Ibid.
11. J. Hoberman, 'Independent nation with films to match', *New York Times*, 18 September 2014. Available at <http://www.nytimes.com/2014/09/21/movies/a-survey-celebrates-georgias-rich-film-tradition.html> (last accessed 10 January 2016).
12. Kaleem Aftab, 'Georgian cinema: the former Soviet Bloc nation is now a movie making hot spot', *The Independent*, 6 October 2015. Available at <http://www.independent.co.uk/arts-entertainment/films/features/georgian-cinema-the-former-soviet-bloc-nation-is-now-a-movie making-hot-spot-a6683351.html> (last accessed 10 January 2016).
13. Anon., 'Focus Georgia', *Visions du Réel*, <http://www.visionsdureel.ch/en/docm/focus/> (last accessed 10 January 2016).

14. Young-Woo Kim, 'Three women under one sky – the power of Georgian women filmmakers', BIFF, 22 September 2014, <http://biff.kr/artyboard/board.asp?act=bbs&subAct=view&bid=9612_22&page=1&order_index=no&order_type=desc&list_style=list&seq=33546> (last accessed 10 January 2016).
15. In addition to her Georgian documentaries, she visited Russia in 2008 to film *Durakovo: Village of Fools* to profile Mikhail Morozov, the director of a rehab clinic and a grassroots conservative activist.
16. Salomé Jashi, interview with the author, 27 September 2015.
17. Anon., <http://www.sakdoc.ge/> (last accessed 10 January 2016).
18. NSC 2011, quoted in T. German, 'Heading West? Georgia's Euro Atlantic path', *International Affairs*, 91/3, 2015, pp. 601–14, p. 608.
19. German, 'Heading West?', p. 608.
20. Jessica Stites Mor, *Transition Cinema: Political Filmmaking and the Argentine Left since 1968* (Pittsburgh, PA: University of Pittsburgh Press, 2012), p. 10.
21. Zaza Rusadze, 'The identity and place of contemporary Georgian cinema', *Kinokultura*, Special Issue 12. Available at <http://www.kinokultura.com/specials/12/rusadze-identity.shtml> (last accessed 10 January 2016).
22. Sudeshna Barman, 'BARE interviews: Nino Kirtadze', *BARE Magazine*, 23 April 2015. Available at <http://www.baremagazine.org/bare-interviews-nino-kirtadze> (last accessed 27 January 2016).
23. Andrew Barry, *Material Politics: Disputes Along The Pipeline* (Oxford: Wiley Blackwell, 2013), p. 2.
24. Interview with the author, 27 September 2015.
25. Salomé Jashi, interview with the author, 27 September 2015.
26. Nino Kirtadze, interview with the author, 21 November 2015.
27. Tato Khatiashvili, 'Beyond time and space: review of Bakhmaro', *Kinokultura*, Special Issue 12. Available at <http://www.kinokultura.com/specials/12/bakhmaro.shtml> (last accessed 10 January 2016).
28. Anon., 'Nino Kirtadze (Don't Breathe) interview', *Tribute.ca*. Available at <http://www.tribute.ca/interviews/nino-kirtadze-dont-breathe/director/103831/> (last accessed 27 January 2016).

Filmography

Ikh Tsartsvo/Their Kingdom (Nutsa Gogoberidze and Mikhail Kalatozov, USSR, 1928).
Dites à Mes Amis Que Je Suis Mort/Tell My Friends That I'm Dead (Nino Kirtadze, 2004).
Un Dragon Dans les Eaux Pures du Caucase/The Pipeline Next Door (Nino Kirtadze, France, 2005).
Mati Vertmphreni/Their Helicopter (Salomé Jashi, Georgia/UK, 2006).
Ert-Erti Ministeri/A Mr Minister (Salomé Jashi and Giorgi Tsiqarishvili, Georgia/Holland, 2008).
Altzaney (Nino Orjonikidze and Vano Arsenishvili, Georgia, 2009).
Something About Georgia (Nino Kirtadze, Georgia/France, 2009).
Dadumebulebi/Speechless (Salomé Jashi, Georgia, 2009).
Lideri Koveltvis Martalia/The Leader is Always Right (Salomé Jashi, Georgia, 2010).
Bakhmaro (Salomé Jashi, Georgia/Germany, 2011).
Five Days of War (USA/Georgia, Renny Harlin, 2011).
La Faille/Don't Breathe (Nino Kirtadze, France, 2014).
Who's Afraid of Feminism in Georgia? (Ia Barateli, Georgia, 2013).

Mandarinebi/Tangerines (Zaza Urushadze, Estonia/Georgia, 2013).
Simindis Kundzuli/Corn Island (Giorgi Ovashvili, Georgia/France/Czech Republic/Kazakhstan/Hungary, 2014).
Ogasavara (Tato Kotetishvili, Georgia, 2015).

11. *PROFESSION: DOCUMENTARIST*: UNDERGROUND DOCUMENTARY MAKING IN IRAN

Lidia Merás

Profession: Documentarist (Herfeh: Mostanadsaz, 2014) is an illustrative example of the feminisation of Iranian civil society in recent decades. Azadeh Kian documents how women filmmakers, as well as writers and publishers, emerged in significant numbers among the urban, educated, middle classes from the 1990s onward.[1] In the last twenty years fertility rates have dropped in Iran, from an average of seven births per woman to two, a figure comparable with most industrialised countries. By 2008, the number of female university students outnumbered male students by 60 per cent.[2] The filmmakers of *Profession: Documentarist* are representative of this new social group of highly educated women who have benefited from a more active participation in society. Although all of the contributors are women filming in Iran, the documentary does not provide viewers with a privileged view of the specific challenges that women directors endure there. Even if these directors have been concerned with gender issues in the past, it would be inaccurate to claim that *Profession: Documentarist* deliberately supports a feminist agenda.[3] The film is for the most part a testimony to the hardship of underground documentary filmmaking in post-revolutionary Iran. Directed by seven filmmakers, it is a diary-style documentary that reflects the challenges of pursuing the vocation of the documentarist in Iran from an autobiographical perspective.[4] It explores the professional barriers involved, and captures the turbulent mood in Iranian society under the presidency of Mahmoud Ahmadinejad (2005–13). Along with the accustomed financial limitations that most filmmakers endure, the directors face the difficulties of working in the aftermath of the Islamic Revolution and the defeat of the reformist Green Movement, namely: harsh censorship laws and the menace of political retaliations. *Profession: Documentarist* thus honours the resilience of Iranian filmmakers, creators unable to get a filming permit after the general election of 2009, who overcome their professional frustration by working together.

With a title that alludes to Michelangelo Antonioni's *Professione: reporter* (1975), the film was co-directed by documentary filmmakers born between 1963 and 1984. Unlike other national cinemas, there are very few examples of collective authorship in Iranian documentary filmmaking.[5] In this regard, *Profession: Documentarist* is unusual. The group effort can only be explained by the political and economical circumstances, in this case aggravated by US and EU sanctions on Iran at the time the film was made. At a screening of the film at London's ICA in March 2014, Shirin Barghnavard, co-director and co-producer of the documentary, confirmed that the project emerged from sharing accounts with other colleagues of the difficulties of realising their ideas.[6] Although economic hindrances are common to filmmakers worldwide, conditions for documentary filmmakers in Iran deteriorated under the hardline presidency of Ahmadinejad. Increased pressure on documentary filmmakers left many out of work and depressed. The origin of the documentary was, in fact, a series of informal meet-ups organised around food and cooking, the main objective of which was to provide mutual support during these difficult times.

Profession: Documentarist consists of seven segments, each preceded by the given name of its respective director, that last between eight and thirteen minutes; a variation that reveals a flexibility in developing the stories. The segments differ in style but certain topics reappear throughout the film. The documentary continues the tradition within Iranian cinema of filming in real locations,[7] but instead of open spaces or filming inside an automobile *à la* Abbas Kiarostami, three of the shorts exhibit the interiors of modern, liberal, middle class domiciles. These are indistinguishable from Western homes but, interestingly, some of the director-narrators comply with the filmic convention that urges women to wear the hijab in private spaces – even if in everyday life they would not do so. However, these domestic settings are not used for their association with traditional female tasks. Instead, the directors present themselves videoconferencing, using mobile phones, deleting messages from an answering machine, packing personal belongings and, above all, filming. Interestingly, when they film themselves at home they are always alone. Their solitude, especially the absence of partners or children, prevents any visible differentiation of traditional gender roles, reaffirming their status as filmmakers.

Although the preference for filming at home can be easily explained (it is one of the few spaces filmmakers can use without requiring the permission of the authorities), the compliance of wearing the hijab adds a certain ambivalence

Figure 19 Segment 'Sepideh' by Sepideh Abtani.

to the clandestine status of the film. It indicates that a few of the filmmakers seemingly avoided being too confrontational; perhaps this was in the hope that the film could eventually be released or, if confiscated, repercussions might be less severe. In any case, the themes addressed in *Profession: Documentarist* condemned the documentary to a modest local audience of mostly private screenings, in spaces not dissimilar to those depicted. Nonetheless it has been widely screened abroad and won both the Best World Documentary prize at Jihlava Documentary Film Festival (Czech Republic) and the Tim Hetherington Award at Sheffield Doc/Fest.[8]

Profession: Documentarist draws upon a wide variety of sources (including archive footage, computer games, mobile phone recordings from recent demonstrations, home movies, and still photographs) to give a sense of Iran's convulsive history, which has so profoundly impacted on the lives of these directors. Although they belong to different generations, the seven filmmakers share similar methods of documenting the course of history. Each of these highly personal stories is deeply connected with Iran's past. The film is a multilayered documentary constructed around the uncertainties of pursuing an artistic career, while at the same time reflecting on war, political repression and nostalgia. In the best tradition of Iranian cinema, the film is also self-reflexive, foregrounding the nature and boundaries of filmmaking.

Each director is also the protagonist of their own segment, each depicted alone, reflecting on their work as an extension of their existence. 'Filmmaking is my life', declares Sahar Salahshoor. 'Last year I didn't make a film and it is as though I didn't live.' This association of filmmaking with living is a guiding principle of this collective film, in which the biographies of the directors are linked to their roles as filmmakers. The ways in which the directors' personal experiences can be extrapolated to the lives of many Iranians is also a key element of the film. The film directors in *Profession: Documentarist* are all presented as witnesses to a turbulent historical period in Iran, and confronted with their own anxieties regarding their role as documentary filmmakers. This ensemble film will be examined as a case study based on the historical, social and national contexts within which contemporary female documentary film-makers now at work in Iran.

THE HOUSE IS BLACK AND A BRIEF HISTORICAL CONTEXT OF IRANIAN CINEMA

In 1962, the poet Forough Farrokhzad[9] directed *The House is Black* (Khaneh siah ast), a landmark film which was recently voted as one of the top twenty-five documentaries of all time in a worldwide poll conducted by *Sight and Sound* magazine.[10] It is a medium-length film about life in a leprosarium near Tabriz. Preceding the Iranian New Wave, *The House is Black* has since been a primary influence among documentary filmmakers in Iran. The film went beyond its initial institutional aim of raising awareness about the living conditions of lepers; the shocking sight of disfigured faces and limb deformities finds a powerful counterpoint in the recitation of sacred texts and Farrokhzad's own poems, voiced by the author, transforming her documentary into an unforgettable cinematic experience.

Many post-revolutionary Iranian filmmakers, especially those working in documentary, have rejected flattering representations of their society and have instead sustained the interest in dealing with social issues. These are the heirs to Farrokhzad's legacy. As filmmaker Rakshan Bani-Etemad states: '[. . .] the roots of our cinema – the source of the progressive force of our cinema – are found at the very heart of our society'.[11] Farrokhzad's seminal work paved the way for the directors featured in *Profession: Documentarist*, who would adopt elements of her filmmaking style, such as the use of a female voice-over (their own voices) to talk about contemporary concerns. The influence of Farrokhzad's film on *Profession: Documentarist* can also be recognised in the 'dirgelike tone', similar to that attributed by Jonathan Rosenbaum to *The House is Black*.[12]

However, the historical context has changed dramatically since the years of the Iranian New Wave. In only five decades, Iran has undergone express Westernisation, revolution, radical Islamisation, war and numerous attempts at reform. It is necessary to take this tumultuous history into account in order to get a better sense of its repercussions on film culture today. The Islamic Revolution in particular had a major impact on Iranian cinema. Between

1978 and 1979 almost half of Iran's cinemas were destroyed by fire.[13] One isolated but dramatic case is the Cinema Rex fire in the city of Âbâdân, where more than 400 cinemagoers were burned alive inside by religious extremists. Ayatollah Khomeini's initial aversion to cinema was justified as part of the more general aim of purifying Iranian society of influences from the West, as well as protecting Iranians from the pervasive effects of the Shah's decadent dictatorship. Not surprisingly, *filmfarsi* was the first victim. This popular genre, which customarily exposed scantily clad female dancers to the male gaze, was banned and most of *filmfarsi*'s talent, especially its actresses, lost their jobs.[14] During the early years of the revolution, these seductive dancers were replaced by new characters, relegating women to marginal roles, including chaste sisters, obedient wives, and devoted mothers, in accordance with Iran's new sharia laws.[15]

Ironically, the regime that was overruling women's rights could also claim to be responsible for the emergence of a considerable number of female directors. As Saeed Zeydabadi-Nejad points out, an interesting side-effect of the 'purification' of the film industry was that it cleared the way for women from a religious background to gain access to the film industry.[16] Interested in making use of cinema as a tool to propagate the new values of the Islamic Republic, the authorities would later relax their policies and accept more women on both sides of the camera. The role of women on screen changed from that of passive, almost invisible subjects to strong characters and heroines in some cases.

The evolution is evident in many contemporary documentaries made by women. Access to a career in the film industry allowed the largest and arguably most affected social group in the aftermath of the Islamic Revolution to address issues that primarily affected them. For instance, in the documentary *Divorce Iranian Style* (Kim Longinotto and Ziba Mir-Hosseini, 1998), the camera follows four women fiercely defending their rights. The film defies the perceived notions of Muslim women as subjects without agency. At the same time, it reveals how difficult it is for women to make their rights effective under the Sharia law. In *Our Times* (Ruzegar-e ma, 2002), Bani-Etemad also gives voice to women; in this case, the female candidates running for the presidency in Iran's 2001 elections. Although aware that they have zero chance of being elected, they all express how they became involved in politics in order to make women's concerns visible. Surprisingly, both *Divorce Iranian Style* and *Our Times* were approved by the government. However, *Our Times* was never released in Iran. *Divorce Iranian Style* had better luck but the directors had to spend twenty months of Kafkaesque negotiations to get permission to film the trials, prior to the shooting.[17] As Ziba Mir-Hosseini affirmed, the main obstacle was that the Iranian government has a very different perception of what kind of 'reality' is 'suitable for filming'.[18] In her film, she argues, the women documentarists' points of view are presented as closer to the people's everyday experience and therefore often represent a counter-discourse to the official representation of reality:

> The most often heard [voice] is that of the law: authoritarian and patriarchal, and increasingly out of touch with people's aspirations and experiences. But there is also an egalitarian voice in everyday life, seldom heard by outsiders. This is the voice women express, and we wanted it to be heard.[19]

Though it cannot be claimed that Iranian women filmmakers prefer documentary over fiction, documentary is a format especially suited to the themes the filmmakers of *Profession: Documentarist* address. As a consequence, many women filmmakers interested in illuminating different aspects of society that affect the lives of women in Iran are compelled to go underground. Choosing documentary, they turn everyday images into subversive material.

Directors working in Iran have to adjust their productions to the 'shifting red lines' of censorship.[20] For those filmmakers who dare to cross those lines, after negotiations or efforts at deluding censors have failed, the options are to work abroad or else produce their films underground.[21] *Profession: Documentarist* was never censored. Its filmmakers simply avoided the Center for Documentary and Experimental Film, the governmental institution that finances and regulates the production of documentaries. Therefore, the film had no distribution through the usual channels: national television (Iran owns a state documentary channel) or the Cinéma Vérité Film Festival (Cinema Haghighat), which specialises in documentary. One of the reasons for the clandestine status of *Profession: Documentarist* is that it specifically engages with the struggle of documentary filmmakers during the emergence of the Green Movement, a grassroots reform movement that emerged in Iran in 2009. Pedram Khosronejad has written on the importance of independent documentary filmmakers during the crisis that followed the disputed elections of June 2009, when extremist candidate Mahmoud Ahmadinejad was re-elected as President of Iran despite being accused of electoral fraud.[22] Supporters of the moderate Mir-Hossein Mousavi protested all around the country in the largest demonstrations since the Revolution. While the authorities tried to prevent media coverage of the demonstrations (including blocking mobile phone access, blogs and social media), 'every single person in the streets who had a cell phone became a citizen journalist and reported on the crisis day by day'.[23] During these tense days, many independent documentary filmmakers also felt it was their duty to record what was happening. Among them was Rakhsan Bani-Etemad, who acted as a spokesperson on behalf of 120 independent documentary filmmakers.[24] In a manifesto, she accused the official media of dividing the country and warned about a potential outbreak of violence.²⁵ A few months later, many compilation films would emerge which used mobile phone footage and amateur videos of the demonstrations, such as *The Green Wave* (Ali Samadi Ahadi, 2010) and *The Silent Majority Speaks* by Bani Khoshnoudi (2010–14). *Profession: Documentarist* also contains some of these recordings, aimed at preserving a historic event for subsequent generations.

Wars, Revolution and the Role of the Documentary Filmmaker

The function of the documentary filmmaker and their responsibility in documenting historic events is central to the conception of *Profession: Documentarist*. Focusing on different political periods – the Iran–Iraq War and the Islamic Revolution respectively – the segments 'Shirin' and 'Sepideh' (Figure 19) are especially committed to dealing with the professional and ethical duties of the independent filmmaker. Filmed during a tense period when an American intervention onto Iranian soil was a prominent threat, the first short reflects on the moral duty of the filmmaker to document war. Shirin Barghnavard asks whether she would be able to record the conflict if the prospect of war was to materialise. In the opening sequence, taken from a video game, American soldiers are approaching the Gisha Bridge, a spot in Tehran close to where she spent her childhood.²⁶ Since the surroundings of Gisha in the videogame have been designed to match the real location exactly, the game visualises the possible attack. While the video console shows the imaginary US attack, the filmmaker's voice-over evokes her childhood memories of her former neighbourhood, which Barghnavard associates with the time it was bombed by Saddam Hussein's airforce during the Iran–Iraq War (1980–8).

The overlapping of this former war child's voice with the simulated images reminds us of the silenced inhabitants of Tehran. Although they remain invisible in the videogame, they now return as ghosts haunted by their memories, to anticipate the scenario of a new battlefield. As a media professional, Barghnavard feels both the urge and a commitment to register historical events, but fears the personal risks for her loved ones: 'I think if there will be another war, would I stay to document it? Or perhaps I wouldn't even let my husband, a cameraman, film anything?'²⁷ As with other sections of the film, Barghnavard's short combines archive images (e.g., military parades, TV recordings of Iraqi bombings) with home movies. She keeps asking what a new war in Iran would look like on screen, and who would record it. But her film has already answered that question. As long as documentarists can hold a camera, war images will no longer be the privilege of governments, and used for the purposes of propaganda, or a wicked form of entertainment. They will serve to portray the sorrow of ordinary people as much as they will depict the vulnerabilities of independent filmmakers.

PROFESSION: DOCUMENTARIST

Figure 20   Segment 'Sahar' by Sahar Salahshoor.

BEFORE NIGHT FALLS:
POLITICAL REPRESSION IN POST-REVOLUTIONARY IRAN

Given that the documentary filmmaker's job is to create unsolicited documents of life in Iran, they defy prefabricated notions of what should be shown on screen. Certain images might be interpreted as dangerous by the government, in that they could compromise orthodox representations of religion, pervade local traditions or harm national pride. In the segments made by Firouzeh Khosrovani and Sahar Salahshoor (Figure 20) the viewer discovers some of the subtle methods employed by the regime to pressure filmmakers. Both segments consist of a first-person account filmed at home. No archive footage is provided this time to tell their stories, and the filming takes place during an unspecified lapse before dawn, probably to convey the everyday oppression of underground filmmakers. 'Your films worry us', Firouzeh Khosrovani recalls an interrogator telling her. In her eight-minute film, we learn about the state's tactics of intimidation designed to make filmmakers feel as if they are under surveillance.

The setting in Sahar Salahshoor's film is almost identical to Khosrovani's. The depiction of a comfortable, well-equipped, yet claustrophobic home suggests once more the idea of the intrusiveness of the Iranian totalitarian state, able to inculcate distress even in the most intimate spaces. Salahshoor films in her apartment where, again, the narrator-protagonist packs her belongings. She has cancelled her thirtieth birthday party and has decided to move from her flat. The reason is that from her apartment she can see Evin Prison, notorious for its political prisoners.[28] Salahshoor senses the proximity of the

177

jail, which makes her feel locked up, confined within the walls of her own house. Even the window's muntins remind us of prison bars. The domestic space of the sitting room is thus visually compared to the institutional space of the prison, where some of her friends are incarcerated. The daily sight of Evin Prison, whose walls she is not allowed to film, has affected her frame of mind. It prevents her not only from celebrating her birthday, but also from filming and even from looking into the future. Salahshoor's film documents the paralysing effect of not being able to ignore the regime's oppression. While the camera shows her packing, her voice-over announces the decision to move: 'I will free myself from the place I've been imprisoned in or where I've imprisoned myself.' But the final shot of the empty flat in darkness suggests that she will not be any freer in her new home, unless she learns to look the other way.

Look Back or Move Forward

The Islamic Revolution marked a turning point in the individual freedoms of secular Iranians. If under the Shah the streets of Tehran were full of youngsters in miniskirts while pious women were humiliated in public for wearing the chador, the early 1980s saw the reversed scenario. Sharia law was enforced, and the clergy made compulsory the observance of a dress code especially strict for women, as were the penalties for its infringement. At different moments, Farahnaz Sharifi and other directors of *Profession: Documentarist* contrast colourful home videos and family pictures with the dark, monotonous clothing of women fully covered outside their homes, imposed after the triumph of the Islamic Revolution. In one of the seven segments, Sepideh Abtahi seems fascinated by the images of her late aunt Maryam, a leftist militant supporter of the Revolution. In a home video recorded before the hijab was made compulsory, Maryam's uncovered hair transports us to a lost paradise in which feminine beauty was exposed to the camera without care.

In addition to the new dress code, many forms of entertainment such as music and dance, now seen as trite and corruptive, had to be eradicated from the public sphere.[29] Farahnaz Sharifi's film is a nostalgic tour of the pre-Revolutionary years through popular music, depicted here as an escape from the rigorous lifestyle enforced by the mullahs. She pays special tribute to actress and pop star Googoosh, who enjoyed enormous popularity in Iran until her career was cut short by the Revolution. Under Khomeini all female performers were banned from singing.[30] As a result, most of her colleagues left the country, but Googoosh remained in Iran, sharing the fate of many women whose careers were equally ruined.[31] In her film, Sharifi illustrates the ban by showing archive footage of a colourful TV show from the 1970s in which Googoosh's voice is faded out, replaced by an intrusive beep until she is completely silenced. Googoosh stopped singing for two decades, yet her music was still widely listened to in private by those who would dwell in the past through her music. Dance and music performed by women only can happen in private spaces. Therefore, home movies featuring family celebrations contain images of all that is forbidden in Iranian cinema: the voices of female performers, men and women socialising and dancing together, and women not wearing the hijab. Making and watching home videos, as much as participating in those dances, are forms of escapism that allow people to break away from the moral restrictions of outdoor activities. Sharifi revisits these earlier recordings to express her longing for the times when it was not necessary to hide her admiration for Googoosh. Her piece is also an illustration of the capacity of art to survive in almost any hostile environment, and its power to make life under these conditions a bit more bearable.

Female Documentary Filmmakers in Post-revolutionary Iran

Profession: Documentarist thus provides an exemplary illustration of the sociohistorical framework in which female documentary filmmakers operate in contemporary Iran. The primary objective, as the title attests, is for the directors to present themselves as documentary filmmakers – or 'documentarists', as they prefer to say. These professionals pay little attention to consciously grounding their discourse in a feminist discourse. In fact, a curious feature of this film about the difficulties of pursuing the profession of filmmaking made by middle class women filmmakers, is the absence of narratives about the work–life balance. For instance, the filmmakers do not appear as mothers or mothers-to-be; only childless Nahid Rezaei refers to this particular subject merely to reaffirm her life choice as a career woman, over what she imagines would be 'a quiet life of a plump mom with a few children, doing cooking and sewing'. The fact that a film entirely made by women, in a country where women's rights are limited, does not specifically challenge gender inequality might bewilder some spectators. But the primary focus of the film is the role of the documentary filmmaker beyond any gender perspective. The directors have positioned themselves as film professionals as well as narrators of the current situation in Iran from the perspective of the urban, secular citizen. The female gaze can nevertheless be traced in the iconisation of Googoosh, and the vindication of her tragic fate as a representative of all women working in the arts, as seen in the sections by Farahnaz Sharifi and Nahid Rezaei, as well as in the construction of Abtahi's aunt into a romantic heroine of the Revolution.

Even if these seven directors have no doubt benefited from the renewed visibility of women in Iranian civil society, it is not evident whether *Profession: Documentarist* represents an image of Iran which is all that distinctive from that of their male colleagues. What the film mainly reflects is that these women directors profess and address the audience as if their tasks were identical to those of the male filmmakers. In fact, they have no special interest in relating the difficulties of their job to any particular 'women's issue' or feminist discourse. This would explain the scarcity of allusions to the work–life balance, and the absence of a critical discussion as to whether a higher degree of oppression is experienced for the mere fact of being women filmmakers. Instead, each of the directors appears in front of the camera as the central character of their stories, capturing the atmosphere of struggle they share with their fellow countrymen and women. If there is anything feminist in the film it is precisely that the universality of their plight is recognised by an all-female team. And it is from this polyphonic chorus of female voices that the voice of modern Iran, so often misrepresented in Western media, is articulated.

Profession: Documentarist is also a powerful reminder of the ability of documentary filmmaking to keep track of the devastating effects of historic events on ordinary lives. The segments explore national traumas (war, revolution) along with personal ones. As the film reveals, the personal and political are profoundly interconnected. It is also interesting to note that the different elements coincide through a number of narrative and aesthetic resources. For instance, most segments look to the pre-revolutionary years with nostalgia. Making use of archive and found footage, home videos and family pictures, the documentary continually maintains the parallels between historical episodes and the present. Despite the unfavourable circumstances these filmmakers and their colleagues find themselves in, the sequences shot behind the scenes, sharing food and personal concerns, turn the film into a sort of group therapy. The filmmakers joined forces to make a film that would prevent them from abandoning their vocation. The documentary itself, then, becomes both the means and the result of their mutual support.

In the first monologue of *The House is Black* Farrokhzad recites: 'There is no shortage of ugliness in the world. If man closed his eyes to it, there would be even more.' Each of these seven shorts confirms that documentary filmmakers are indispensable, never hiding from us all that is ugly and evil in our societies, without knowledge of which we would be condemned to endure even darker times.

Acknowledgment

I am very grateful to Ehsan Khoshbakht, who took the time to carefully read and comment on the completed manuscript. All images in this chapter have been reproduced with permission of Shirin Barghnavard.

Notes

1. Among the female directors Kian mentions are Tahmineh Milani, Pouran Derakhshandeh, Manijeh Hekmat, Marziyeh Meshkini, Samira Makhmalbaf,

Nikki Karimi and Rakshan Bani-Etemad. Azadeh Kian, 'Social and cultural change and the women's rights movement in Iran', in Annabelle Sreberny and Massoumeh Torfeh (eds), *Cultural Revolution in Iran. Contemporary Popular Culture in the Islamic Republic* (London: I. B. Tauris, 2013), p. 52.
2. Ibid. p. 43.
3. Past films dealing with gender issues were, for instance, Sahar Salahshoor's film about a female taxi driver, *Behind the Wheel of Life* (2007); or Firouzeh Khosrovani's *Iran, Unveiled and Veiled Again* (2012).
4. Farahnaz Sharifi, Firouzeh Khosrovani, Mina Keshavarz, Nahid Rezaei, Sahar Salahshoor, Sepideh Abtahi and Shirin Barghnavard.
5. *The Silent Majority Speaks* (2010–14) appeared to be a contemporary exception. Released under the pseudonym 'The silent collective', in 2013, Bani Khoshnoudi claimed its authorship. In her introduction to the film at ICA London in 2016, she justified her initial decision of hiding under a collective name for fear of retaliation and her desire to keep travelling to Iran.
6. Essay Film Festival, ICA, London, 28 March 2014.
7. Mehrnaz Saeed-Vafa, 'Location (physical space) and cultural identity in Iranian films', in Richard Tapper (ed.), *The New Iranian Cinema: Politics, Representation and Identity* (London: I. B. Tauris, 2013), p. 200.
8. The film has been screened at the Amsterdam Film Festival, BAFICI, the Zurich Film Festival, IDFA and the Essay Film Festival (London).
9. Farrokhzad, one of the greatest Iranian poets of the twentieth century, was a controversial figure among traditionalists. Married at seventeen and divorced a few years later following rumours of infidelity, her poems were silenced for a decade after the triumph of the Islamic Revolution. Poetry is a popular art form among Iranians and, despite the ban, the average Iranian could recite her works years after her tragic death at age thirty-two in a car accident.
10. 'Critics 50 greatest documentaries of all times', *Sight and Sound*, September 2014.
11. Bani-Etemad in Shiva Rahbaran, *Iranian Cinema Uncensored: Contemporary Film-makers since the Islamic Revolution* (London: I. B. Tauris, 2015), p. 238.
12. Jonathan Rosenbaum, 'Radical humanism and the coexistence of film and poetry in *The House Is Black*', in Jonathan Kahana (ed.), *The Documentary Film Reader: History, Theory, Criticism* (Oxford: Oxford University Press, 2016), p. 475.
13. Saeed Zeydabadi-Nejad, 'Beyond gender: women filmmakers and sociopolitical critique', in Annabelle Sreberny and Massoumeh Torfeh (eds), *Cultural Revolution in Iran*, p. 112.
14. Ibid. p. 113.
15. Ibid.
16. Ibid. p. 116.
17. The making of *Divorce Iranian Style* has been documented by co-director Ziba Mir-Hosseini, 'Negotiating the politics of gender in Iran: an ethnography of a documentary', in Tapper (ed.), *The New Iranian Cinema*, p. 167.
18. Ibid. p. 167.
19. Ibid. p. 198.
20. Saeed Zeydabadi-Nejad, *The Politics of Iranian Cinema. Film and Society in the Islamic Republic of Iran* (Abingdon: Routledge, 2010), p. 30.
21. Recent examples from female documentary filmmakers of the Iranian diaspora are the fascinating *Jerry & Me* (Iran/United States, 2012), by Mehrnaz Saeed-Vafa, and *My Stolen Revolution* (Nahid Persson Sarvestani, Iran/Sweden, 2013).
22. Pedram Khosronejad, 'Some observations on visual representation of the 2009 presidential election crisis', *Iranian Studies*, 4/3, 2011, p. 396.

23. Ibid. p. 400.
24. The icon of the Green Movement was also a woman. On 20 June 2009, only one day after Bani Etemad read the manifesto, an amateur recording captured the death of philosophy student Neda Agha-Soltan. Shot by a sniper, the video circulated on the Internet turning her into the martyr of the Green Movement.
25. An English translation of the manifesto can also be found in Khosronejad, 2011, p. 401. The video is available on YouTube, <www.youtube.com/watch?v=lFx-8QHi5d8> (last accessed 1 October 2016).
26. Naficy notes that videogames were used by the US government as a means of propaganda against the Islamic Republic. Hamid Naficy, *A Social History of Iranian Cinema, vol. 4. The Globalizing Era, 1984–2010* (Durham, NC: Duke University Press, 2012), p. 291.
27. Shirin Barghnavard's husband, Mohammad Reza Jahanpanah, is the cinematographer of *Closed Curtain* (Pardé, 2013), by Jafar Panahi.
28. The 1979 Revolution was initially a popular uprising supported by a heterogeneous amalgam of Marxists, nationalists, Islamists and other disaffected groups that opposed Mohammad Reza Pahleví's authoritarian regime and its feared SAVAK national police force. From his exile in Paris, Shia leader Ayatollah Khomeini would unite the opposition against the Shah and become, after Pahleví's fall, the Supreme Leader in the newly founded Islamic Republic of Iran. Once Khomeini came to power, disenchantment soon followed among secular sympathisers. Left militants and other dissident groups (e.g., Kurds) were tortured, killed or incarcerated. See Michael Axworthy, *Irán: Una historia desde el Zoroastro hasta hoy* (Madrid: Turner, 2010) [first published as *Iran: Empire of the Mind*, London: Penguin, 2008], pp. 296–313.
29. 'Since the majority of religious people associated it with promiscuity and frivolous attitudes towards life, dance became the most demonised art form after the revolution [. . .]. However, [. . .] despite all prohibitions, dance remained popular as a house-bound activity in spaces that were away from the direct gaze of officials.' Parmis Mozafari, 'Dance and the borders of public and private life in post-revolution Iran', in Annabelle Sreberny and Massoumeh Torfeh (eds), *Cultural Revolution in Iran*, pp. 99–100.
30. The prohibition on showing female singers persists. In the last short, Nahid Rezaei notes that censors cut a sequence in a previous film in which a schoolgirl sings a song by Googoosh.
31. Farhad Zamani explored the phenomenon and cultural significance of the actress and pop diva in the documentary *Googoosh: Iran's Daughter* (2000).

Filmography

Behind the Wheel of Life (Poshte Farman-e Zendegi) (Sahar Salahshoor, Iran/UK, BBC World Service Trust, 2007).
Closed Curtains (Pardé) (Jafar Panahi and Kambuzia Partovi, Iran, Jafar Panahi Film Production, 2013).
Divorce Iranian Style (Kim Longinotto and Ziba Mir-Hosseini, Iran/UK, Twentieth Century Vixen, 1998).
Googoosh: Iran's Daughter (Farhad Zamani, USA, Atash Productions, 2000).
Iran, Unveiled and Veiled Again (Firouzeh Khosrovani, Iran, 2012).
Jerry & Me (Mehrnaz Saeed-Vafa, Iran/United States, 2012).
My Stolen Revolution (Min stulna revolution) (Nahid Persson Sarvestani, Iran/Sweden, RealReel Doc, 2013).
Our Times (Ruzegar-e ma) (Rakhsan Bani-Etemad, Iran, 2002).

Profession: Documentarist (Herfeh: Mostanadsaz) (Farahnaz Sharifi, Firouzeh Khosrovani, Mina Keshavarz, Nahid Rezaei, Sahar Salahshoor, Sepideh Abtahi and Shirin Barghnavard, Iran, 2014).

The Passenger (Professione: Reporter) (Michelangelo Antonioni, Italy/Spain/France, Compagnia Cinematografica Champion, Les Films Concordia, CIPI Cinematográfica S.A., 1975).

The Green Wave (Ali Samadi Ahadi, Germany, ARTE, Dreamer Joint Venture, WRF, 2010).

The House is Black (Khaneh siah ast) (Forough Farrokhzad, Iran, Golestan Film Studio, 1963).

The Silent Majority Speaks (Bani Khoshnoudi, Iran, 2010–14).

12. 'REFLECTING THROUGH IMAGES': THE DOCUMENTARIES OF MERCEDES ÁLVAREZ

Linda Ehrlich

On an August afternoon in 2015, I had the opportunity to talk at length with experimental documentarist Mercedes Álvarez on the spacious terraza of Ca la Maria in the heart of Barcelona. This was actually our second meeting; the first had taken place in La Floresta, north of Barcelona, in 2004.[1] Mercedes – the director of two acclaimed documentaries, *El cielo gira* (The Sky Spins, 2004) and *Mercado de futuros* (Futures Markets, 2011) – is a soft-spoken person, with a warmth and intensity as she enters into a discussion about the cinema. In her two full-length documentaries, Mercedes has played a key role in exploring expanded parameters in the documentary mode, both in Spain and beyond.

Mercedes's films compel us to examine the hybrid form of the 'essay film', a style which includes the diary film, the travelogue, the portrait – in other words, somewhere between 'fiction and nonfiction, news reports and confessional autobiography, documentaries and experimental film'.[2] In *The Personal Camera*, Laura Rascaroli describes this 'domain' (a term she prefers to 'genre') as 'irreducibly plural' and 'a cinema of doubt and self-scrutiny'.[3]

Mercedes Álvarez is a member of an influential group of graduates of the innovative MA Programme in Creative Documentary (*Documental de Creación*) at the Universitat Pompeu Fabra in Barcelona.[4] This programme, started in 1998 by curator/scholar Jordi Balló, has produced more than twenty-four films, with graduates such as Isaki Lacuesta, Ricardo Íscar, Neus Ballús, Renate Costa and Ariadna Pujol. In Mercedes's own words, the Pompeu Fabra documentarists tend to look to '*métodos artesanales . . . que en cierto modo nos hermanaban con los pioneros de cinematógrafo'* [craftsman-like methods ... that in a certain way aligned us with the pioneers of the cinema].[5] The approach of this varied group of filmmakers has been named '*Cinema de real* [Cinema of the Real]'. As Spanish filmmaker Víctor Erice notes in his eloquent essay on *El cielo gira,* 'none of these films responds – in subject matter, treatment, and duration – to an established cinematographic or television model'.[6] Below are some highlights from our recent conversation and from readings about the director.

A Woman's Voice

For Mercedes, filming is a way to 'reflect through images', to reflect on landscapes full of meaning (or 'universes' [*universos*], a term she prefers). In her own words, filmmaking allows her to reflect 'before and during, to think along with images' (*pensar con las imágines*). Editing, on the other hand, becomes for her a kind of writing (*escritura*). Her films offer reflections on worlds that are becoming increasingly stripped of meaning and – an even more serious problem – stripped of memory.

Mercedes is both profoundly rooted in one geographical location and open to cross-currents in the world today. Hers is a cinema of objects (manmade and natural) that punctuate, or even define, our lives. While she appreciates the work of documentarists like Michael Moore, Mercedes is aware that she does not want to approach her subjects in an aggressive and accusatory (*acosadora*) manner. She also does not want to replicate a journalistic approach, or to have her films give the same sensation one might have reading a book. We go to her films for their contemplative tone and evocative images.

Citing inspiration from female directors like Chantal Akerman, Farrokh Farokhzad and Agnès Varda, Mercedes is conscious of the flow of the diary as one means of revealing a woman's voice and interior life. To her, this form of narration becomes a means of disclosing intimacy. She notes that the documentary form offers a kind of liberty to women in that they can work with smaller crews. While the digital camera provides greater flexibility and fluidity than working with film, she fears there is also the danger that it can encourage shooting without an initial period of reflection. In fact, she noted that when she starts a film, she is not sure if it will be a documentary or one with actors. She is open to the latter although that has not happened yet.

Early Training

When she began her MA, Mercedes was thinking of working in fiction (and she still maintains some interest in working with actors, professional and non-professional). One of her key influences was Pompeu Fabra professor and documentarist Joaquim Jordà (1935–2006). Other influences on her work include Jean Rouch, Fred Wiseman (who was a guest lecturer during her MA programme), Chris Marker and Pasolini. (She describes Pasolini's *Comenzi d'amore* (*Love Meetings*, 1965) as an example of 'spontaneous, natural filmmaking.')

For her graduation from the MA programme in 1998, Mercedes completed *El viento africano* (*The African Wind*, 1996). For sixteen months following her graduation, she worked as part of the crew and editor for director and UPF instructor José Luis Guerín's *En Construción (Work in Progress*, 2001).[7] She called her work on the Guerín film *'un esfuerzo de reflexión teórica y un ejercicio constante de invención y exploración'* [an effort of theoretical relection, and a constant exercise of invention and exploration].[8] This experience taught her how one could proceed without a written screenplay, to carry on a 'dialogue with reality' (*un diálogo con la realidad*) and how a filmmaker could prepare her gaze 'like a painter'. In our discussion, she noted that working without a script can present a kind of 'vertigo', but it also offers irrepatable situations 'without rushing to establish a thesis or to arrive at a conclusion'.[9] She stressed that it was not just a case of going out and filming whatever crossed one's path.

El cielo gira (*The Sky Spins*, 2004)

In Mercedes's first full-length essay film, we are introduced to a place familiar to the filmmaker, her home region of Soria, and particularly the village of Aldealseñor. 'This is a landscape in which everything is named, every tree refers to a certain family, every village had its own "*novelas*" (imagined stories).'

Mercedes's family left Aldealseñor when she was just three years old, seeking greater opportunities elsewhere. She has returned various times, drawn to the familial house with ties of curiosity and nostalgia. When she decided on the subject of her debut feature film, the village was not just an interesting locale for Mercedes; it was a point of reference for her entire life. As the last person to have been born in Aldealseñor (in 1966), she will always be the child of the village. *El cielo gira* focuses on the world of what will probably be the last villagers, presenting that world through a series of concentric circles, or layers.

At the time of filming *El cielo gira,* only fourteen elderly residents remained, augmented at times by an array of visitors, including a Moroccan shepherd living four kilometers from the village or an (unintentionally) comic car blaring political slogans and trying to attract votes! Other layers included prehistoric dinosaur tracks, an inn from an earlier period now believed by some to be haunted, and the sound of planes passing overhead towards wars in the Middle East, stirring up the village residents' memories of Spanish Civil War times.[10]

Figure 21   Pello Azketa.

During her nine months of filming there (from October 2002 to June 2003), she found that the landscape is actually very open (*abierta*) and full (*amplia*) of subtle fluctuations in the light and in the dramatic movement of clouds. Although she first went there to film with a full crew, she soon saw that this would be an intrusion and so she returned with only two colleagues for the duration of the filming. The reason she edited the film to start with scenes from the autumn months was to show the village as it is during most of the year, when the occasional summer visitor or grown children have returned to the city.

At one point, Mercedes decided to bring into the village an unusual outside force, the painter Pello Azketa (b. 1949). In the 1970s, Pello was part of the Escuela de Pamplona, a group of painters who favoured abstract expressionism and minimalism. The artist's dignified form in the village is accepted easily by the villagers – they ask no questions as he learns his way around the giant elm tree in the village square (Figure 21). Pello's soft-toned landscapes are infused with light, with a lingering tribute to light, because he is going blind.

Like the gradual, but inexorable, fading of the painter's vision, the village of Aldealseñor hovers on a brink that is at once treacherous and precious. Mercedes describes the elderly villagers as fatalistic but with a redeemingly sardonic sense of humour. The sense of instability Mercedes found in Pello's paintings was one of the incentives to bring him into this film about the instability of a village on the verge of disappearing, even as the landscapes continue in their unending cycles of change. In this meditative atmosphere, even an Olympic hopeful who appears in one scene seems to be in no rush. A Moroccan athlete, running his thirty miles per day, represents the new world of international exchanges and immigration.

'Cinco elementos' (Five Elements) is a short film made to accompany the DVD of *El cielo gira* distributed in the US. Its poetic voice-over (by the director) and evocative images inspire reflection on each viewing. Mercedes relates to us how, in the village: '*El tiempo ... se marcha y vuelve ...Todo está al principio*' (Time leaves and returns ... Everything is at the beginning). And she continues: '*También como el tiempo vuelven las palabras. De andar y caminar surgieron las palabras ...*' (Also, like time, words return. From walking around, words appear). Here we find what Mercedes refers to (quoting the poet Antonio Machado) as '*el vértigo de tiempo*' (the vertigo of time). In this vertiginous point of view, a cyclical sense of time mixes with historical/biographical time and with mythic time. '*En la plaza del pueblo, en las noches junto al fuego, he oído contar una y otra vez estas historias como si hubieran sucedido en el día de ayer*' (In the town square, during nights next to the fire, I have heard over and over these stories as if they had happened yesterday).

El cielo gira gained international acclaim, winning one of the three Tiger Awards at the Rotterdam Film Festival and the Buenos Aires International Festival of Independent Cinema, among other prizes. It also won the '*premio al major guión documental del 2005*' from the Premio Escritores y Guionistas de Cataluña (Catalonian prize for writers and screenwriters).

Writer/editor Drake Stutesman[11] writes eloquently about this film:

> I included Mercedes Ávarez's documentary *The Sky Turns [2005]*, in my list of *Sight and Sound's* 2012 international poll of the 50 greatest films in cinema history. Her film accomplished something unique in both the documentary form and in the memoir genre. She structured a film that was polemically personal, yet almost without personal presence, and widely universal, yet focused on a tiny Spanish village (where Álvarez was born) that was slowly becoming deserted as younger people left for a better life. Yet she makes a film that is very much alive with people. She focuses on routines, landscapes, interiors and conversations, often just listening to older people discussing what used to happen and what is happening now.
>
> *The Sky Turns* combines Álvarez's memory and others' memories with a formal, abstracted structure that reveals people's naturally busy routines as somehow unstoppable, even as village life slows as the village becomes more and more empty. With this, Álvarez has no 'conclusion'; instead she deliberately brings the village's changes into the gigantic cycle of life, which is as limitless as the turning sky.

Mercado de Futuros (Futures Market, 2011)

The idea for this film came to Mercedes and her co-screenwriter Arturo Redín in 2007, even before the period known as 'the crisis' was officially announced in Spain in 2008. In preparation, they started reading a wide variety of newspapers, journals and scholarly writings (by anthropologists, urban studies specialists, ecologists) about the current economic situation in Spain. In fact, they even wrote a 'fictional screenplay' of around seventy pages, including lines of dialogue. This helped them visualise a potential film and also to receive a government subsidy.

In *Mercado de futuros*, Mercedes offers an essay style in which the overall themes (over-consumption and the sale of false dreams) could be viewed from different angles (*'abriendo el punto de vista'* [opening the point of view]). Mercedes searched for an approach that differed from the ones already taken by journalists. She noted how, in filming, one theme led to another. Although she spoke with experts on various aspects of the overall topic before filming, she decided not to include expert testimony in the finished film itself, rejecting such sequences as only stressing one point of view. She states emphatically that she is not an expert in any of the theoretical fields she consulted, but she hopes to *'asociar ideas un poco lejanas y buscar entre ellas una asociación con el tema del "espacio y la memoria"'* [to associate ideas that are somewhat distant, and to search across them for an association with the theme of 'space and memory'].

Mercado de futuros invites us to reflect on the years of speculation in real estate; over-construction of houses in Spain, Italy and other Mediterranean countries; the destruction of landscapes, and corruption. Mercedes laments how those trends were accepted by the majority of the people. *'Aceptamos unas cosas que no son aceptables'* [We accept things that are unacceptable]. While filming, she came to identify two kinds of spaces: (1) the new city where the objects for sale are not present and (2) the old city – a marketplace of visible objects full of memories, but in disuse.

Seven alumni from the Master de Documental de Creación of the Universitat Pompeu Frabra assisted with the nine-week filming which took place mostly in Barcelona and Madrid. The first sequence they shot was that of American 'gurus' (inspirational coaches in the business world) in the Expomanagement HSM in 2009 (filmed in Barcelona and in Madrid). She notes that the term 'guru' is a conscious one, stressing 'the pseudo-philosophical, almost religious fervor' of those settings. But at that point, Mercedes and Arturo had no idea where the film was heading. Only later did the opening and ending of the film take shape.

In Mercedes's terms, the scenes of the sales of 'dream spaces' in the *ferria imobilaria* (real estate sales rooms) take place in an area that is 'like a small city', with its doorways, streets, places of leisure. Yet it is also a space that is completely virtual and false. 'In the Ferias they sell an idea of the future' (*venta de sueños*/sale of dreams) ... the future as a form of merchandise. The sense of tension in these scenes, and in the subsequent scenes of the frenzied buying and selling in the Stock Market, is offset by the strangely silent transitional scene of traffic jams filmed without sound. In contrast to such slowness, the vendors in the Real Estate Fairs want time to speed up, to not give people time to think. Mercedes reminds in *Cinco Elementos*: '*la memoria . . . exige un poco de silencio*' (memory demands a little silence).[12]

In our late-afternoon discussion, Mercedes pointed out that the destruction of the landscape by artificial cities is a theme already presented, through different approaches, by directors like Fritz Lang (*Metropolis*), Jacques Tati (*Playtime, Mon Oncle*) and Antonioni (*Red Desert*). She noted that it was difficult to film scenes she did not particularly like, such as the scenes of the '*boom inmobilario*' (housing boom).

There are moments intentionally inserted into the film to add a sense of 'breathing'. At one point, we catch a glimpse of a man tending a small garden adjacent to a busy train track. The scenes with the elderly vendor, Sr Jesús, in the Mercado de los Encants (in the Plaza de las Glorias next to the Torre Agbar) provide a counterpoint ('*un contrapunto perfecto*') and touches of humour, to offset the intensity and tension of the scenes of the real estate sales rooms and the Stock Market. The Yoda-like Sr Jesús is more interested in talking to people and finding out what they need than in exerting himself to satisfy those needs. When a potential customer asks for a particular object, he tends to reply: 'I have it, but it's buried somewhere in my storeroom' (making a gesture to the pile of stuff behind him), and then never getting off his comfortable chair to uncover it!

In another sequence, young men (*Parkours*) (Figure 22) playfully jump over concrete barrels in an abandoned area. They are not explained in the film but they also represent moments of resistance. It turns out that they are part of a political practice, started in France, that helps with the reclaiming of the urban landscape.

Figure 22   *Parkours.*

The finished film actually begins in an apartment in the Ensanche section of Barcelona, the former home of a woman (now deceased) whose life offered layers of memories now at the point of losing their integrity. Mercedes chose that apartment to film specifically because she wanted to record a place with a great library of books, full of classics. Also in the apartment are old dolls that tell of voyages overseas – to Japan and beyond. Later, *Mercado de futuros* wraps up with a shot of those old dolls resting next to the ubiquitous Barbie and Bratz in Sr Jesús's cavernous and eccentric storeroom (a word that is more appropriate than 'shop' since he never seems to want to sell anything!). Here Mercedes is contrasting dolls with 'stories' of memories with dolls as objects of desire and merchandise (*los muñecos como un objecto de deseo, mercancía*).

Although the men who clear away the possessions in the empty apartment treat them with respect, even with admiration at times, they nevertheless efficiently strip the rooms. Later, in the street markets, they throw the books onto the ground 'almost like potatoes' (*casi como patatas*) and people step on them. But then there is one man who gets down on his knees and looks for a special book for himself, helping to break the cycle of meaningless consumption.

As one review of *Mercado de futuros* in *El Público* stated: 'Once again the cinema of Álvarez doesn't go in search of all the answers; rather of deep questions . . . In both of her films she speaks against '*superproducción y consumo*' (overproduction and consumption), '*el future como mercancía*' (the future as a kind of merchandise).[13] The people who try to sell Spanish customers property in Budapest, or Dubai, or Ecuador assert that the land up for sale is a 'blank slate'. But as Mercedes Álvarez painted for us so eloquently in *El cielo gira*, there is no such natural space; rather, our villages overflow with layers of memory. In the city, in contrast, '*ya no es possible experimentar el arte de perderse*' [it is not possible to experience the art of losing oneself].

The complex and mysterious title sequence of *Mercado de futuros,* featuring squid ink and severty-eight drawings, traces a line showing the origins of a city (two intersecting lines), a branch, then a tree, the rooftop of a house, and so on, up to constellations. As in *El cielo gira*, we again see layers of memories and time.

Other Work

In addition to teaching and lecturing, Mercedes Álvarez has written about directors whose work she values, like the Italian filmmaker Ermanno Olmi.[14] In an interview she conducted with the noted Italian documentarist and feature film director, she points out how Olmi's films focus on individual responsibility and on an admonition to '*dialogar . . . con la realidad . . . He aprendido a representar la vida con los materiales de la vida*' [to have a dialogue with reality . . . I've learned to represent life with the materials of life].[15]

Financing and Distribution

Distribution is a problem for any independent filmmaker. *El cielo gira* is distributed in the US by New Yorker Films and *Mercado de futuros* by Icarus Films. Mercedes noted that it is easier to receive government assistance in Spain for first and second films, but not for subsequent ones. With the closing of many art cinema houses in contemporary Spain, she fears, it would be more difficult now to have widespread screenings of her films. 'They think there is no audience for our kind of films, but that is not true', she affirmed. Víctor Erice notes that Canal+ has played a role in many of the projects of the Pompeu Fabra students and alumni.

Fortunately there are festivals devoted to the documentary where films like hers can be shown to an informed audience – festivals like Punto de Vista (Pamplona) and Cinéma du Réel (Paris), as well as film festivals in Switzerland, Locarno, Rotterdam and Tribeca (US). She prefers festivals that are *'más abiertos'* (more open) than ones devoted exclusively to documentaries – festivals that cross artistic boundaries, as *'lugares de reflexión muy importantes'* (very important places for reflection).

Concluding Notes

Mercedes Álvarez's films invite us to contemplate fluidity between modes – documentary, painting , some slightly choreographed moments (like the introduction of the painter Pello Azketa into Aldealseñor). She questions the standard relationship between those established modes of filmmaking, as she sheds light on the relationship between objects, history, economics, and memory.

What is remarkable about Mercedes's work is the consistency of tone, and the mixture of subtlety, social criticism, and the elegiac. Her films gently challenge official narratives of 'progress', without being overly didactic. They point out that, along with times of apparent abundance, comes the destruction of the landscape and the creation of *'barrios fantasmales'* (fantasy/ghostly neighborhoods). 'Why do we just accept these things?', she asks over and over. Mercedes Álvarez is a filmmaker who patiently waits for stories that need to be told – before time erases them or before they erase time.

Acknowledgements

With thanks to Maria Luisa Villalba, Helena Rotés and B & B Ca la Maria (Barcelona). Thanks to Steven Wenz for checking the Spanish translations.

Notes

1. For more information on that meeting, see Linda Ehrlich, 'Three Spanish filmmakers: landscape, recollection, voice', *Senses of Cinema* (2008, online). I will use the director's first name since I have met her several times.
2. Timothy Corrigan, *The Essay Film: From Montaigne, After Marker* (Oxford: Oxford University Press, 2013), p. 4.
3. Laura Rascaroli, *The Personal Camera: Subjective Cinema and the Essay Film* (London: Wallflower Press, 2009), pp. 189–90.
4. For more information, see Beatriz Comella's *Filmar a pie de aula: Quince años de una experiencia docente en la Universidad* (*Filming at the Foot of the Classrom: 15 Years of Teaching Experience in the University*) (Tarragona: Publicaciones Editorial Universitat Rovira i Virgili, 2014) (328 pages). The section on Mercedes Álvarez can be found on pp. 223–31.
5. 'La mirada navega. *El cielo gira*', Valladolid VI Encuentro de Nuevos Autores 2004. 50 Semana Internacional de Cine (13–21), p. 18.
6. Víctor Erice, 'Concerning *The Sky Turns*', originally published in *El País*, 13 May 2005. English translation by Mónica Savirón (January 2012).
7. *En Constucción* received a Goya for Best Documentary Film in 2001, among other awards.
8. Beatriz Comella, *Filmar a pie de aula*, p. 225.
9. Ibid p. 224.
10. The tower of the present-day Palacio dates from the tenth century, the time of Moorish conquests. In the sixteenth century, the palace was built around the tower. According to Mercedes, the legends that surround the palace 'mix true history with imagination. Above all, true stories transmitted orally contain references to ancient inhabitants that remain in the memory of the village as *fantasmas* (ghosts).'
11. Stutesman is a writer, editor of *Framework: Journal of Cinema and Media*, and an adjunct professor at New York University. Personal correspondence.
12. The scenes of the *ferria immobiliaria* were actually the result of two filmings – one in the Barcelona Meeting Point in 2008, and the other in the *Salón immobiliario* of Madrid, 2009.
13. 'Hemos vendido cosas importantes de la vida por baratijas' (We have sold things which are important to life for a cheap amount), *El Público.es*.
14. See 'Olmi llegaba desde muy lejos', *Cahiers du cinéma España* (September 2008), and *Ermanno Olmi: Seis encuentros y otros instantes,* Colección Punto de Vista 3 (January 2008), pp. 200–15.
15. 'Olmi llegaba', p. 7.

SELECT BIBLIOGRAPHY

Aftab, K., ' Georgian cinema: the former Soviet Bloc nation is now a movie making hot spot', *The Independent*, 6 October 2015, <http://www.independent.co.uk/arts-entertainment/films/features/georgian-cinema-the-former-soviet-bloc-nation-is-now-a-moviemaking-hot-spot-a6683351.html> (last accessed 10 January 2016).
Altman, Rick, 'Moving lips: cinema as ventriloquism', *Yale French Studies*, 60, 1980, pp. 67–79.
Anon., 'Focus Georgia', <http://www.visionsdureel.ch/en/docm/focus/> (last accessed 10 January 2016).
Anon., 'Nino Kirtadze (Don't Breathe) interview', *Tribute.ca.*, <http://www.tribute.ca/interviews/nino-kirtadze-dont-breathe/director/103831/> (last accessed 27 January 2016).
Anon., 'Press release: The 19th Busan International Film Festival Special Program in focus: the power of Georgian women filmmakers', 27 August 2014, <http://www.biff.kr/artyboard/board.asp?act=bbs&subAct=view&bid=9611_05&list_style=list&seq=32740> (last accessed 10 January 2016).
Anon., <http://www.sakdoc.ge/> (last accessed 10 January 2016).
Anon., *Who's Afraid of Feminism in Georgia?* [online video] 2015, <https://www.youtube.com/watch?v=vXtgHhVd2T0> (last accessed 9 September 2016).
Astruc, Alexandre, 'The Birth of a New Avant-garde: Le Camera Stylo', in Ginette Vincendeau and Peter Graham (eds), *The New Wave: Critical Landmarks* (London: BFI Book, Palgrave Macmillan, 2009).
Axworthy, Michael, *Irán. Una historia desde el Zoroastro hasta hoy* (Madrid: Turner [first published as *Iran: Empire of the Mind*, London: Penguin, 2010]).
Barman, S., 'BARE interviews: Nino Kirtadze', *BARE Magazine*, 23 April 2015, <http://www.baremagazine.org/bare-interviews-nino-kirtadze> (last accessed 27 January 2016).
Barry, A., *Material Politics: Disputes Along The Pipeline* (Oxford: Wiley Blackwell, 2013).

Barry, Anrew, *Material Politics: Disputes Along The Pipeline* (Oxford: Wiley Blackwell, 2013).
Barthes, Roland, *Camera Lucida*. (London: Vintage Books. 2000).
Barthes, Roland, *Image, Music, Text,* trans. Stephen Heath (New York: Hill and Wang, 1977).
Barthes, Roland, *S/Z*, trans. Richard Miller (New York: Farrar, Straus & Giroux, 1991 [1973]).
Barthes, Roland, *The Fashion System* (Berkeley and Los Angeles, CA: University of California Press, 1990).
Batchen, Geoffrey, 'Snapshots', *Photographies*, 1/2 (2008), pp. 121–42.
Baudrillard, Jean, *Simulacra and Simulation* (Michigan: University of Michigan Press,1994).
Bauerlein, Mark, *The Dumbest Generation: How the Digital Age Stupefies Young Americans and Jeopardizes Our Future (Or, Don't Trust Anyone Under 30)* (New York: Tarcher/Penguin, 2009).
Belleau, Lesley, 'Stretching through our watery sleep: feminine narrative retrieval of cihcipistikwân in Louise Halfe's *The Crooked Gain*', in Neal McLeod (ed.), *Indigenous Poetics in Canada* (Ottawa: Wilfrid Laurier University Press, 2014).
Bénézet, Delphine, *The Cinema of Agnès Varda: Resistance and Eclecticism* (New York: Columbia University Press, 2014).
Berger, John, *Ways of Seeing* (London: Penguin Books, 2008).
Bonner, Virginia, 'The radical modesty of *Les Glaneurs et La Glaneuse*', in Corinn Columbar and Sophie Mayer (eds), *There She Goes: Feminist Filmmaking and Beyond* (Detroit, MI: Wayne State University Press, 2009).
Bordo, Susan, *Unbearable Weight: Feminism, Western Culture and the Body* (Berkeley and Los Angeles, CA: University of California Press, 2003).
Bronfen, Elisabeth and Gabriele Schor (eds), *Francesca Woodman: Works from the Sammlung Verbund* (Cologne: König, 2014).
Brusati, Celeste, 'Stilled lives: self-portraiture and self-reflection in seventeenth-century Netherlandish still-life painting', *Simiolus: Netherlands Quarterly for the History of Art*, 1990, pp. 168–82.
Bruzzi, Stella, *New Documentary: A Critical Introduction* (London and New York: Routledge, 2000).
Butler Judith, *Giving an Account of Oneself* (New York: Fordham University Press, 2005).
Butler, Judith, 'Performative acts and gender constitution: an essay in phenomenology and feminist theory', *Theatre Journal*, 40/4, 1998, pp. 519–31.
Butler, Judith, *Bodies That Matter. On the Discursive Limits of 'Sex'* (New York and London: Routledge, 1993).
Butler, Judith, *Gender Trouble. Feminism and the Subversion of Identity* (London: Routledge, 1990).
Cariou, Warren, 'Edgework: Indigenous poetics as re-placement,' in Neal McLeod (ed.), *Indigenous Poetics in Canada* (Ottawa: Wilfrid Laurier University Press, 2014).
Cheung, Ruby, *New Hong Kong Cinema: Transitions to Becoming Chinese in 21st-Century East Asia* (New York and London: Berghahn, 2015).
Chion, Michel and Claudia Gorbman, *The Voice in Cinema* (New York: Columbia University Press, 1999).
Cixous, Hélène, 'The laugh of the Medusa', in Keith Cohen and Paula Cohen (eds), *The Portable Cixous*, trans. Marta Segarra (New York: Columbia University Press, 2010).
Condee, Nancy, *The Imperial Trace: Recent Russian Cinema* (Oxford: Oxford University Press, 2009).

Cooley, Heidi Rae, '"Identify"-ing a new way of seeing: amateurs, moblogs and practices in mobile imaging', *Spectator*, 21/1, 2004, pp. 65–79.
Cooley, Heidi Rae, 'It's all about the fit: the hand, the mobile screenic device and tactile vision', *Journal of Visual Culture*, 3/2, 2004, pp. 133–55.
Cooley, Heidi Rae, 'The autobiographical impulse and mobile imaging: toward a theory of autobiometry', in *Workshop Pervasive Image Capture and Sharing: New Social Practices and Implications for Technology at Ubicomp*, 2005, v, 11–14, <http://www.ht.sfc.keio.ac.jp/~tailor/ubicomp/mirror/ubicomp2005web/Ubicomp%202005/www.spasojevic.org/pics/PICS/autobiographical_impulse_and_mobile_imaging.pdf> (last 6 accessed 14 September 2014).
Corrigan, Timothy, 'The commerce of auteurism: a voice without authority', *New German Critique* 49, winter 1990.
Daniel, Sharon (2011), 'Collaborative systems: redefining public art', in Margot Lovejoy, Christiane Paul and Victoria Vesna (eds), *Context Providers: Conditions of Meaning in Media Arts* (Chicago, IL: University of Chicago Press, 2011).
Daniel, Sharon (n.d.), *Public Secrets*, <http://www.sharondaniel.net/#about-1> (last accessed 7 January 2017).
Daniel, Sharon (n.d.), 'Inside the Distance', <http://www.sharondaniel.net/#inside-the-distance> (last accessed 7 January 2017).
de Beauvoir, Simone, *The Second Sex*, trans. Constance Borde and Sheila Malovany-Chevallier (London: Vintage, 2010 [1949]).
de Lauretis, Teresa, *Figures of Resistance: Essays in Feminist Theory* (Urbana and Chicago, IL: University of Illinois Press Chicago, 2007).
de Lauretis, Teresa, *Technologies of Gender: Essays on Theory, Film and Fiction* (Bloomington, IN: Indiana University Press, 1987).
Debord, Guy, *Society of the Spectacle* (London: Rebel Press, 1992).
Demetriov, S., 'Rising from the ashes? The difficult (re)birth of the Georgian state', *Development and Change*, 33/5, 2002, pp. 859–83.
Doane, Mary Ann, 'The voice in the cinema: the articulation of body and space', *Yale French Studies*, 60, 1980.
Elgersma, Christine, '9 social media red flags parents should know about', 2016, <https://www.commonsensemedia.org/blog/9-social-media-red-flags-parents-should-know-about> (last accessed 16 October 2016).
Entwistle, Joanne, *The Fashioned Body: Fashion, Dress and Modern Social Theory* (Cambridge: Polity Press, 2000).
Fraser, Nancy, *Fortunes of Feminism: From State-Managed Capitalism to Neoliberal Crisis* (New York: Verso, 2013).
Gaden, Georgia and Delia Dumitrica, 'The "real deal": strategic authenticity, politics and social media', *First Monday*, 20/1, 5 January 2015.
Geraghty, Christine, 'Continuous serial – a definition', in Richard Dyer et al. (eds), *Coronation Street* (London: BFI, 1981).
German, T., 'Heading West? Georgia's Euro Atlantic path', *International Affairs*, 91/3, 2015, pp. 601–14.
Gill, Rosalind and Andy Pratt, 'In the social factory? Immaterial labour, precariousness and cultural work', *Theory, Culture & Society*, 25/7–8, 2008, pp. 1–30.
Gill, Rosalind, 'Beauty surveillance: the digital self-monitoring cultures of neoliberalism', forthcoming in *European Journal of Cultural Studies* (London: Sage, 2017).
Gill, Rosalind, 'Postfeminist media culture: elements of a sensibility', *European Journal of Cultural Studies*, 10/2, 2007, pp. 147–66.
Goffman, Ervin, *Gender Advertisements* (New York: Harper Torchbooks, 1987).
Grant, Catherine, 'www.auteur.com?' *Screen*, 41/1, 2000, pp. 101-108, esp. 107.

Guengerich, Galen, 'Galen Guengerich: 'selfie' culture promotes a degraded worldview', *Washington Post*, 31 January 2014, <http://www.washingtonpost.com/local/galen-guengerich-selfie-culture-promotes-a-degraded-worldview/2014/01/31/cb444130-8942-11e3-916e-e01534b1e132_story.html> (last accessed 10 September 2014).

Hawkes, Gail, *A Sociology of Sex and Sexuality* (Maidenhead: Open University Press, 1996).

Hochman, Nadav and Lev Manovich, 'Zooming into an Instagram city: reading the local through social media', *First Monday*, 18/7, 2013, <http://firstmonday.org/ojs/index.php/fm/article/view/4711> (last accessed 15 September 2014).

Hollinger, Karen, *Feminist Film Studies* (London and New York: Routledge, 2012).

hooks, bell, *Talking Back: Thinking Feminist, Thinking Black* (Boston: South End Press, 1989).

Jamieson, Lynn, 'Personal relationships, intimacy and the self in a mediated and global digital age', in Kate Orton Johnson and Nick Prior (eds), *Digital Sociology – Critical Perspectives* (London: Palgrave Macmillan, 2013).

Jashi, S., Interview with the author, 26 September 2015.

Johnston, Claire (ed.), *The Work of Dorothy Arzner* (London: BFI, 1975).

Johnston, Claire, 'Women's cinema as counter-cinema', in Claire Johnston (ed.), *Notes on Women's Cinema* (London: Society for Education in Film and Television, 1975). Reprinted in: Sue Thornham (ed.), *Feminist Film Theory: A Reader*. (Edinburgh: Edinburgh University Press, 1999).

Johnston, Claire, 'Women's cinema as counter-cinema', in Philip Simpson, Andrew Utterson, and K. J. Shepherdson (eds), *Film Theory : Critical Concepts in Media and Cultural Studies*, vol 3 (New York: Routledge, 2004), pp. 183–192.

Jones, Amelia, 'The 'eternal return': self-portrait photography as a technology of embodiment', *Signs*, 27/4, 2002, pp. 947–78.

Juhasz, Alexander, *Women of Vision: Histories in Feminist Film and Video* (Minneapolis, MN: University of Minnesota Press, 2001).

Keller, Jessalynn, *Girls' Feminist Blogging in a Postfeminist Age* (London and New York: Routledge, 2016).

Kelsey, Robin and Blake Stimson (eds), *The Meaning of Photography*, The Clark Symposium (Williamstown, MA and New Haven, CT: Yale University Press, 2008).

Khatiashvili, T., 'Beyond time and space: review of *Bakhmaro*', *Kinokultura*, Special Issue 12, <http://www.kinokultura.com/specials/12/bakhmaro.shtml> (last accessed 10 January 2016).

Kian, Azadeh, 'Social and cultural change and the women's rights movement in Iran', in Annabelle Sreberny and Massoumeh Torfeh (eds), *Cultural Revolution in Iran. Contemporary Popular Culture in the Islamic Republic* (London and New York: I. B. Tauris, 2013).

Kim, Young-Woo, 'Three women under one sky – the power of Georgian women filmmakers', BIFF, 22 September 2014, <http://biff.kr/artyboard/board.asp?act=bbs&subAct=view&bid=9612_22&page=1&order_index=no&order_type=desc&list_style=list&seq=33546> (last accessed 10 January 2016).

King, Humay, 'Matter, time, and the digital: Varda's *The Gleaners and I*', *Quarterly Review of Film and Video*, 24/5, 2007, pp. 421–29.

Kirtadze, N., Interview with the author, 21 November 2015.

Kiviat, Katherine and Scott Heidler, *Women of Courage: Intimate Stories from Afghanistan* (Salt Lake City, UT: Gibbs Smith Publisher, 2007).

Lahiji, S., 'Chaste dolls and unchaste dolls: women in Iranian cinema since 1979', in R. Tapper (ed.), *The New Iranian Cinema: Politics, Representation and Identity* (London: I. B. Tauris, 2002), pp. 215–26.

Levin, Adam, 'The selfie in the age of digital recursion', *InVisibile Culture: An Electronic Journal of Visual Culture*, 20, 2014.
McCall, Sophie, *First Person Plural: Aboriginal Storytelling and the Ethics of Collaborative Authorship* (Vancouver: University of British Columbia Press, 2011).
McLeod, Neal (ed.), *Indigenous Poetics in Canada* (Ottawa: Wilfrid Laurier University Press, 2014).
McNay, Lois, *Gender and Agency: Reconfiguring the Subject in Feminist and Social Theory*. (Cambridge: Polity Press, 2000).
McRobbie, Angela, 'Notes on the perfect', *Australian Feminist Studies*, 30/83, 2015, pp. 3–20.
McRobbie, Angela, *The Aftermath of Feminism. Gender, Culture and Social Change* (London, Thousand Oaks, New Delhi and Singapore: Sage, 2009).
Maracle, Lee, *Sojourner's Truth and Other Stories* (London: Press Gang Publishers, 1990).
Marwick, Alice E., *Status Update: Celebrity, Publicity, and Branding in the Social Media Age* (New Haven, CT: First Edition, 2013).
Mayne, Judith, *The Woman at the Keyhole: Feminism and Women's Cinema* (Bloomington and Indianapolis, IN: Indiana University Press, 1991).
Mir-Hosseini, Ziba, 'Negotiating the politics of gender in Iran: an ethnography of a documentary', in Richard Tapper (ed.), *The New Iranian Cinema. Politics, Representation and Identity* (London and New York: I. B. Tauris, 2013).
Mirzoeff, Nicholas, *How To See The World* (London: Penguin, 2015).
Murray, Susan, 'Digital images, photo-sharing, and our shifting notions of everyday aesthetics', *Journal of Visual Culture*, 7/2, 2008, pp. 147–63.
Naficy, Hamid, *A Social History of Iranian Cinema, Vol. 4. The Globalizing Era, 1984–2010* (Durham, NC: Duke University Press, 2012).
Naficy, Hamid, *An Accented Cinema: Exilic and Diasporic Filmmaking* (Princeton, NJ: Princeton University Press, 2001).
Nichols, Bill, 'The voice of documentary', *Film Quarterly*, 36/3, 1983.
Nichols, Bill, *Representing Reality* (Bloomington, IN: Indiana University Press, 1991).
Pedicini, Isabella, *Francesca Woodman. The Roman Years: Between Flesh and The Film* (Rome: Contrasto, 2012).
Phelan, Peggy, *Unmarked: The Politics of Performance* (London: Routledge, 1993).
Power, Nina, *One-Dimensional Woman* (Winchester: O Books, 2009).
Prei, Carrie and Maria Stehle, *Awkward Politics: Technologies of Popfeminist Activism* (Montréal/Kingston: McGill-Queen's University Press, 2016).
Rahbaran, Shiva, *Iranian Cinema Uncensored: Contemporary Film-makers since the Islamic Revolution,* (London and New York: I. B. Tauris. 2015).
Ravetto-Biagioli, Kriss, 'Anonymous social as political', *Leonardo Electronic Almanac*, 19/4, 2013, pp. 179–95.
Renov, Michael, *The Subject of Documentary* (Minneapolis: University of Minnesota, 2004).
Robbins, Kevin, 'The virtual unconscious in post-photography', *Science as Culture*, 3/1, 1992.
Rocamora, Agnes, 'Personal fashion blogs: screens and mirrors in digital self-portraits', *Fashion Theory*, 15/4. 2011.
Rocamora, Agnes, *Fashioning the City: Paris, Fashion and the Media* (London: I. B. Tauris, 2009).
Rosenbaum, Jonathan, 'Radical humanism and the coexistence of film and poetry in *The House Is Black*', in Jonathan Kahana (ed.), *The Documentary Film Reader: History, Theory, Criticism* (Oxford: Oxford University Press, 2016), pp. 473–76.

Ruby, Jay, 'Speaking for, speaking about, speaking with, or speaking alongside: an anthropological and documentary dilemma', *Journal of Film and Video*, 44/1–2, 1992, pp. 42–66.
Rusadze, Z., 'The identity and place of contemporary Georgian cinema', *Kinokultura*, Special Issue 12, <http://www.kinokultura.com/specials/12/rusadze-identity.shtml> (last accessed 10 January 2016).
Said, Edward, *Orientalism* (London, Penguin, 1977).
Sherlock, Amy, 'Multiple expeausures: identity and alterity in the 'self-portraits' of Francesca Woodman', *Paragraph*, 36/3, 2013, pp. 376–91.
Shohat, Ella and Robert Stam, *Unthinking Eurocentrism: Multiculturalism and the Media* (London: Routledge, 1994).
Sight and Sound, 'Critics 50 greatest documentaries of all times', *Sight and Sound*, September 2014, <http://www.bfi.org.uk/sight-sound-magazine/greatest-docs (last accessed 13 January 2016).
Silverman, Kaja, *The Acoustic Mirror: The Female Voice in Psychoanalysis and Cinema* (Bloomington and Indianapolis, IN: Indiana University Press, 1988).
Sontag, Susan, *On Photography* (London: Penguin, 1979).
Spivak, Gayatri, 'Can the subaltern speak', in Carrie Nelson and Lawrence Grossberg (eds), *Marxism and the Interpretation of Culture* (Chicago, IL: University of Illinois Press, 1988).
Spivak, Gayatri, *An Aesthetic Education in the Era of Globalization* (Cambridge, MA: Harvard University Press, 2012).
Stites Mor, J. *Transition Cinema: Political Filmmaking and the Argentine Left Since 1968* (Pittsburgh, PA: University of Pittsburgh Press, 2012).
Townsend, Chris, *Francesca Woodman* (London: Phaidon Press, 2007).
Trachtenberg, Alan, *Classic Essays on Photography* (New Haven, CT: Leete's Island Books, 1980).
Trinh T. Min-ha, *Framer Framed: Film Scripts and Interviews* (Routledge: London, 1992).
Truffaut, François, 'A certain tendency in French cinema', *Cahiers du cinéma*, 31, 1954, pp. 15–29, reprinted in Scott MacKenzie (ed.), *Film Manifestos and Global Film Cultures* (Berkeley and Los Angeles, CA: University of California Press, 2014), pp. 133–44.
Turkle, Sherry, *Alone Together: Why We Expect More from Technology and Less from Each Other* (New York: Basic Books, 2012).
van Dijck, José, *The Culture of Connectivity: A Critical History of Social Media* (Oxford and New York: Oxford University Press, 2013).
Waugh, Thomas, *The Right to Play Oneself: Looking Back on Documentary Film* (Minneapolis, MN: University of Minnesota Press, 2011).
White, Patricia, *Women's Cinema, World Cinema: Projecting Contemporary Feminisms* (Durham, NC and London: Duke University Press, 2015).
Winston, Brian (ed.), *The Documentary Film Book* (London: British Film Institute, 2013).
Wolf, Larry, *Inventing Eastern Europe: The Map of Civilisation on the Mind of the Englightenment* (Stanford, CA: Stanford University Press, 1994).
Wolf, Naomi, *The Beauty Myth* (London: Vintage Books, 1991).
Woodward, Sophie, *Why Women Wear What They Wear* (Oxford/New York: Berg, 2007).
Zeydabadi-Nejad, Saeed, 'Beyond gender. women filmmakers and sociopolitical critique', in Annabelle Sreberny and Massoumeh Torfeh (eds), *Cultural Revolution in Iran: Contemporary Popular Culture in the Islamic Republic* (London and New York: I. B. Tauris, 2013).

Zeydabadi-Nejad, Saeed, *The Politics of Iranian Cinema: Film and Society in the Islamic Republic of Iran* (Abingdon and New York: Routledge, 2010).

Zimmerman, Patricia, 'Flaherty's midwives', in Dianne Waldman and Jill Walker (eds), *Feminism and Documentary*, vol. 5 (Minneapolis, MN: University of Minnesota Press, 1999).

Zimmermann, Patricia, *Reel Families: A Social History of Amateur Film* (Bloomington, IN: Indiana University Press, 1995).

INDEX

Abirafeh, Lina, 146
Abortion of Others (Gallo), 114, 115–18
absence, and the voice, 74; *see also* death/absence
Abtahi, Sepideh, 178
accented cinema, 157–8
adolescence *see* teenagers
Afghanistan, documentaries, 137–55
Afghanistan: 10 Years On (Sadat), 140
After 10 Years (Sadat), 143, 149–50
After 35 Years (Sadat), 140
ageing, 85–96
agency, 59; *see also* voice, and agency
Agger, Ben, 104
Ahmadinejad, Mahmoud, 170, 171, 175
Alcohol Years, The (Morley), 72–4, 80
alterity, 51, 104
Álvarez, Mercedes, 184–93
Amsterdam, migrant women, 125, 127, 129–30
Angel (Woodman), 105
Angry Inuk (Arnaquq-Baril), 63–7
animal rights groups, 65, 66
Antonioni, Michelangelo, 171, 190
Apna Haq: Our Right (2013), 133
Arbor, The (Barnard), 78–80

archetypes, 15, 23–34, 40–6, 116–17
archives, 80, 87–9, 176
Argentina, transition films, 157, 161
Armitage, Simon, 76
Arnaquq-Baril, Alethea, 63–7
Arsenishvili, Vano, 160
asylum seekers, 127, 128, 133
auteurism, 77, 138–9, 159
authenticity, 23–34; *see also* performativity
autobiography, 10–12, 16–20, 51, 73–4, 107, 170
Azketa, Pello, 187

Bakhmaro (Jashi), 165–6
Balló, Jordi, 184
Bani-Etemad, Rakshan, 173, 175–6
Barclay, Barry, 64
Barghnavard, Shirin, 171, 176
Barnard, Clio, 78, 79
Barthes, Roland, 2, 39–40, 49, 59, 71, 89, 102
Bashir, Maria, 140, 144, 146–9
Baudrillard, Jean, 96
'Beauty Face' (app), 104
Beneath the Veil (2001), 148

201

Berger, John, 108–9
Bernardet, Jean-Claude, 120
bias, 126
Black Lives Matter, 127
blogs, 38–53
Body Anxiety (2015), 31
Boltanski, Luc, 46–7
Boluk, Stephanie, 60
Bombay Beach (Ha'rel), 76–8
Bondebjerg, Ib, 145
Boxing Girls of Kabul, The (2012), 148
Brazilian documentaries, 114–24
Bröckling, Ulrich, 51
Brossard, Nicole, 58
Bruzzi, Stella, 79, 80
Bühler, Melanie, 26
Burqas behind Bars (2013), 148
Butler, Judith, 40, 43–4, 100, 106, 107
'Buyer, Walker, Rover' (2013), 29

cameraphones, 13–14, 104, 175–6
cameras, 108, 111, 126–7, 185
Canada, Inuit filmmaking, 63–7
caregiving, 95–6
censorship, Iranian, 175
Cheung, Ruby, 157
Chiapello, Ève, 47
child marriage, Afghanistan, 144, 145, 146
childbirth, 114–24
child-woman, fashion imagery, 42–3
Chion, Michel, 70
choreography *see* dance
Chun, Wendy, 15
cielo gira, El (Álvarez), 185, 186–8
Cinco elementos (Álvarez), 188, 190
'*Cinema de real*', 185
Citron, Michelle, 60
Cixous, Hélène, 58–9
class, 114–15, 116, 120, 123, 146
close-ups, 117, 140, 145, 164
collaboration, 70–2, 75, 77, 130; *see also* relationships
collective authorship, 172–3
collective memories *see* family memories
colonial legacies, 64
commemoration, 101, 102

commercialisation, 71
Common Sense (website), 16
Condee, Nancy, 157
consciousness, 39, 64; *see also* unconscious
consumption, problems of, 58, 189, 191
Cooley, Heidi Rae, 13
Corn Island (Ovashvili), 159
criminal justice system, 61–3, 118–19
critical theory, 72

dance, 76–8, 174, 179
Daniels, Jill, 74
Daniels, Sharon, 60–3
Darling, Jesse, 30, 33
Darling-Wolf, Fabienne, 151
Day in Her Life, A (Lin), 129–30, 132
de Lauretis, Teresa, 3, 124
Dean, Aria, 32
death/absence, 78–81, 101, 102–3, 107, 111, 160
disappearance, 4, 18, 101, 165, 187
Displaced Daughters (Lin), 132
distance/proximity, 122–4, 145
distribution, Spanish film, 192
Divorce Iranian Style (Longinotto, Mir-Hosseini), 174
Doane, Mary Ann, 80
domestic violence, 129, 132–3, 143–51
Don't Breathe (Kirtadze), 159, 160, 166
drag performance, 43–4
Dreams of a Life (Morley), 80–1
drug use, 48, 61, 146
Dunbar, Andrea, 78–80
Durer, Albrecht, 11
Dutch non-ethnic communities, 127, 128, 131
Dziapshipa, Anna, 160

Eastman, George, 13
editing, 72, 73, 91–2, 95, 116, 117–18, 121
embodiment, 33, 34, 57, 87–90, 95, 110
empire rhetoric, 142, 151
entrepreneurship, 50, 51, 141
Erice, Victor, 185, 192
Escuela de Pamplona, 187

essay films, 184, 186–91
European Union, ban on seal products, 65
Excellences and Perfections (Ulman), 23–37
experimental documentary, 78–81, 167

Facebook, 26
family memories, 84–99
Farrokhzad, Forough, 173, 180
fashion blogs, 38–53
Fellini, Federico, 159
female gaze, 179; *see also* gaze
feminine archetypes *see* archetypes
feminisation, 129, 170
feminism/feminist
   commodified/apolitical, 45–6
   film studies, 129
   narratives of, 33
   urban/rural, 157
Feminist Approach to Technology, 130
'f/f' (Ulman), 30
fiction films, Georgian, 159, 160
film festivals, 159, 172, 175, 188, 192
film production, women in, 72
filmfarsi, 174
filmmaking equipment, 72, 73; *see also* cameras
filmmaking techniques, 70–83, 90–2
financing film, 71, 192
First Number (Sadat), 140
Fisher, Caitlin, 60
FitzSimons, Trish, 71–2, 73, 81
Five Days of War (Harlin), 161
Flickr, 14, 16
forced marriage, Afghanistan, 144, 145
Fourth Cinema, 64
Fraser, Nancy, 46
Freud, Sigmund, 15

Gallo, Carla, 114, 115–18
Gaprindashvili, Lela, 157
gaze, 44, 103–4, 107–11, 179
gender identity, 40–4, 59
gender stereotypes *see* archetypes

Georgia, post-Soviet, 156–69
Geraghty, Christine, 18
Gevinson, Tavi, 46–51
Gibson, Sarah, 71
Giddens, Anthony, 40
Gill, Rosalind, 10, 46, 51
girlhood, politics of, 46–51
Girls (Werneck), 114, 115–16, 118
Gleaners and I, The (Varda), 57–60
Goffman, Erving, 40, 43
Gogoberidze, Nutsa, 160
Google Earth/Street View, 19
Googoosh, 178–9
Graham, Mark, 142, 145, 151
Grant, Catherine, 139
Green Movement, Iran, 175
Green Wave, The (Ali Samadi Ahadi), 176
Guerín, José Luis, 186

Half Value Life (Sadat), 140, 143, 145, 146–9
Ham, Julie, 133
Ha'rel, Alma, 76
hashtags, 16–17, 18, 23, 30
Heidler, Scott, 148
Hello Kitty is Dead (Lin), 126
hijab, 127, 132, 171–2
Hill, Brian, 76
Hirsch, Ann, 31
history, and witnessing, 88
History and Memory (Tajiri), 12, 84–99
HIV prevention programme, 61
Hollywood films, Asian women in, 126
home movies, 172, 176, 178, 179
Hong Kong, 128, 130, 157
House is Black, The (Farrokhzad), 173, 180
housing boom, 189–90
human trafficking, 127, 128, 129

I am a Girl (2013), 148
I Could No Longer Play (Woodman), 110–11
identity, 26–31, 33–4, 40–1, 104; *see also* archetypes; performativity

identity politics, blogs, 38–51; *see also* Afghanistan, documentaries; Álvarez, Mercedes; Iran; transition
improvisation, 75–6, 78, 186
India, 127, 130
Indigenous film, 63–7
Indonesia, 131, 133
Inside the Distance (Daniel), 62
Instagram, 9–22
   as autobiography, 10–12, 16–20
   Excellences and Perfections, 23–37
   and photography, 12–15
Institute for Women's Empowerment (IWE), 131
interactive new media documentaries, 60–3
interactivity, 66–7
Internet, 18, 26, 40, 60–3, 140–1; *see also* Instagram
interviews, 72–6, 78, 80, 125–34
intimacy *see* distance/proximity
Inuit culture, 63–7
Iran, underground documentary, 170–83
Islamic Revolution, 173–4, 176, 178–9

Jackson, Shelly, 60
Japanese American internment, WWII, 85–94
Jashi, Salomé, 156–69
Johnston, Claire, 126
Jones, Amelia, 11–12
Jordà, Joaquim, 186
Juhasz, Alexandra, 79
justice, historical/social, 93, 96
justice system, 61–3, 118–19

Kalatozov, Mikhail, 160
Karzai, Hamid, 144
Keller, Jessalynn, 48, 49
Khatiashvili, Teo, 166
Khidasheli, Keti, 157
Khomeini, Ayatollah, 174, 178
Khosrovani, Firouzeh, 177
Kian, Azadeh, 170
King, Homay, 58
Kirtadze, Nino, 156–69

Kiviat, Katherine, 148
Kotetishvili, Tato, 160
Kvezereli, Bakur, 163

labour
   emotional/sex, 125, 126, 127, 128, 129–30
   informal, 125, 126, 129, 133
   new forms of, 47
   unions, 131
Land, Charles, 13
landscapes, destruction of, 189, 190, 192
Lang, Fritz, 190
Leader is Always Right, The (Jashi), 163–4
Leahy, Gillian, 71
lepers, 173
Lesage, Julia, 73, 81
Levin, Adam, 13
life expectancy, Afghanistan, 144–5
Lifting the Veil (2007), 148
Like Water Through Stone (Rocha), 114, 115, 120–4
Lin, Vivian Wenli, 125–34
Lonely Girl (2013), 31
long shots, 143–4, 165
Longinotto, Kim, 174
Love Crimes of Kabul (2011), 148
Loving Work (Lin), 126
Lunbeck, Elizabeth, 15–16

male gaze, 44, 103–4; *see also* gaze
'Man Repeller' (Medine), 41–6, 50
Manovich, Lev, 16
Maori culture, 64
Maracle, Lee, 66
marginalisation, 60, 63, 74, 120, 125–6, 127, 138
Margvelashvili, Giorgi, 161
Matwick, Alice, 51
McCall, Sophie, 59, 64
McCracken, Ellen, 45
McDougal, David, 78
McNay, Lois, 59
McRobbie, Angela, 49, 50, 104
mediation, in justice system, 62–3
Medine, Leandra, 41–6, 49–51

memes, 16–17
memoir genre, 188
memory
  family memories/trauma, 84–99
  see also archives
Mercado de futuros (Álvarez), 188–91, 192
Mesquita, Claudia, 123
migrant women workers, and VOW Media, 125–33
Milk and Iron (Priscilla), 114, 115, 118–19
Miller, Daniel, 27
Mir-Hosseini, Ziba, 174–5
mise en scéne, 120, 124
miss_etc, 19
mobile phones, filming, 13–14, 175–6
Moist Forever (Ulman), 29
montage, 91, 121
Morley, Carol, 72–4, 80–1
Morrissey, Trish, 11
motherhood, 85–96, 114–24
motifs, 91–2
mourning, 102, 160
movement, metamorphosis, 105–6
Mr Minister, A (Jashi), 160, 163
Museum of Modern Art (MOMA), New York, 159
music, 76, 124, 145, 178–9

Naficy, Hamid, 157–8
narcissm, 15–16, 103–5
narrative(s), 18–19, 107; *see also* voice
Nash, Kate, 67
nationalism, Georgian, 163–4
neoliberal capitalism, 46–7
neoliberalism, and postfeminism, 49–51
Nepal, and VOW Media, 130, 133
Netflix, 19
Netherlands, immigrants to, 127, 128, 131, 132–3
Nichols, Bill, 19, 71

objectification, 110–11, 126
Olmi, Ermanno, 191
On Being An Angel (Woodman), 105
1,2,3? (Sadat), 140, 143–6

online database, 60–3; *see also* Internet
orality, Inuit, 63, 66
Orjonikidze, Nino, 160
otherness, 122, 142
Our Times (Ruzegar-e ma), 174

Pant, Pooja, 128, 129, 133
Pedicini, Isabella, 101, 105
performance, workshops, 75
performativity, 23, 24–30, 33, 34, 40–4, 101, 108, 110
Peter, Aaju, 64–5, 66
Phelan, Peggy, 27, 40, 101
photography, 105, 111
  and commemoration, 101, 102
  history, 11–13
  as performative, 39–40
  witnessing, 126–7
  see also fashion blogs; Instagram; selfies; self-portraits
Photoshop, 131
photostreaming, 16–20
Pipeline Next Door, The (Kirtadze), 161, 162–3, 166
police violence, 127
political repression, Iran, 177–8
Pompeu Fabra documentarists, 184–6
pop culture, 46–9, 50
porn industry, 126
portraits *see* selfies; self-portraits
postcards, Georgian project, 156–7
postfeminism, 10, 45–6, 50–1
Power, Nina, 46
pregnancy/childbirth, 114–24
Priscilla, Claudia *see Milk and Iron*
prisoners, mothers as, 118–19
prisoners, political, 177–8
Profession: Documentarist (Herfeh: Mostanadsaz, 170–83
'progress', narratives of, 192
Provinelli, Elizabeth, 86
Public Secrets (Daniel), 61–3

Rabinowitz, Paulan, 78
race, and second-wave feminism, 31–2; *see also* Inuit culture; marginalisation

205

radio documentary, 131–3
rape, 117
Rascaroli, Laura, 184
Ravetto Biagioli, Kriss, 17
Raymond, Claire, 108, 111
realism, 78
reality television, 75–6
record keeping, 84–99
Redín, Arturo, 188
relationships, 26, 105, 107, 119–20, 123
  and voice/identity, 59, 73–4, 75, 76
  see also collaboration
Renaissance, 11
Renov, Michael, 73
responsibility, individual, 191
Rettburg, Jill Walker, 18
Rezaei, Nahid, 179
Riches, Harriet, 107
Riggs, Marlon, 12
Rocha, Marília, 120–4
Roell, Annemeike, 66
Rogers, Bunny, 27
'Rookie Magazine' (Gevinson), 46–9, 50
Rose Revolution, Georgia, 158, 159, 163, 167
Rumbelow, Saul, 74, 75
rural/urban feminism, Georgia, 157
Rusadze, Zaza, 159, 162
Russian films, and Post-Soviet era, 157

Sadat, Alka, 137–55
Sagynbaeva, Elzira, 146
Said, Edward, 142
Sakashvili, Mikhail, 158–9, 160, 164
Sakdoc Film, 160–1
Salahshoor, Sahar, 172, 177–8
Scandalishious (Hirsch), 31, 33
Schneemann, Carolee, 32
Scholz, Trevor, 15
Sconce, Jeffrey, 19
scriptrix narrans, 59–69
seal hunting, 64–6
Self Made (Wearing), 74–6, 78
selfhood, performance, 111

'selfie feminism', 31–2
selfies, 9–22, 26, 40, 103–5
self-portraits, 2–3, 11–12, 40, 48; see also subjectivity
self-surveillance, 10, 20, 47
serial narratives, 18–19
'settler' education, 66
'Seventeen Magazine', 48
sex workers, 125, 127, 128, 129–30, 132
Sharia law, 174, 178
Sharifi, Farahnaz, 178–9
Sherlock, Amy, 102, 108
Shevardnadze, Edward, 158
Signs that say (Wearing), 74
Silent Majority Speaks, The (Khoshnoudi), 176
Sky Spins, The (Álvarez), 186–8
Sluis, Katrina, 33
Slumdog Millionaire (2008), 142
social justice, 60–3
social media see blogs; Instagram; selfies
Something About Georgia (Kirtadze), 164, 165
Sontag, Susan, 102
sound/soundtrack, 79–80, 91, 163, 165; see also music; voice
Soviet Union, 157, 158
Space (Woodman), 105, 106
Spain, economic crisis, 188–9
'speak about/nearby', 119–20, 121
Speechless (Jashi), 164–5
Spivak, Gayatri, 139, 142
standardisation, 29–30
stereotypes, 15, 23–34, 40–6, 116–17
Stites Mor, Jessica, 157, 161
Stutesman, Drake, 188
'Style Rookie' (Gevinson), 46
subjectivity, 32, 103–11
suicide, 4, 101, 143
Surname Viet (Trinh T. Minh-ha), 75
surveillance, 10, 20, 33, 47, 177

Taiwan, 128, 133
Tajiri, Rea, 12, 84–99
Tangerines (Urushadze), 159

Tati, Jacques, 190
Tatsuno, David, 89
teenagers, 16, 133
    in Georgian 'patriot' camps, 163–4
    pregnancy, 115–16, 121
    and prostitution, 128
    see also selfies
Their Helicopter (Jashi), 165
Their Kingdom (Gogoberidze, Kalatozov), 159–60
time/temporality, 105, 165–6, 188
Tongues Untied (Riggs), 12
Townsend, Chris, 108
transition, 101, 156–67
trauma, national, 180
trauma, transgenerational, 84–94
Trinh T. Minh-ha, 58, 75, 79
truth, 76, 78, 79–80, 105, 106, 126
    historical, 88, 90, 92
Tulving, Endel, 96
Twitter, 14, 16, 46

Ulman, Amalia, 23–37
unconscious, 73, 86
UNICEF, media workshops for, 125
Untitled (Woodman), 109–10

van Dijck, José, 14
Varda, Agnès, 57–60
ventriloquism, 73, 75, 76
video games, 176
Vietnamese-American actors, 75
Vincent, Joyce Carol, 80–1

violence, 107–8, 110–11, 117, 143–55;
    see also domestic violence
visibility, 3, 29, 31–4
Visualizing the Voices (project), 133
voice
    and agency, 58–60, 63–6, 70
    hybrid practices, 70–83
Voices of Women (VOW) Media, 125–34

We are Postmodern (Sadat), 140
Wearing, Gillian, 74–6
Web 2.0, 15
websites, 41–6, 125; *see also* Internet
Wenli Lin, Vivian, 125–34
Werneck, Sandra *see* Girls
Western ideologies, 139, 142, 148
White, Patricia, 139
'Who's Afraid of Feminism in Georgia?' (2013 project), 156–7
Wilders, Geert, 132
Wilke, Hannah, 32
Wire, The (2002), 18, 19
Wisdom Gone Wild (Tajiri), 94–6
With Love From Taiwan (Lin), 133
witnessing, 96, 127
Woodman, Francesca, 100–13

YouTube, 18, 31, 140, 145

Zeydabadi-Nejad, Saeed, 174
Zimmerman, Patricia, 13, 72, 77
Zuckerberg Mark, 26

EU representative:
Easy Access System Europe
Mustamäe tee 50, 10621 Tallinn, Estonia
Gpsr.requests@easproject.com

www.ingramcontent.com/pod-product-compliance
Lightning Source LLC
Chambersburg PA
CBHW051058230426
43667CB00013B/2348